CRISIS INVESTING FOR THE YEAR 2000

CRISIS INVESTING FOR THE YEAR 2000

HOW TO PROFIT FROM THE COMING Y2K COMPUTER CRASH

L. JAY KUO

AND

EDWARD M. DUA

A BIRCH LANE PRESS BOOK
PUBLISHED BY CAROL PUBLISHING GROUP

A Birch Lane Press Book
Published by Carol Publishing Group
Birch Lane Press is a registered trademark of Carol Communications, Inc.

Editorial, sales and distribution, rights and permissions inquiries should be addressed to Carol Publishing Group, 120 Enterprise Avenue, Secaucus, N.J. 07094.

In Canada: Canadian Manda Group, One Atlantic Avenue, Suite 105, Toronto, Ontario M6K 3E7

Carol Publishing Group books may be purchased in bulk at special discounts for sales promotion, fund-raising, or educational purposes. Special editions can be created to specifications. For details, contact Special Sales Department, 120 Enterprise Avenue, Secaucus, N.J. 07094.

Manufactured in the United States of America
10 9 8 7 6 5 4 3 2 1

Library of Congress Cataloging-in-Publication Data

Kuo, L. Jay.
    Crisis investing for the year 2000 : how to profit from the coming
  Y2K computer crash / L. Jay Kuo and Edward M. Dua.
        p.   cm.
    Includes bibliographical references and index.
    ISBN 1-55972-518-4
    1. Investments. 2. Year 2000 data conversion (Computer systems)
  I. Dua, Edward M.   II. Title.
  HG4521.C66   1999
  332.6—dc21   99-19462
                                                           CIP

CONTENTS

INTRODUCTION

An engineer at a major U.S. food processor reported that its ware-house's automatic safety system destroyed millions of dollars worth of product when the computers mistakenly believed that the food— which would expire in "00"—was nearly 100 years old.[1]

When General Motors and Chrysler ran independent tests to see what problems the Year 2000 bug might cause at their manufacturing plants, they turned the clocks forward to the new millennium and encountered numerous surprises, from security systems locking down all the plant doors to robotics freezing in mid-operation.[2]

Produce Palace, a grocery chain in Warren, Michigan, sued its cash register vendor, TEC of America, contending its entire computer sys-tem and ten of its cash registers crashed every time a credit card with a year 2000 or higher expiration date was swiped. TEC has agreed to settle the case for $250,000.[3] Trial lawyers have begun to see the Year 2000 bug as the biggest litigation bonanza in history.

October 17, 1973. One of the most important dates of the 1970s. Can't place the date? Rewind twenty-five and some odd years and just imagine that, on that day, you happen to be passing by a secluded hotel in the Middle East, and notice dozens of limousines and armed guards camped out front. "What's going on?" you ask a bellboy in your best Arabic. He replies (in English, thank goodness) that the ministers of some group called OPEC are having a meeting. "They are going to cut off the oil," he says with a grin, drawing a finger ominously across his throat. The people around him nod solemnly.

Being an astute investor, you understand the implications. You quickly send a telegram to your broker in New York and instruct him to sell most of your equities, except of course the oil stocks. You move the proceeds into oil futures and keep the rest in cash.

Boy, are you glad you did. The oil embargo that results from that fateful OPEC meeting sends oil prices sky-high, shocks world markets, and is the catalyst for a global recession. Gas lines form outside service stations. Inflation soars as the sudden spike in oil prices raises costs for manufacturing, utilities, transportation, and just about every other sector. From its peak in 1973 to its low at the end of 1974, the Dow Jones drops *40 percent* in a bear market lasting twenty-three months. Real GDP drops over 3.4 percent from high to low during the same period. Investors who are long in the markets get slaughtered. But not you. You make out like a bandit.

Fast forward to 1999. You're an informed investor. You know about the Year 2000 Bug—how computers processing only the last two digits in dates will interpret "1/1/00" as the beginning of 1900 instead of 2000 and could crash at the turn of the millennium. You appreciate the economic consequences of worldwide, simultaneous computer system failures. You even know that the acronym-obsessed *digerati* have dubbed the Year 2000 Bug "Y2K" for short. And you realize that investors ignore this Y2K phenomenon at their own peril, since a wholesale breakdown of information systems could make a simple oil embargo look like a practice drill.

So, like other smart investors, you've begun to adjust your portfolio to make sure you don't miss the millennium boat, or at least that you don't flounder in its wake for years. Perhaps you've even put together a scheme to make some quick money out of the crisis. You've got a plan, right?

If the answer is no, you are not alone. Maybe you haven't sat down to consider the consequences that Y2K will have on your portfolio. Maybe you haven't had time to think about how Y2K will affect prices, interest rates, and the economy in general. Or maybe you just don't believe all the hype out there, and you lump Y2K together with all the other apocalyptic predictions swirling about the year 2000. It is tempting, and perhaps falsely comforting, to think that the people who created this problem are going to solve it, that the world will go on as usual, and that nothing extraordinary is going to happen in less than a year.

If you've picked up this book because you are a little worried there may be a kernel of *truth* to all the doom and gloom, and you are genuinely concerned that Y2K could end up eating your finances come the turn of the century, then congratulations. You're already ahead of the game. If you still need some convincing, what we have to say in this book will leave little room for doubt.

Come On, How Bad Could It Possibly Be?

When most people think about computer bugs, the words *inconvenience* and *delay* often come to mind. Computer problems hardly ever are associated with *crisis* let alone *disaster*. Send in the computer people, wait a few hours, and problem solved, right? After all, if Y2K is just about two little digits, how could this result in something that could shake the economy to its core?

The sad truth is, while the calculations some computers can perform in a single second would take hundreds of humans years to do, they still aren't really very *smart*. When computers encounter data anomalies, such as unrecognizable dates, they often crash, or get themselves into a loop, or start to spew garbage data.

Back in 1996, for example, computer controls at Comalco Ltd.'s smelters in Australia and New Zealand weren't programmed to recognize 1996 as a leap year. So when on December 31 they were instructed to process the three hundred sixty-*sixth* day of the year, they simply shut the system down. Parts overheated and had to be replaced at a cost of half a million dollars.[4]

The Y2K bug will result in similar date calculation problems though likely more serious and certainly more widespread than what Comalco experienced with its smelters. Y2K tests conducted at U.S. manufacturing facilities resulted in some alarming results.

Take Consolidated Paper, Inc., a company that makes high-end glossy paper for magazines and annual reports. The *Wall Street Journal* reported that the company has catalogued some 30,000 items that must be checked and that potentially need to be brought into Year 2000 compliance. Here is an excerpt from that article that illustrates the magnitude of the problem:

Dale Wroblewski steps to the controls of a giant paper cutter in the Consolidated Papers, Inc., mill here [in Wisconsin Falls] and resets the time to 11:59 p.m. and 30 seconds on Dec. 31, 1999.

Thirty seconds later, the screen goes haywire, displaying the date as 1/01/00 and spitting out a line of gibberish every second. The paper cutter continues to clatter, but Mr. Wroblewski has lost the ability to control its razor-sharp knives or the wheels that are advancing paper at a rate of almost seven feet a second.[5]

The article went on to report that Consolidated had "uncovered winders that won't wind, wrappers that won't wrap, and color adjusters that won't adjust, among other prospective problems at its eleven mills in Wisconsin and Minnesota."[6] Even in Consolidated's newest mill, which opened in 1992 at a cost of $492 million, Y2K problems abound: "One set of computers controls the flow of pulp. A second regulates the fine movements of the paper-making machines. A third minds the boiler and drive system, while a fourth continually monitors the paper as it's made, feeding back information used to adjust the other three systems." All of these systems had be checked for Y2K. The price tag on the fix? A cool out-of-pocket charge of $26 million.

The Sober Truth

The fact is, any computer or embedded microprocessor that thinks "00" means "start the century over" *will* crash or process bad data after January 1, 2000—or even sooner—unless the problem is fixed. Multiply this over the millions of at-risk systems out there, and you have a technological nightmare. This could be bad. It could be *very* bad. Computers pervade our society, and our economy is highly dependent upon information technology, as much or more than it depended on oil in 1973. Y2K will be remembered as a pivotal event in the history of technology, markets, and the global economy. Such events only occur once or twice in a lifetime. The question you should be asking yourself is whether you want to be ready for Y2K, or just another victim of it.

Many computer systems will fail

Sure, it's possible that the whole thing could be a bust—the biggest nonevent in recent history. But are you prepared to take that chance? After all, no one will know how bad Y2K will be until sometime after the stroke of midnight at the end of 1999. But if you pay attention to what the experts are saying, the damage could be extensive. And sometime in late 1999, it is *highly* likely that stock prices will move down sharply in *anticipation* of the crisis as companies and governments start admitting that they have not completed fixes on their computer systems and as the media starts to expose the dangers of Y2K.

Already, the *New York Times* is running full-page feature stories on Y2K, and CNN has begun to air a chilling series entitled "Countdown to the Millennium Bug." An ominous USA Today/Gallup Poll taken in December 1998 revealed that 16 percent of Americans intended to withdraw *all* of their money from the banks, and another 31 percent planned to withdraw a large sum of cash.[7] Just as Americans lined up at gas stations during the second oil crisis in 1979 in the *mistaken* belief that oil imports were going to dry up, the likelihood of public overreaction over Y2K cannot (and will not) be ignored. Given the swell of public interest and fear that will mount in 1999, it is hard to see how markets could *fail* to react as we draw nearer to the fateful hour.

If the resulting economic impact is as bad as the chaos resulting from the oil embargo—and stocks fall as far—we are talking about a Dow in the vicinity of the *mid-5000s*. We certainly hope Y2K will not be this bad; but the one thing we *can't* say is that something that awful has never happened before.

By the way, if you feel your portfolio is unprepared for Y2K, you're in good company. The average investor hasn't taken a hard look at how Y2K will affect the economy and his or her investments. But as the end of the millennium draws near, investors trying to stay ahead of the looming crisis are mostly left with unanswered questions. What industries and equities are at risk? How will Y2K affect earnings and share prices? Can investors take measures to protect their assets? What about interest rates and inflation, or (gulp) the risk of a global recession? And can I make money from the crisis?

What investors need to know

Without this book, to begin to answer these questions you would otherwise need to read, process, and make sense of the mountains of Y2K information out there today. You would hear everything from alarming predictions of worldwide Y2K-induced recession[8] to confident reassurances that Y2K will be little more than an after-party eco-nomic hiccup.[9] The most common refrain you would encounter is that while there will be disruptions, no one can tell you where they will likely occur or how bad they will be.[10] Small help, that. Individual investors trying to get a handle on how Y2K will affect their portfolios understandably have come away with headaches.

This book will go a long way toward easing Y2K frustration and anxiety for investors. We've gathered volumes of information from Y2K experts, industry leaders, and top economists, and distilled them down, taking out the techno-speak and the media hype. This book puts the Y2K problem into its proper perspective and provides read-ers with a simple way to understand and predict the impact of Y2K. We demystify Y2K so that individual investors are able to make informed decisions. Whether you are a cautious investor protecting your nest egg or an aggressive player hoping to multiply your assets, the facts and recommendations on Y2K investing contained in this book should prove invaluable.

But Wait—Can't They Just Fix It?

A common assumption among investors and the public at large is that all of the world's Y2K problems will be fixed in time. They won't. There is no antivirus software or debugger in existence that can do the job completely. This means that, in most cases, computer code has to be checked line by line for two-digit date references, meaning painful labor costs.

Line-by-line checking is not a simple or straightforward task. Soft-ware programs, especially on older "legacy" systems, are notoriously sloppy. The stuff programmers input is often called "spaghetti code" because of its overly complex and tangled structures. Spaghetti code frequently results from "patch and update" programming, where existing programs and software were modified piecemeal over the years to run on ever more sophisticated machines.

Add to this problem the fact that computer programmers rarely made clear when or how they were *using* date references in their pro-grams. In computing, a date or other piece of data is often given a *variable*—a symbolic name that is referred to later in the program. Pro-grammers can choose whatever variables they want. But instead of using clear variable names such as "age of borrower" or even "YR," they might use a favorite pet's name or a name of an old girlfriend. Today's debuggers, therefore, often can't for the life of them figure out what the former programmer was talking about.[11] And many of the old programmers aren't around any longer to help out. Those that *are* still working are being paid a lot of money to undo the problem they helped create years ago.

Other dates are often hidden among other data and are particularly thorny to fix. The *New York Times* ran a story covering the efforts of Public Service Electric and Gas Co. (PSE&G) to rid its millions of lines of computer code of Y2K. One anecdote reveals the difficulty of finding and repairing Y2K bugs:

> One day this summer, Mrs. Zavlyanova was inspecting a tiny 523-line segment. A special computer program had already quickly scanned all 523 lines, picking out eighteen with numbers that could be dates.
>
> One of those lines contained the name of a twenty-five-digit serial number. Suspicious, Mrs. Zavlyanova zeroed in on this segment and there it was: a millennium bug! Six of the digits in the serial number referred to a date: two for the month, two for the day, and only two for the year.
>
> Now the question was how to repair it. The utility wanted to expand the serial number to twenty-seven digits, adding two digits to represent the year. But such an expansion was not as easy as it sounded, because it would throw off the position of the other numbers. A number that was in position 15, which might have stood for, say, a customer's geographic location, would move to position 17, which the program might react to as if it refers to the meter reader's route number. So expanding the serial number could require changes to many other lines in the program. . . .
>
> "Y2K work isn't as easy as a lot of people think," said Mrs. Zavlyanova, who has on her desk a certificate praising her as a top performer. "There are all kinds of complications that come up."[12]

Even if many or even most of the Y2K bugs infesting millions of systems worldwide can be found and repaired, often the repair itself creates additional unforeseen difficulties and bugs. Some experts predict that new problems introduced by software programmers attempting to fix Y2K problems will plague companies well into the year 2000. Seemingly harmless changes (such as the one favored by PSE&G in the story above) could produce other glitches unrelated to Y2K. Industries are only now beginning to talk in terms of needing IVV programs, standing for "Independent Verification and Validation," where the fixes implemented by companies are themselves checked and in many cases fixed. The cost of this process is uncertain, but some experts have suggested that it may be around 25 percent of what has already been spent.[13]

It comes down to this: Bill Gates won't be firing any silver bullets that can kill this technological bugbear. Indeed, it has recently come to light that even venerable Microsoft is not immune from Y2K bugs. Microsoft has admitted that even its Windows 98 operating system would display the incorrect date in the year 2000 and after in certain "rare scenarios."[14]

Only dedicated, line-by-line debugging, coupled with comprehensive testing of all systems, stands a chance of eliminating Y2K from a company's computers and automated processes. For a lot of reasons you'll read about in this book, many companies are not going to make it in time.

So Are You Saying the Sky Is Falling?

You may already have read or heard some Y2K predictions that are truly apocalyptic in nature: planes falling out of the skies, nationwide blackouts, food riots, and even nuclear missiles launching accidentally. Survivalist supply stores have had a banner year, in part due to millennium bug hype.[15] In some ways, the exaggeration of the crisis has undermined legitimate calls for decisive action from industry and the government. We can't say with *absolute certainty* that the doomsayers are flat-out wrong. In our view, however, most of the hysteria around Y2K is overblown, largely unsupported, and often irresponsible. If everyone bought into them, the ensuing panic would be worse than the problem.

Doom and gloom— not helpful

Don't get us wrong. There *will* be Y2K-related disruptions, ranging from the inconvenient (elevator malfunctions, security systems locking out workers) to the worrisome (bank errors, late or missing government checks) to the potentially life-threatening (hospital equipment failures, overburdened air traffic control). People will no doubt be talking a lot about their personal travails with Y2K. Like El Niño and the O.J. trial, Y2K will be the subject of choice in broadcast and print media, the buzz around water coolers, and the target of comedians' monologues for many months as January 1, 2000, comes and goes.

We are also certain that a lot of money will be made and lost as a result of Y2K. The price tag on the Y2K fix alone may top *$600 billion worldwide*, with another potentially more massive cost in post-Y2K litigation. The Gartner Group, a respected Y2K consulting firm, places the total cost somewhere between $1 and $2 *trillion*—or around $300 for every person on the planet.[16] There will be business failures, and in some sectors the situation will be quite chaotic. Eventually, though, the situation will right itself, and computers will once again be our silent assistants rather than our lurking assassins. But for an unpredictable period of time, investors who have the foresight to protect their assets and bet against hard-hit sectors will be thankful they took action.

There are, naturally, those critics who pooh-pooh the notion that Y2K will have a serious impact on markets and the economy. Some suggest that the gravity of the situation is being exaggerated by unscrupulous consultants trying to scare corporate America into throwing money at a nonexistent problem. We only wish they were right, that all of the money and time being spent is a monumental waste of resources. In general, however, markets and major companies do not make irrational economic choices, especially on such a scale and in so universal a manner. To our knowledge, not a single chief information officer of any major corporation has come forward and said, "What's the big fuss all about? We don't have a Y2K problem in our systems." To the contrary, most CIOs admit that they wish they could have started solving their Y2K problems earlier, and that the scope of the problem weren't so large.

So if others scoff at your interest in and concern over Y2K, remember that you are not alone in your preparations. Every major U.S. company with any sense is concerned and is taking action.

The Glitching Hour?

A common misperception is that the Y2K problems will occur worldwide *on* January 1, 2000, starting in Australia which, due to the
arrangement of world time zones, Australia will be the first continent
to pass into the year 2000, before hitting like a wave in Asia, Europe,
and then the Americas. The fact is, glitches relating to the millennium
bug will precede the changeover to 2000, and investors should not be
caught off guard.

Y2K problems actually began to crop up years ago. For example,
warranty claims on cars sold in 1996 were rejected at one company
when computers insisted that the four-year or higher
warranty periods in fact had expired in "00"—nearly
100 years ago. One U.S. television network had to
rewrite its long-term advertising and associated air-
time scheduling software because it couldn't accept
programming slotted beyond 1999. An insurance company even
began to bill newborns for insurance coverage as early as 1977, when
the computers examined twenty-three-year prepaid policies and concluded that further premium payments should be collected starting
in "00"—or 1900. Talk about a lapsed policy.[17]

*Y2K problems
are already
cropping up*

A survey conducted in April 1998 by Cap Gemini America noted
that 37 percent of the nation's largest corporations had by that time
already experienced some kind of Y2K-related failure.[18] By the end of
1998, Cap Gemini reported that *most* survey respondents had experienced some kind of Y2K failure, and that *98 percent* expected more
failures through 1999.[19] And early failures of some systems on January
1, 1999, due to computers' confusion over how to interpret "99"
(which means "end of file" to some systems) may be a precursor of
what we can expect on a much larger scale in 2000. Taxi meters in Singapore stopped working at noon. Some defibrillators and patient
monitors used at hospitals began to calculate the date and time incor-
rectly, raising the specter of misdiagnoses and legal liability. Swedish
airport security computers failed at midnight, fouling up the issuance
of temporary passports.[20] These problems are concededly minor and
easily remedied, but the fact the date-related foul-ups are already
occurring is quite troubling—something akin to finding out that
indeed there is a fault line running directly beneath your home.

It is clear, then, that businesses will spend much of the rest of

1999—and of course all of 2000 and perhaps beyond—dealing with Y2K-related foul-ups, and that the likely impact of Y2K on markets and economies will become more apparent the closer we get to the end of the millennium.[21]

We would not be surprised in the least, for example, if the following or similar headlines appeared in late 1999:

- FAA: Y2K Will Ground Thirty Percent of Flights
- Feds Move to Shore Up Bank Reserves
- Regulators Force Preemptive Shutdown of Nuclear Plants Over Y2K Worries
- State Hospitals Told No Medicaid Payments till Mid-2000
- Yen Collapses As Extent of Japan's Millennium Bug Problems Revealed
- Gold Breaks $400/oz. as 2000 Nears

While these hypothetical headlines lack some of the drama and spectacle of those proffered by Y2K doomsayers, for investors these kinds of news stories would be nothing short of bombshells. When you adjust your investment portfolio, remember that business and markets are forward-thinking, and computer systems such as accounting and planning software are designed with that in mind. Business and consumer expectations will shift as the extent of computer problems and lack of industry preparedness becomes more apparent. Smart investors will also be forward-thinking and adjust their portfolios long before events overtake the market. This book can't be a crystal ball, but it can offer a commonsense guide, alerting the investor to danger signs and opportunities arising out of Y2K within critical business systems. Now is the time to assess and to act.

Another common misperception is that all of the Y2K problems that haven't made themselves known in 1999 will occur on January 1, 2000, making that a day that will not soon be forgotten. Most experts predict, however, that while the actual day of January 1, 2000, will see scattered occurrences of Y2K, most glitches will become evident sometime later as programs fail or bad data accumulates and is discovered. We expect that, just as the world breathes a collective sigh of relief after it is assumed the worst is past, two or three weeks later we all will experience the true, potentially awful impact of the Millennium Bug.

A Simple Question

If you're like most small investors, you have a lot of your money in one or more mutual funds, either through direct investments or through a 401K or other pension plan. Have you ever examined those quarterly statements you get from your fund manager—the ones that describe in detail the industries and areas in which your mutual fund is invested? If you're like most investors, you get the brochure in the mail and promptly toss it.

The next time you get one of these statements, *read it carefully.* Exactly where is your money invested? A mutual fund is typically diversified across U.S. equities and bonds. It might have around 60 percent in stocks, another 30 percent in bonds, and the rest in cash, looking like this:

Asset Allocation

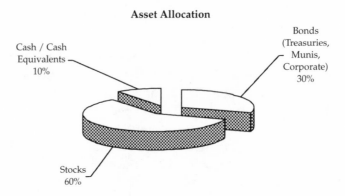

And among stocks, a portfolio allocation usually is diversified among sectors. It might look something like this:

Sample Diversified Equity Portfolio

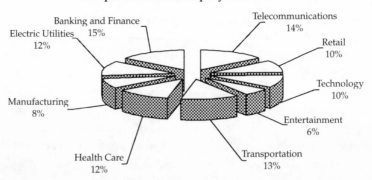

Look okay to you? Well, after you're through with this book, you would *never* stay invested in a fund like this. This book will show you why sectors like transportation, health care, utilities, banking, telecommunication, and even municipal bonds should be avoided by Y2K-minded investors, at least until after the crisis is past. If you want some specific ideas on the kinds of portfolios you can construct to prepare for Y2K, you'll find them at the end of this book in chapters 10 and 11.

Our Plug on the Bug

Our approach doesn't dwell on individual companies' efforts to beat the bug, though this is certainly an important factor. Rather, we believe the real focus should be on how Y2K will impact the *complex business systems* in which companies participate. Throughout this book, we'll talk a lot about these complex business systems as we examine some key at-risk industries. We'll show why certain systems are far more vulnerable to Y2K than others, and we'll give you practical advice on where your money should and definitely should *not* be when Y2K strikes.

And strike it will. We predict Y2K will have a serious if not devastating impact on certain sectors of the economy, with spillover effects on every other sector. We commend you as an investor for taking the first step of considering advance measures. Armed with the information and commonsense advice from this book, investors can and should get through the Y2K crisis safely, and in some cases even make a handsome profit.

No Company Is an Island

A lot of attention has been paid to the Y2K-compliance efforts of major corporations. In plain English, "Y2K-compliance efforts" means what is being done to debug systems by fixing two-digit date formats in computer code, as well as replacing faulty equipment and computer chips. Some investors and analysts (including us) have spent countless hours poring over public SEC filings of major public companies to try to determine who leads and who lags in Y2K compliance spending. When all their research is complete, these people might *wrongly* conclude that companies with the right level of money, foresight, and nose-to-the-grindstone debugging and testing will weather the millennial storm. Surveys have shown that investors appear *more* likely to move their money to companies that have demonstrated that their *own* systems are Y2K compliant, perhaps in the mistaken belief that no amount of huffing and puffing by the big, bad Y2K wolf will blow down well-built Y2K houses. We wish the problem were that simple.

While it is clear that many businesses have done a remarkable job preparing for Y2K—and would have faced certain disaster had they done nothing—there unfortunately are limits to what a single company in today's interdependent business world can do. *This is because Y2K is not really something any one company can fix for itself.*

Most companies are used to dealing with their own problems. They have systems in place to supervise, check, and recheck their own operation failures. When serious problems arise with outside vendors and suppliers, companies have always had the option of taking their business elsewhere, or as a last resort, to settle the matter in court.

The Y2K problem is different. To deal effectively with Y2K, a company must not only turn a critical eye *inward*, it also must look *outward* at all of its business relationships and then be sure every partner, every link in the system, is fixing its own problems and is also "Y2K-compliant," or as close to compliant as possible. In some cases, such as where the "noncompliant" partner is the government, or where there are thousands upon thousands of independent noncompliant suppliers, this may be next to impossible.

Not nearly enough attention has been paid to the threat Y2K poses to companies' complex business systems. A company earning praise from analysts, the media, and government oversight committees for its Y2K-compliance efforts has usually demonstrated comprehensive and well-organized efforts at solving its *internal* Y2K problems. It started by building a Y2K crisis response team. It then hired hundreds of programmers to pore over millions of lines of computer code to find and fix any pesky two-digit date references. It has assessed and tested all "mission-critical" computers and equipment with embedded microchips. It has finished upgrading or phasing out any internal system that might go haywire starting January 1, 2000. It has spent tens or even hundreds of millions of dollars and is now resting comfortably on its laurels. Such a company, while admittedly well ahead of most others around the globe, might then assure its shareholders that it is on top of the crisis and that investors have nothing to fear. If you happen to be one of these shareholders, *don't* be lulled into complacency.

More than anything, investors should understand that Y2K is an insidious, fundamental assault upon the complex business systems we describe in this book. Whether a company is a Fortune 500 conglomerate or a mom-and-pop corner store, it will have frequent, necessary contact with other parties. Customers, suppliers, vendors, distributors, and shippers are the obvious contacts. Companies also rely daily upon utilities, local and long-distance telephone companies, and financial institutions to provide uninterrupted service. Businesses further count on government to enforce laws and regulations, approve new drugs, make our skies safe for flying, collect our taxes, and pay entitlements to millions. Further, companies depend increasingly on the global nature of business to tap into new markets, to provide greater choices in vendors and suppliers, and to benefit from cheaper labor and imports. The true danger from Y2K is that it threatens to disrupt these interactions and all the economic benefits that companies derive from them.

There are many links in today's complex business chains

This book will provide investors with an in-depth analysis of the kinds of complex business system failures we think have a high chance of occurring as a result of Y2K. In today's world, such failures translate directly into higher costs, lower profits, and depressed share prices. Where the risk of complex business system failures are significant, we will show how conservative investors can avoid getting burned, and how more aggressive investors stand to benefit.

The Pain Ain't the Same

One inescapable reality is that Y2K will impact certain business systems much more profoundly than others. Our first task in this book is to identify sectors that are most at risk from Y2K. Of course, the easiest and perhaps most basic question is what preparations, if any, are under way within a sector to diminish Y2K's impact. Sectors that are far behind others in their Y2K fixes are going to be thrashed by investors when their lack of readiness becomes more apparent. Thus, at a minimum, investors should be aware of what sectors are Y2K laggards.

But our inquiry can't stop there. Most at-risk sectors—with a few notable exceptions—are doing what they can to beat the bug. To make determinations of Y2K vulnerability among these sectors, we identify those sectors where Y2K will likely cause chaos *beyond* the nuisance of malfunctioning elevators, erroneous billing, and other operations headaches, or where the frequency of such commonplace problems actually threatens to fundamentally affect core operations. The vulnerability could arise from a reliance on what are called just-in-time operations, the presence of critical bottlenecks in operations, a need for extremely conservative procedures due to safety concerns, or the tendency of the sector to receive more than its share of public scrutiny, just to name a few causes.

From there, the question becomes more difficult, involving an analysis of the Y2K risk to complex business systems within a given industry. We have two simple but important points to make. First, business systems at major companies are nearly completely automated, and human intervention is not only rare, but considered undesirable. Second, business systems are increasingly interdependent, both within and across sectors.

We all know that business systems over the past few decades have moved decisively toward computer automation as the norm rather than the exception. The transition has been so universal that we hardly notice how dependent we have become on computers as we approach the end of the millennium. Business today is transacted electronically, usually without any need for cumbersome and mistake-prone human intervention. The astonishing speed and computerization of commerce has permitted the development of just-in-time operations, which allow companies to reduce inventories while streamlining production. Automation has also allowed firms to slash the number of jobs while increasing the productivity of the remaining workers. Entire new industries have arisen to support our computer-based business infrastructure.

Y2K RISK FACTOR
Automation

On top of automation, businesses have also learned to springboard off of other businesses' efficiencies and competitive advantages. This is how interdependence begins. Carmakers farm out the manufacturing of parts to thousands of smaller, more efficient shops. National supermarket chains import fresh fruit from growers in South America during winter. Phone companies and cable companies merge to bring the Internet and telecommunications to us through our television sets. Mail order companies sell their customer lists to other catalogers, and we get all that junk mail. The result is an ever increasing web of connectivity and a greater sophistication and interdependence among businesses.

Y2K RISK FACTOR

Interdependence

Automation and interdependence have permitted many companies to do more with less, in many cases meaning increased earnings and soaring stock prices. Companies today, particularly large corporations, are creatures whose lifelines are computerized, mind-bogglingly interdependent business systems. Indeed, as we discuss in chapter 1, computer automation and business interdependence have been the fuel for the economic engine of growth in the United States. But sever the connections, and the engine grinds to a halt.

As we show, some sectors are clearly more automated than others. They are therefore more at the mercy of vendors, suppliers, shippers, and various service providers. More ominously, some sectors are completely reliant on the government to get its act together. Others have extensive global operations that are at risk from inaction overseas. In such cases, no matter how much effort companies in these sectors put into Y2K compliance, all their work could be for nothing because forces beyond their control may still bring about economic ruin.

We have identified key sectors of concern to investors and broken them down into chapters 2 through 6, covering air transport, health care, electric utilities, banking, and telecommunications, respectively. We assess the danger Y2K poses to share prices and earnings of publicly traded companies in these sectors, as well as pointing out specific Y2K risks within each sector that lead us to especially disfavor it.

Chapters 7 and 8 discuss the global Y2K crisis and the larger economic outlook under Y2K, and chapter 9 provides readers with some ideas for opportunities in sectors that could actually benefit from the Y2K crisis.

Chapters 10 and 11 set out our investment strategies. We provide risk-adverse readers with investment strategies for *protecting assets* from the devastation of Y2K while showing risk takers how to turn crisis into opportunity by *building wealth* (perhaps *significant* wealth) during the Y2K crisis.

Read Our Book, But Think for Yourself

The Y2K situation is unpredictable in many ways, and no investment guide can give 100 percent assurances. But in our view, it is possible to weigh the *relative* risks of disruptions across various industries and make investment decisions based on those risks. Could we be wrong? Of course. The important thing to remember is that we think the *chances* of disruptions or even a meltdown in the industries we've identified are higher than in other industries, and investors should— and will—take that into account.

One final word: We recognize that each small investor's situation is different with respect to investment goals and acceptable levels of risk, so we can't give you specific investment advice on when or how much to buy, sell, or hold. We provide some sample portfolios and investing strategies at the end of this book, but only you know what use you should make of the information contained in these pages.

Only a handful of people could have known about the 1973 OPEC oil embargo before it happened. With Y2K, investors can prepare themselves and their portfolios for the crisis. There is still time. Every investor *knows* that Y2K is out there, just around the bend. This book gives you the second piece of the puzzle by explaining the likely effects of Y2K and providing investment strategies. But only you can complete the plan and take appropriate measures to protect your assets and build wealth through the Y2K crisis.

ONE

THE MISSING NAIL: HOW Y2K THREATENS COMPLEX BUSINESS SYSTEMS

For want of a nail, the shoe was lost
For want of the shoe, the horse was lost
For want of the horse, the rider was lost
For want of the rider, the battle was lost
For want of the battle, the kingdom was lost
All for the want of a nail.

—Proverb, attributed to Benjamin Franklin

When 3,400 UAW Local 659 workers walked out of their Flint, Michigan, metal stamping plant on June 5, 1998, they knew what the fallout for General Motors would be. The Flint plant produces doors, hoods, fenders, and engine cradles used at more than half of GM's North American plants. By striking, the Flint workers knew that they would deprive GM of some of its most basic parts and that it would not be long before production at other GM plants would grind to a standstill. Indeed, it was predicted that plants from Fort Wayne, Indiana, to Arlington, Texas, would face parts shortages within four days and would begin to send thousands of workers home.[1]

One week after the start of the strike, eight assembly lines in fact had halted completely and three other parts plants partially shut down. More than twenty-five thousand workers were idled across the United States. And that was just the beginning. After that week the situation started to really spiral out of control.

On June 11, GM received the bad news of another work stoppage,

1

this one at its nearby Delphi Flint East plant. The Delphi plant complex makes electronic instrument clusters consisting of speedometers, tachometers, fuel gauges, and other parts. It also makes engine components, such as spark plugs, fuel pumps, oxygen sensors, fuel and oil filters, air meters, and cruise control parts. These components are used in nearly every vehicle made by GM. The two strikes combined to make the production of cars and trucks next to impossible. GM management was determined not to give way, and it dug in for a long, bitter summer.

By July, twenty-six of GM's twenty-nine assembly plants and over one hundred of its auto parts plants in North America and Singapore were out of operation, crippling about 95 percent of GM's total production and affecting more than 160,000 workers.[2] Shortages of models in dealerships across the United States ensued. At the height of the work stoppage, some 193,000 workers were affected. In short, the workers in two plants in Flint, Michigan, succeeded in halting nearly all of the operations of the world's largest automaker. When the strike finally ended on July 29—after over seven weeks—the cost to the company was a whopping $2 billion in lost production.[3]

For Want of a Nail

So what does all this have to do with Y2K? The Flint strikes are a good example of how a failure at one point in a complex business system—the proverbial "missing nail"—can result in a cascade of failure throughout the system. This is the true, if less visible, threat from Y2K. Like the Flint strikes, Y2K's effect will be felt by entire business systems, slowing and in some cases completely halting supply, production, distribution, and sales for entire companies.

Unlike the Flint strikes, however, Y2K will not go after single, isolated points in a manufacturing system. GM was ultimately able to restore production because the break in the supply chain could be contained in the two plants in Michigan. When those strikes were resolved, the system swung back into operation. To round out the proverb, GM was able to find a spare nail to tack the horseshoe back on the horse's hoof in time for its rider to go to battle to save the kingdom. But what if the problem wasn't just with a single nail in the horseshoe? What if the horseshoe itself was still in inventory or lost in transit, the horse was feeble from lack of feed, the tannery had sent the wrong size saddle, and half of the soldiers had no ammunition? How would GM have kept from losing the kingdom? This is the question that Y2K presents to industries relying heavily on interdependent manufacturing systems, which are at risk of multiple failures.

We Aren't Talking Dominos

When people talk about the domino effect, they usually picture a single line of dominos, with the first one tipping over to start the whole process going. One failure leads to another failure which leads to another. In reality, manufacturing system failures don't always occur in straight lines. Usually, a single failure in a complex system will cause several other failures to occur at around the same time. Picture a ring instead of a line, a water drop on a still pond causing a ripple effect.

Even this doesn't tell the whole story, however. When the first Flint strike occurred, within a week not only car assembly plants but also other parts plants were affected. This is because when the assembly plants lacked doors, fenders, and engine cradles, they couldn't make finished cars, so they could no longer make use of other parts. Rather than having these parts pile up in inventory, GM made the decision to slow or idle other parts plants.

So, instead of a ripple on a pond, we have something more like a detonation, where a single well-placed explosion can cause a major cascade effect. As demolition experts know, however, if one pack of dynamite can cause one side of a building to go, two or more packs can bring the whole thing down in a cloud of dust. This is what we call the "multiple detonation" effect.

The multiple detonation effect can be seen in the GM strike example. When workers from the first Flint plant struck, this caused disruptions in eight out of the twenty-nine GM assembly plants within the first week. When the second Flint plant shut down, the damage increased threefold and spread to nearly all of GM's plants. While GM had some other sources for the parts in short supply—for example, instrument clusters made in Reynosa, Mexico, and other manufacturers of spark plugs across the United States—the parts were insufficient in number or variety to keep GM operations running.[4]

So when people talk about the Y2K domino effect, think instead of multiple Y2K detonations—lots of little bombs going off all over the system. Then ask yourself how long it will take the structure to collapse completely.

Ghosts in the Machines

GM and other carmakers know that if Y2K went unfixed, it would be as if poltergeists were running the plants rather than GM foremen. Y2K problems would affect several, if not all, of GM's primary assembly sites simultaneously, snarling production with a litany of problems from the silly to the severe. Hard to believe? When GM ran initial tests in its worldwide facilities, technicians found Y2K problems in every facility. In some cases robotic devices simply froze up.[5] When Chrysler ran a test at its Sterling Heights Assembly Plant, turning the clocks forward to midnight of December 31, 1999, the security system promptly kicked in, locking everyone inside the plant for several hours.[6]

Here's an example of what might happen within a distributed manufacturing system like GM's. Let's suppose that the Delco Electronics plant in Delnosa, Mexico, sends a critical shipment of components to the Chevy Lumina plant in Oshawa, Ontario. When the parts are received, a computer reads a bar code on the parts which, due to oversight, is not Y2K-compliant because it still uses two digits to represent the current year. The computer is looking for parts for the new Lumina models rolling out in the fall of 2000, but the delivered Delco parts register as "old" parts (in fact, 100 years old). Without explaining why, the computer refuses to accept the shipment, and a clerk in shipping and receiving dutifully repacks them and sends them back to Mexico with a note saying they are the wrong parts.

Y2K will impact distributed manufacturing systems

When the parts get back to Mexico, a clerk shelves the components as defective and sends out a new shipment. The same problem occurs in Oshawa, and the parts are returned. This time the clerk manually checks the parts and sends a note insisting that they are correct. This goes back and forth a couple more times. By this time, the Delnosa plant has received rejects from across the country, and the supply of these components is critically low. In fact, this problem is not an isolated one since the supplies of hundreds of other parts have run low, and in desperation the Oshawa plant curtails production sharply while it tries to sort out the mess. This in turn causes suppliers of parts for Chevy Luminas across the country to shut or slow down, and, well, you get the picture.

Sound comical? Businesses aren't laughing. This example is actually a real one, based on the experience of British food retailer Marks and Spencer, whose orders for corned beef with an expiration date of 2000 went back and forth between its stores and the vendor so many times that the astonished Marks and Spencer wound up with no corned beef on its shelves and yet tons of perfectly good corned beef were destroyed.[7]

This is why GM is spending over $500 million to solve its Y2K problems.[8] Indeed, GM has taken the highly unusual step of offering its Y2K consultant a *bonus* of $75 million if EDS can ensure that GM's operations are "capable of continued operation before, on, and after January 1, 2000, without causing significant business disruption."[9]

While GM's internal Y2K nightmares are significant and costly, the true wild card lies with its independent parts suppliers, which number near 100,000 and often lack the resources to perform the kind of Y2K fixes required. According to GM's information systems spokesman, the company will have to check and test "interchange interfaces" (also called "electronic data interchange") with suppliers at 40,000 critical supply sites and find "workarounds" if it can't be sure the suppliers' programs are Y2K-compliant.[10] In plain terms, GM is worried that its computers won't be able to communicate electronically with those of its vendors, and therefore some sort of backup plan will be necessary.

But even if such "workarounds" succeed, this means only that GM business systems can continue to include noncompliant suppliers in the production chain for the time being. It does *not* mean that those suppliers will actually be able to provide the needed parts, as suppliers may face their own set of Y2K nightmares. From this alone it is clear that there are a lot of nails that could be found wanting when GM fights the Y2K battle.

Interdependence Exposed

The GM example underscores our theme in this book, that U.S. companies have become entirely *dependent* on interdependency, and that this has left them particularly susceptible to Y2K-related failures. GM was vulnerable to the Flint plant strikes because of its own success. As part of an aggressive long-term strategy to lower costs and increase productivity, GM, like other automakers, has gradually decentralized manufacturing operations to take advantage of regional efficiencies. It has contracted with tens of thousands of small, independent vendors to provide parts and services. It has automated as much of its manufacturing and business systems as possible. Under constant pressure from shareholders, it has slashed jobs where possible to improve its bottom line. As a result, GM is no doubt now a leaner, more competitive company than before the computer revolution and the exponential rise of business interdependence.

But GM's new, streamlined manufacturing model now contains dangerous bottlenecks, as the strikes at the parts plants in Flint demonstrate. GM must be prepared to deal with disruptions in supply at key junctures or face system-wide shutdowns, since failure at critical supply points such as Flint means complete systems failure for all of GM.[11] The Flint situation can be compared to a clog in an artery, in a system where every major blood vessel must function properly for the organism to remain healthy.[12]

Y2K will result in clogged business arteries

This phenomenon isn't limited to GM, of course. Specialization, complexity, and interaction—the engines of economic growth—always mean greater susceptibility to disruption. "There isn't quite as much forgiveness in the economy," notes Stanford University economist Paul Romer, "but the trade-off is well worth making."[13]

Unfortunately, GM's experience with labor strikes don't really qualify it to deal with a problem like Y2K. Even the most complex systems tend to break down only in single, easily discerned ways. Neither GM nor any other company has ever had to deal with the possibility of multiple failures across all systems. Y2K's uniquely maddening quality is that, while the reason for glitches throughout a distributed manufacturing system may be the same (i.e., the inability of the computer to distinguish between 1900 and 2000), the *effects* of each glitch will be decidedly unique and will require individual attention.

Where's the Upside?

Some analysts suggest that examples like the GM strike actually indicate that Y2K will not cause significant loss of share value in major companies, since GM has shown that it can survive disruptions in its production, even on as large a scale as the Flint shutdowns. Y2K, the argument goes, can be likened to a one-time charge against earnings associated with a layoff of excess workers, an acquisition of another company, or the cost of automation upgrades.

While there is some merit to this argument, it misses an essential point. The high costs of restructuring, acquisition, or automation are acceptable to Wall Street precisely because there is a payoff in increased long-term productivity and efficiency and lower long-term costs. The perverse consequence of Y2K is that companies that have expended large amounts of money in the past to automate and integrate their systems will be hardest hit, while receiving little to nothing by way of increased efficiency or lower costs in return. In short, Y2K is almost pure maintenance. There is not much upside.

Wall Street clearly supported GM's get-tough policy toward the United Auto Workers (UAW), keeping GM's stock price relatively stable—a 5.6 percent dip over the course of the strike— *At least you* because most analysts concurred that a successful reso- *can get tough* lution of the strike would mean GM could continue its *with strikers* long march toward manufacturing automation, increased outsourcing of parts to independent shops, and a decrease in the number of workers on the payroll.[14] In other words, the cost of the bloodying fight was worth the prize, which to GM management was the sustained development and use of cheaper, faster, and proven successful business systems that could replace fallible, less productive, and strike-prone humans.

But what if the prize itself became the root of the problem? What if these same business systems, gleaming bright and fully automatic, were the *cause* of a precipitous drop in production? What would Wall Street say about a sharp rise in costs and an equally sharp drop in earnings brought about by the same systems that were supposed to buoy profits and productivity? Analysts may be asking these very questions when Y2K begins its full-scale assault upon interdependent systems.

We'll Do Things the Old-Fashioned Way

In the most serious cases, Y2K may so critically impact business systems that it will cause some companies to completely abandon the benefits they have enjoyed from automation and interdependence.

A return to manual operations?
Many companies foolishly assume that if the system crashes, they can "go back to paper" or "do things by hand" again. The problem is, going back to the days before computers ran everything usually means hiring back the people that companies were able to lay off in downsizing. There simply isn't a good way to measure the economic cost of hiring back this many people, just to try to do what a company used to accomplish with a lot fewer hands. Where would they find these people? Where would they put them?

Other companies, whose own Y2K compliance efforts are more or less as comprehensive as can be expected, believe they can erect Y2K fortresses—a kind of cordon sanitaire—to protect their systems against the noncompliant barbarians outside the walls. Again, this is tantamount to surrendering the hard-won benefits of interdependence gained over the last twenty years. If a company chooses simply not to do business with noncompliant vendors, it must either make up the difference itself or find new vendors. Inevitably, this will drive up costs, since the number of Y2K-compliant vendors will inevitably be smaller, perhaps markedly so.

It's A Question of Risk

The sad reality is that companies can't go back to how things were without significant—perhaps insurmountable—costs. We predict Y2K will cause a shake-out among businesses, ruthlessly punishing the unprepared, the interdependent, and the terminally automated.

Naturally, there will be some companies that are able to muddle through the crisis with only a minimum of disruption to manufacturing operations. A few companies won't have to sacrifice much in the way of their gains from prior investments in automation and decentralization of production, either because they are lucky or because their partners, vendors, and customers are all relatively Y2K bug free.

But a smart investor looks at major trends and probabilities and rarely bets against them. When Y2K strikes, do you want your money tied up with companies whose existence is dependent on the error-free functioning of complex manufacturing systems? Companies whose very strategy for profitability has been to automate and disperse every aspect of production? Companies that have already shown they are vulnerable, even from a single, isolated break in the routine?

Getting the JIT-ters: The UPS Strike of 1997

The Flint strikes demonstrate how a break in the supply chain for key components can shut down production at other plants in a matter of a few days. Like other industrial leaders, GM had come to rely heavily upon just-in-time delivery of parts as a way to reduce costly inventories. JIT operations are undoubtedly the direct offspring of the automation and business systems revolution of the past two decades. The growth of JIT processes has spawned whole new industries promising overnight deliveries of letters, packages, supplies, and parts. It has also left these same industries—and those that depend on them—highly vulnerable to breakdowns in business systems.

The U.S. experienced a nationwide taste of the crippling effect of a system failure on JIT-dependent businesses during the United Parcel Service strike of 1997. In our view, the UPS strike provides a useful model and a small-scale precursor for how Y2K might affect JIT systems in the year 2000.

On August 4, 1997, with only a few days' notice, approximately 185,000 UPS employees walked off their jobs, leaving only UPS managers to handle the estimated twelve million parcels and letters processed daily by the company. According to a UPS spokesperson, this amounted to about 5 percent of the U.S. gross national product simply not moving.[15] Other carriers—such as Federal Express and Airborne Express—quickly proved incapable of handling all of the extra load, as their commitments necessarily were with their existing customers.

Catalog businesses with mail order deliveries were among the first to feel the impact. Within that industry, the specialty food catalogers—those most dependent on JIT deliveries—were among the hardest hit, when food went undelivered and was left spoiling in UPS warehouses.

Take the case of Clambake Celebrations, operating out of Cape Cod, Massachusetts. That company had shipped some $15,000 worth of orders over the weekend before the strike, and when the food was stranded, it was a total loss. Company president Jo-Von Tucker made the decision to stop all shipments. Customers

Information technology business operations suffer first and hardest

cursed and cried foul. Those who had ordered for special occasions were sorely disappointed. As the strike dragged on, Tucker began to substitute more costly but enduring items such as lobsters for the more perishable steamers and mussels. The substitutions were expensive, and her shipping costs went up. She and other food catalogers were understandably concerned that they might not be able to endure a prolonged strike entailing limited shipments, slow delivery, restricted product lists, and the financial risk of spoilage.[16]

Hospitals were also scrambling to make do. Many found that basic supplies—such as catheter trays, IV sets, blood plasma, and pharmaceuticals—were stranded somewhere in the pipeline.[17] Perishable medications—such as certain IV antibiotics—were at particular risk. Fortunately, the effect on hospital care, while tangible, was somewhat offset by UPS's policy (and the agreement of other major carriers) to prioritize shipments of critical hospital supplies.

Other effects of the strike, while not life-threatening, caused widespread inconvenience, delays, and economic hardship. For example, schools opening for the fall semester found they lacked textbooks. Simon and Schuster on average ships 34 million college textbooks and some 273 million other books annually to K–12 schools, libraries, and general bookstores, with a sizable percentage going by UPS.[18] Its busiest months are August and December, prior to the start of school semesters, but for many schools, the books would not arrive in time if the strike were to continue.

Businesses began to lay off employees as they realized they were unable to ship products, as shipping costs for what they *could* get out rose dramatically, and as losses from undelivered time-sensitive shipments began to mount.[19] Vendors were unable to get products into warehouses for the fall season. Small businesses were especially susceptible to loss of daily deliveries and shipments, and in the course of the strike, some six hundred of them reported going out of business as a result.[20]

Fortunately, most businesses were able to get by with only modest pain from the temporary drop in delivery volume for goods. After an initial strain, other delivery companies and the U.S. Postal Service were able to take up some of the extra demand. The strike itself proved short-lived—a total of just fifteen days. Soon afterward, the wheels of commerce began to turn again in the JIT delivery business.

Y2K and JIT Operations

Unlike a strike at a single major carrier like UPS, Y2K threatens to cut the legs out from under JIT operations by attacking every vulnerable point in the system. This includes computer programs that track the status of orders, hand-held bar code readers of delivery staff, embedded chips on the assembly and packaging lines of vendors, and even the air traffic system that manages the air cargo planes of the carriers. The trouble with JIT operations is that they are only as fast as their slowest component. The system must literally run like clockwork to make deliveries on time. In other words, it won't matter if Federal Express has wiped out all its Y2K problems and is able to internally process all its shipments on time if its planes are stuck in Hong Kong because a malfunction in the baggage handling computers has delayed air traffic by days. (Lest this example seem far-fetched, it is based on an actual crisis, as we discuss later in this chapter.)

Under Y2K, businesses accustomed to JIT deliveries will need to make significant allowances for likely delays. Consumers will have to do without the reliability of having their packages delivered absolutely and positively overnight. Companies that stake their very existence upon JIT deliveries may face the cold reality that, until the Y2K bug is eradicated, commerce simply doesn't operate at that speed anymore, and they could well go out of business.

In our view, if Y2K becomes infamous for any single woe, it will be for *delays*. When a computer malfunctions and an order is delayed, it requires a live human to track down the problem and correct it. Anyone who has ever had a package or letter lost in the system can imagine what would happen if tens of thousands of tracking errors occurred in the system every day, or if (heaven forbid) the system had to fall back to manual operations.

But our dependence on error-free, JIT delivery goes beyond a simple appetite for overnight letters and fresh specialty foods. JIT delivery has reduced and in some cases eliminated the need for expensive warehousing or duplication of parts for manufacturers. A loss of faith in JIT dependability brought on by Y2K failures would lead many companies to stock up on essential supplies and parts, in part reversing the efficiencies in inventorying so hard-won over the years. Because the health and growth of the economy is a direct function not only of how much is produced, but of *how quickly* and *how often* what is produced changes hands, it is not hard to see how a drop in the availability of JIT delivery would lead to a slowdown in the economy as a whole.

Silence From the Skies

The GM and UPS strikes show how production or service shutdowns in one part of a business system can cause a system-wide meltdown when certain levels of business interdependencies are achieved. When a glitch occurs in a technologically sensitive system, however, the effects are often instantaneous and even more widespread. A recent, vivid example of this phenomenon occurred when a single satellite positioned high over the United States spun out of control, cutting off service for millions of pager customers and causing other satellite-dependent systems to crash.

On Tuesday, May 19, 1998, at 6:18 P.M. EDT, the spacecraft control processor onboard PanAmSat's Galaxy IV satellite experienced "an anomaly" which caused it to begin to rotate and lose its fixed orientation relative to earth, according to PanAmSat's press release issued the following day. Apparently, the automatic switch-to-backup system also failed, and the satellite, which had been launched in 1993, spun hopelessly out of orbit.

The satellite outage knocked out service to nearly 90 percent of pager users in the United States.[21] This translates into about 36 to 40.5

million users affected, according to PageNet, the nation's largest service provider.[22] Hospitals were the most seriously impacted, as they typically utilize pagers to contact doctors in the event of emergencies. Some doctors stayed overnight at hospitals in case they were needed, and hospitals resorted to alternative methods—including old-fashioned loudspeakers—to summon surgeons to operating rooms.[23]

In addition to silencing the pagers, the satellite failure cut off transmissions for some broadcasters, including the first transmission of that night's CBS evening news program, the Warner Brothers Network, and National Public Radio. "When our feed went down, we paged the manager of our twenty-four-hour classical music program, but he of course never got it," chuckled one public radio programming director in Minnesota. Most broadcasters were able to reroute their systems through other satellites, phone lines, or, in the case of NPR, through live Internet audio feeds.[24]

Also affected were investors relying on real-time stock market data from Data Transmission Network Corp. and Bonneville Communications, which both reported breaks in their service.[25] Most television weather broadcasts were unable to show viewers their standard moving weather maps and resorted to downloading still images off the Internet.[26] Seventy affiliates of the Network Indiana radio network lost that Tuesday's basketball playoff game between the Indiana Pacers and the Chicago Bulls.[27] Many Powerball lottery players worried about missing the next day's record $175 million drawing when live broadcasts from over eighty-eight stations had to be rerouted.[28] Self-service gas pumps equipped with automatic credit card readers were knocked off-line, including around 5,400 of Chevron's 7,700 units.[29] Banking networks and automatic teller machines across the country froze up.[30] In short, for one day, we got to experience a small taste of what life might be like at the beginning of the new millennium.

All the Eggs in One Basket

The outage was a wake-up call to many about our society's dependence on technology, the fragility of the communications network, and our vulnerability to failures of critical systems. Why did such a huge percentage of our pagers rely upon a single satellite? In this case, it seemed to make good economic sense at the time. The Galaxy IV satellite, in geosynchronous orbit directly over Kansas at 99 degrees west longitude, could reach the entire lower forty-eight states and parts of Canada. Located smack in the middle of the country, it made communications between the East and West coasts easy.[31] In addition, pager transmissions take up very little of the available bandwidth on a satellite, compared with, say, television signals. So PanAmSat went aggressively after the pager market for the Galaxy IV, knowing that it would have plenty of room left for other customers.[32]

Sometimes it all comes together at a single failure point

Besides, there had never before been a nationwide service outage for pagers, according to industry spokespersons.[33] With a backup system on board, the chance for a system-wide failure must have seemed remote. In the unlikely event of failure of both the system and its backup, critical transmissions could be rerouted so that service interruptions would be only temporary. Consumers that were affected could fall back on alternate satellites or even land-based transmissions.

With all this in mind, it doesn't seem unreasonable (except in hindsight) to place our reliance on a single system. In any case, argued industry defenders, the Galaxy IV glitch had been short-lived. Pager service at large providers such as AirTouch and MobileCom was restored within a day.[34] Previous large-scale system crashes (such as the prior month's single-frame relay outage at one of AT&T's high-speed data networks—which also shut down pager services and impacted credit card authorizations and Internet traffic) had been inconvenient but not catastrophic.

Sadly, failures like Galaxy IV may be all too common in the year 2000. The inescapable conclusion from the Galaxy IV lesson is that single-point failures in high-tech systems are capable of crashing the whole system, just as a pinpoint strike at GM was able to halt production for months. As a society, we have been willing to tolerate the risk of occasional system-wide disruptions in exchange for the convenience and relatively low cost of the service provided.

But what if consumers were to lose confidence in such systems due to repeated Y2K-related failures? We have all felt the frustration of walking up to an ATM only to discover that it is out of service, or have cursed at our cable provider when "technical difficulties" interrupted our favorite ballgame. What if every other ATM at any given time might be out, or worse, might miscalculate our balances after we withdraw money? What if advertisers couldn't rely on programmers to get their messages out to the promised audience? What if doctors could never know whether their pagers would be working that day? Computers, communications systems, and other networks are only useful so long as they are reliable. The reality is, if we can't depend on them, many people will conclude we are better off without them.

Can't We All Just Get Along?

A few bold optimists believe that the risk to high-tech systems from Y2K is overblown. They argue that if one path in an advanced computer or telecommunications system is cut off due to a technical failure, there are a lot of other paths, so the system is usually up and running again in a short time. Companies will deal with the situation as they deal with, say, a power outage. The vast dispersion and sheer complexity of systems—so the thinking goes—act as insurance against a complete meltdown, and companies inevitably will find ways through the morass. Said one analyst, "There won't be a domino effect [from Y2K], because there are lots of switches throughout the system that will put on brakes."[35]

How many little fires can we stamp out at once?

We think this gets the problem backward and winds up seriously understating the threat. Y2K will not be so merciful as to limit its impact to a single wayward satellite or mainframe computer—as has been the case with the types of system failures to which we are accustomed. Where systems are dispersed, operators may find it impossible to quickly locate the source of a failure brought about by Y2K, or it may be difficult to coordinate repair efforts effectively. Systems operators also may be so busy trying to keep other systems running that they don't have time to address the problem at its source. In any event, as the Galaxy IV example shows, systems are not as efficiently distributed as we might imagine, since there are often critical bottlenecks through which otherwise dispersed systems must pass.

Moreover, the more complex the system, the more likely it is to be vulnerable to paralyzing glitches, as complexity usually means greater synchronization and interdependence. Just ask the poor folks at Hong Kong's new Chep Lak Kok Airport. The sparkling new $20 billion facility was highly touted as the most advanced in the world. The airport had been under pressure to open by early July 1998, in conjunction with Present Clinton's visit to China, even though not all the systems had been tested. Almost immediately after the airport opened, a host of nightmares arose when the ultrasynchronized systems were crippled by a glitch in—of all things—

Just ask people in Hong Kong about their new airport

the baggage-routing software. Terminal screens went black, passengers missed flights, and *every other piece* of luggage was lost. The operations of Hong Kong Air Cargo Terminals Ltd. had to be unceremoniously rerouted to the seventy-three-year-old former airport facility, at a cost of billions of dollars in spoiled or late cargo. Analysts glumly predicted that the fiasco would shave another 0.1 percent off the region's battered GDP.[36]

The Hong Kong airport fiasco, while not Y2K-related, may be a harbinger of the havoc that Y2K could wreak. It also brings into serious doubt the argument by some analysts that more complex systems are by their very nature safer, more reliable systems. On the contrary, greater complexity, and thus greater interdependency, appears to multiply the damage from single-point failures.

A Few Last Words

In this chapter, you probably noticed that we provided examples of breakdowns of business and high-tech systems that were decidedly not Y2K-related. There were two reasons for this. First, we think these types of breakdowns are easier to understand because we have all seen them happen before. They provide a good starting point for our discussion about interdependent, automated systems while giving us a preview of what we might expect come the turn of the millennium. Second, we would have loved to have provided lots of examples of Y2K failures, but it's not the year 2000 yet, so at best we can only let you know about the results of some preliminary tests and what experts have predicted.

You now have examples of the impact of single-point failures within a manufacturing system, within a business system dependent on JIT deliveries, and within a complex, high-tech communications system. We have discussed why we believe Y2K will present an even greater threat to systems than these failures because of the likelihood of multiple, rather than single, glitches. And we hope we've got you thinking in terms of Y2K's impact on whole systems rather than within isolated malfunctioning computers.

In subsequent chapters, we'll extend our observations and conclusions about Y2K's threat to particular business systems, and we'll show you why we think complex systems within certain industries are particularly vulnerable to Y2K. If by now you aren't convinced that investors in these industries are at risk, the subsequent chapters should persuade even the most optimistic of investors.

TWO

THE PLANE TRUTH: WHY Y2K WILL GROUND THE EARNINGS OF MAJOR AIRLINES AND AIR COURIER COMPANIES

The airplanes aren't going to fall out of the sky. The issue is whether they will take off.

—Tom Brown, Airline Transport Association[1]

The senior manager of industry operations at the International Air Transport Association put it mildly when he wrote that the nature of the airline industry made its Y2K problems "special."[2] In our view, airlines and air courier companies are the true poster children for Y2K, destined to bear a painfully disproportionate share of the business world's Y2K woes. While it is our hope and belief that airline safety will not be compromised as a result of Y2K, we would be surprised if planes aren't left sitting on runways when the crisis hits as a result of delays and serious service disruptions. Our take: If the air carriers don't fly, their stocks won't either.

What is it about the air transport industry that makes it so special in the world of Y2K? The IATA itself has identified four characteristics: round-the-clock service, the high-profile nature of the industry, major use of automated systems, and high intra-industry integration.[3] To these, we would add our observations that the industry is also highly dependent on thousands of small vendors and on stable, low fuel prices; its aircraft must rely on local airports to operate effectively;

and it is at the mercy of the FAA and international air traffic control systems.

What consequences do the above characteristics have for air transportation and Y2K? How do these characteristics set the airline and air courier industry apart from others? The discussion in this chapter should convince you that air transport equities are in for more than a little turbulence.

Can't Stop the Clock

In the introduction to this book, we noted that certain industries are inherently more susceptible to Y2K, over and above anticipated nuisances such as malfunctioning elevators and sprinkler systems. Air transport is just such an industry because it is one of the most *time-sensitive* of industries around—indeed, people usually choose flying over driving, and overnight air delivery instead of ground freight, in order to save

Y2K RISK FACTOR
Time Sensitivity

time. Airlines and air courier companies conduct incredible JIT operations, and they do so twenty-four hours a day, 365 days a year. Delay is the industry's chief enemy. Service disruptions and delays immediately result in lost profits and miffed customers and, were they to become systemic problems, would seriously impact upon bottom lines in the air transport sector.

Delayed flights don't necessarily mean passenger cancellations, but they may still result in immediate losses. As a simple example, when planes are kept circling in the sky, they use up more jet fuel. While this is presently only a periodic occurrence, usually due to bad weather, if it were to become a system-wide phenomenon, with each plane having to spend, say, 10 to 20 percent more time in the air than usual, the cost to airlines would be considerable given the relatively high cost of fuel as a percentage of operating costs.

Other costs of service disruptions and delays may be less obvious. Take our earlier example of the Hong Kong airport fiasco, where cargo services were seriously disrupted for weeks. It turns out that Northwest Airlines lost nearly one million dollars in just the first few days of the crisis, not because passengers demanded refunds, but because it found itself unable to load extra cargo on its regularly scheduled passenger flights.[4] This practice is common when the volume of passenger baggage permits the simultaneous transportation of commercial cargo. Northwest apparently determined that it couldn't delay its passenger flights while it waited for the cargo handlers to get their act together, or couldn't accept time-sensitive cargo shipments when passenger flights were so delayed. In either case, Northwest lost cargo customers.

This illustrates another important point about disruptions to air service. Unlike work stoppages at a manufacturing facility, where current losses are often offset through increased future productivity and worker overtime, the airlines and air courier companies are offering a *service*, and therefore sales can't always be deferred. There are simply just so many days in a year, and just so many resources (e.g., airport runways and gates) to go around. Once an opportunity to provide service is lost, it usually can't be made up. Worse still, if service is significantly impacted, there may be additional costs associated with making it up to the customer, such as putting up passengers in hotels, issuing free tickets and vouchers, replacing lost luggage, or reimbursing for spoiled cargo. While these costs are usually minimal, if Y2K has a sustained, system-wide impact, they would certainly figure into short-term earnings.

As we touched on in the previous chapter, Y2K will be a nasty pest for air transport because it will cause delays in a previously well-run JIT system. Unlike delays caused by bad weather, which customers may grumble over but will ultimately forgive, Y2K-related delays will be widespread, persistent and, over time, confidence-shaking. Below, we'll discuss how we think Y2K will affect critical services for airlines and air courier companies. For now, our basic point is that if Y2K-related delays become sufficiently serious, the industry will lose its reputation as offering a reliable, time-saving way to travel. Until the Y2K bug is squashed, the public may adjust travel plans to more local destinations and elect more reliable modes of transportation, and companies may find alternative means of shipping their cargo. This would have a serious short-term impact on airline profitability.

The enemy is delay

Always in the Headlines

The airline industry often bemoans the fact that it is a high-profile industry, meaning it gets constant attention and scrutiny from the media and the public. News stories about bad weather across the nation inevitably feature miserable passengers huddled in drafty airports. Airplane crashes, though relatively rare compared to other accidents, are always top-of-the-news, with fire trucks blaring and lights flashing.

With Y2K, things are no different for the beleaguered airlines. The International Air Transport Association lamented that "speculation on the impact of the year 2000 on the airlines is much more 'sensational' than for other industries."[5] Whether from congressional hearings, talk shows, media commentaries, or books like this one, airlines seem to get more than their share of the Y2K worries.

Not surprisingly, Y2K concerns in air travel center around safety. We are happy to report that after researching this subject exhaustively, we don't believe that air travel within the United States will be a major safety issue. For starters, the Federal Aviation Administration and airline insurers are unlikely to let a plane get off the ground if there is the slightest chance the airline (or the FAA for that matter) has not addressed its mission-critical systems. The Department of Transportation has already told a Senate committee that it may ban U.S. airline flights to and from certain countries whose air traffic control systems are not bug free.[6] The airlines themselves will tend to err on the side of safety. One carrier—Dutch airline KLM—has declared that it will self-enforce "no-fly" zones in regions considered dangerously noncompliant. KLM is working with its partners, including Northwest and Continental, on a "Global Millennium Compliance Forum" to identify global Y2K danger spots.[7] And three of Britain's leading tour operators announced they simply will not fly any travelers to any destinations on either December 31, 1999, or January 1, 2000.[8]

In any case, it may well be that by the time the year 2000 rolls around the airlines won't need to curtail flights or limit their destinations. The public may be so alarmed about the prospect of unsafe skies that few will be on those flights, even over the normally busy New Year's holiday. Notwithstanding *Empty planes?* the FAA's cheery assurances (discussed and criticized below), the public appears to be taking a wait-and-see attitude before risking air travel. A USA Today/Gallup Poll conducted in late 1998 revealed that 47 percent of Americans probably would avoid flying on or around January 1, 2000.[9] As an IATA spokesperson stated, "Given the industry's total devotion to ensuring a safe air transport system, it is more likely that flights will be canceled for commercial reasons due to low passenger booking. No company is going to fly empty aircraft around the world if traffic disappears due to customer perceptions and fears."[10]

But whether the planes don't fly because Y2K has crashed their systems, or because the airlines themselves won't take the risk of flying, or because the public is in effect voting with their feet (or in this case, with their cars), the resulting impact on airline profitability is the same. No passengers, no profits.

Both the air transport industry's need to prioritize safety and its inherent JIT nature identify it as a prime candidate for our list of industries with which Y2K-minded investors should proceed cautiously. Furthermore, as we show below, the industry also happens to be among the most highly automated and interdependent of all industries, which in our minds makes it doubly clear that Y2K will plague airline and air courier stocks in the coming year.

On Autopilot

Airlines helped pioneer our society's transition to the computer age. American Airlines and IBM took the bold step of introducing high-performance reservation systems to the industry

Y2K RISK FACTOR
Automation

as early as 1965. It's hard to believe, but up to that point reservations were still being written by hand and often were simply tacked to large boards for tracking purposes. Computerization was pretty much the only way to keep up with the development of high-powered jets, which could handle greater numbers of passengers.[11]

By the 1970s, computer reservation systems became distributed among independent travel agents, allowing airlines to cut back on

169,000 flights
each day

reservation staff. Today, computers now not only record and track reservations, but also control flight schedules, baggage handling systems, passenger boarding, flight paths, weather reporting systems, maintenance schedules, and frequent flier program accounts, among their many tasks. The system works well enough to allow 169,000 flights to take place daily in the United States.[12]

SABRE Rattled

To handle this number of flights and passengers, highly sophisticated systems are needed. Of course, as we have seen with other automated systems, a single computer problem can cause major disruptions to entire operations. A good example of this is the recent mishaps of the SABRE travel reservation system, which is 84 percent owned by American Airlines and which handles billions of reservations a year for American and dozens of other airlines. On the morning of June 25, 1998, the system went off-line for three hours when a series of circuit breakers were tripped at SABRE's underground data center in Tulsa, Oklahoma. In a situation eerily similar to the Galaxy IV satellite outage discussed in the previous chapter, the circuit breakers failed to switch automatically to an alternative source, despite the Sabre Group having invested millions of dollars in emergency preparedness and the presence of double and triple redundancies in the system.[13]

American Airlines and more than forty other carriers, as well as travel agents in more than 40,000 offices, were unable to make reservations, sell tickets, call up passenger information, or access flight schedules. The SABRE system usually processes hundreds of thousands of flights per day, and enters data for countless airlines, hotels, and car rental companies in over seventy countries. With the system down, ticket counter and gate agents had to take passengers at their word if they were traveling using American's "ticketless" service.[14]

Less than a week later, the system crashed again, this time as a result of an unspecified software glitch. This outage lasted twice as long as the prior week's and occurred during peak traffic hours, at around 5:00 P.M. Central Standard Time. American's airport agents, bag handlers, and other operators used manual systems for check-in, flight boardings, and baggage handling, all of which are normally automated.[15]

Neither of the outages affected SABRE's automated flight operations systems, which American and other airlines rely on to manage the movement of aircraft and personnel. But that system, too, had crashed the previous October for around ninety minutes, leaving passengers waiting at gates and sitting on planes. Pilots could not get flight plans and fuel information from the computer system, so they couldn't take off.[16]

The three system crashes within a year of each other are troubling—

particularly because SABRE hadn't suffered a similar problem since 1989, when the system went down for thirteen hours. (The other recorded outage occurred in 1982, when an opossum ate through a power line in Tulsa.) The disruptions were less serious in those years because airlines were less dependent on computers for daily operations.[17]

SABRE currently is facing significant Y2K challenges. With over 200 million lines of mainframe code—much of it date-sensitive given the nature of the travel business—SABRE will have its work cut out. In addition to solving its own problems, SABRE will have to ensure that the 1,500 external data feeds with which SABRE shares information are also compliant. To make matters worse, SABRE promulgated new standards in December 1997; at least some of SABRE's electronic data interchange partners are unlikely to have adopted these new standards. SABRE must be able to process data in both the old and the new formats and make sure the data interchange is completely "integrated," meaning that its computers can still communicate with all the outside computers. Further, SABRE's business is forward looking and takes reservations as much as 333 days in advance.[18] As a result, it rushed to complete its upgrades by June, 1998—six months ahead of most companies—and began its testing by that time.[19] (Interestingly, SABRE had not disclosed the nature of the "unknown software problem" that had crashed its system for six hours on June 30.)

200 million lines of code

Gotta Spray Everywhere

In addition to passenger service-related systems, airlines now use computers on board aircraft to conduct many critical flight operations. According to Dutch airline KLM—one of the more candid airlines when it comes to Y2K issues—there are up to 160 date-dependent systems on a typical commercial aircraft.[20] Two-digit dates crop up in flight management computers and in internal navigation systems. Noncompliant systems could cause aircraft to fail preflight inspections, causing significant delays. Many airline systems contain date-dependent embedded microprocessors will have to be replaced.

Computers and embedded chips are also omnipresent in airline engineering, maintenance, training, and catering centers. Airlines are finding they need to conduct top-to-bottom, comprehensive reviews of all their systems. Given the magnitude of the task, some airlines have admitted that their systems cannot possibly be 100 percent compliant, and that some noncritical systems will be missed or skipped.

Most of us are familiar with advertisements by companies in the air courier business, like Federal Express, boasting how office employees can now use custom software to track their shipments, and how in this manner, one person can do what it used to take a whole office to get done. This is because Federal Express and other carriers now use bar codes, customer account numbers, and other data to keep track of their shipments. This is basically a necessity, given the volume of priority shipments that take place daily. Unfortunately, this also makes companies like Federal Express extremely vulnerable to Y2K. Indeed, in a report on Y2K prepared by Merrill Lynch, Federal Express was singled out due in part to its "information intensive" nature.[21]

In short, in thinking about Y2K's affect on automation in air transport, keep in mind that the *reason* the industry moved early to computer systems was to keep up with demands upon the services provided. In other words, *they couldn't do their jobs without computers.* This should give any Y2K-minded investor pause.

In fairness, large airlines have been relatively well-organized and dedicated to fixing their internal Y2K problems. For example, United Airlines reported in mid-1998 that it had completed 60 percent of its Y2K upgrades on its mainframes. Of its 40,000 computer programs, 11,000 of them required changes. United plans to complete those fixes in 1998 and test applications through 1999.

Y2K Readiness in Air Transport

American Airlines pledged publicly that it would check every piece of equipment—"from flight simulators to fax machines"—and is similarly confident that its own systems will be ready by the end of 1999.[22] It has budgeted $160 million, according to the International Air Transport Association.[23] Delta is similarly geared up for the Y2K fight. "We want to be as comprehensive as possible because missing one thing could mean a whole system going down," admitted one corporate communications manager at Delta. Delta has an internal team of four hundred—as well as outside consultants—to identify, assess, and correct systems that have already been affected.[24] Delta has set aside $125 million for its Y2K fixes.[25] And Federal Express by mid-1998 had costs of around $120 million—or fifty cents a share—to squash its internal bugs.[26]

Hundreds of millions for the fix

Before You Put Your Seat-Back Down . . .

Lest these assurances set your mind at ease, remember that we don't believe that *internal* fixes are the key to whether Y2K will cause a company's operations to falter and profits to nose-dive. Internal fixes by at-risk companies are classic "necessary but not sufficient" actions. Airlines also must contend with the fact that they are highly interconnected and interdependent, both with one another and with their vendors and suppliers.

Y2K RISK FACTOR
Interdependence

Hanging Together

Unlike other industries where information is often a closely guarded trade secret, airlines commonly share information with one another. Indeed, data sharing is essential among airlines to ensure safety through coordinated flight plans, to provide high levels of customer service, and to efficiently make use of limited resources (e.g., runway and air space). Nearly all of the data sharing occurs electronically, given the sheer amount of information that must be shared in a limited amount of time.

The problem with systems that must share data, of course, is that the data has to be accurate and complete. All it takes is a single non-compliant computer feeding wrong dates into the system, or turning itself off out of confusion, and the whole system could crash. The culprit will have to be located, isolated, and repaired or replaced. Unfortunately, this takes time and requires manual checking, meaning—you guessed it—delays.

The level of interconnectivity among airlines is in part a function of the number of players in the system. Many people might have difficulty naming two dozen airlines operating in the United States; in fact, there are 290 of them. The smaller airlines—like smaller enterprises everywhere—will face difficulties bringing their operations into full compliance given the high cost of replacement or repair. Some international airlines—particularly those based in developing countries—will be similarly ill-prepared for Y2K. These airlines could well feed corrupt data into the system, or could suffer a system crash, making everyone else's operations slow down. Our prognosis is that

290 airlines
flying our skies

even if the major airlines can get their systems to be mostly bug free, air traffic will be snarled up by delays associated with smaller airlines and international carriers. Think of the system like a complex super-highway, where traffic is used to going at fifty to sixty-five miles an hour. What happens when a semi jackknifes, or even if one small car breaks down in the middle of the road? Everyone suffers from the resulting jam.

Vendor Vulnerability

On top of worrying about each others' compliance efforts, the airlines and air courier companies have to be concerned about the state of Y2K preparedness of some 17,000 vendors who provide goods and services to the industry. Some of the large vendors (such as the Boeing Company, which makes most of the fleet, and Honeywell, which supplies instrumentation and other electrical components) have the resources to assist the industry in its Y2K remedial work. But as large, complex companies, such vendors face their own internal Y2K issues.

For example, Honeywell's Y2K manager admitted he feared that "some plants will have trouble operating and will have to shut down. Some will run at a reduced scope. I expect considerable system outages during December 1999 through February 2000."[27] Boeing is confident that its own systems will be fine, but it has expressed concern over its 920 suppliers, some of which are the sole vendors for parts in its planes. In 1997, Boeing faced production bottlenecks and severe parts shortages, causing shutdowns of its 747 and 737 production lines for about a month. Delays eventually cost Boeing $3 billion in pretax charges.[28]

Most of the vendors, however, are small operations without large information technology budgets. This concerns us, and it should concern the airlines and any other large businesses dependent on thousands of smaller suppliers. Surveys have shown that small and mid-sized businesses remain woefully unprepared for Y2K. A study conducted by Wells Fargo and the National Federation of Independent Business revealed that some five million small businesses are at risk. Of those businesses surveyed, 21 percent admitted their operations are "very dependent" on automated processes, while another 27 percent said they were "somewhat dependent." Notwithstanding this fact, a full three-quarters of small businesses had taken *no action* to address the potential risk, and half of businesses *did not plan to act* before Y2K problems occurred.[29] Other surveys back up these alarming statistics. The National Association of Securities Dealers—the people who run NASDAQ—surveyed 5,600 members in early 1998 and found that 61 percent of small companies responding didn't even have a plan at that time to address Y2K.[30]

What accounts for this inaction? "There is a surprising lack of urgency," said IBM's manager of global small and medium business initiatives in a statement to the House Small Business Committee. "Some think they are ready, some think they have plenty of time, and some feel the issue is all hype and they will not be affected."[31] Another problem, of course, is money. Y2K hardware upgrades are expensive, and hiring software programmers to fix code is not realistic for many smaller firms.

Airlines and air courier companies have to contend with the fact that they interact with thousands of at-risk small business vendors.

Thousands of vendors at risk

As part of their compliance efforts, most airlines have sent out questionnaires to their vendors. But while SEC regulations recently have required large publicly traded companies to disclose possible Y2K problems, lawyers for smaller vendors, fearing liability, often advise those companies not to make additional assurances about Y2K compliance. The result is that industries like the airlines that are highly dependent on small to mid-sized vendors can't be certain that their supply chains are not at risk from Y2K disruptions.

Fuel to the Fire

Any airline executive will tell you that the fortunes of air transport rise and fall with the cost of jet fuel. Most airline profits have been sky-high lately because the cost of a barrel of oil is near rock bottom. Jet fuel accounts for between 15 and 25 percent of an airline's operating costs. In fact, the airline industry saves $170 million every time the price of a gallon of fuel drops just one penny.

Y2K *ADDED* RISK FACTOR
Fuel Supplier Noncompliance

In 1996, the price of jet fuel was around 70 cents per gallon. In 1997, the price had fallen around 10 percent, and projections for 1998 were around 52 cents a gallon, for savings of about $1.9 billion over the prior year. (In case you're wondering, the airlines haven't passed much of these savings onto customers, given the strong economy and high demand for travel.)[32]

But what threat does Y2K pose to jet fuel? A study by Science Applications International Corporation revealed that many top oil-producing nations such as Venezuela, Nigeria, Mexico, and Saudi Arabia are at least six months to two years behind the United States in efforts to address Y2K problems.[33]

Large international oil companies are faced with the monumental task of bringing their worldwide operations into compliance. Y2K risks exist in equipment in operating units like production fields, refineries, and pipelines, and a good number of the equipment must be replaced or repaired.[34] This often means obtaining the cooperation of foreign vendors, which are even farther behind the United States in Y2K remedial efforts. Refineries and other operations must be able to obtain spare parts. Vendors must be able to provide compliant data. Chevron has over 12,000 vendors for its shipping division alone,[35] and has stated publicly that it does not expect all systems to be compliant by 2000.[36]

In short, oil prices may spike during the Y2K crisis as a result of a drop in supply. We think there is a sufficient risk of a rise in the price of fuel to pose a threat to fuel-sensitive industries such as airlines and utilities. If we are correct, say goodbye to stratospheric earnings for the airlines.

Not All-Systems-Go

Airports assume critical responsibilities in air transport operations such as fuel systems, loading bridges, baggage claims, and the access control systems that monitor entry from the terminal to the airfield. They operate much like miniature cities, with a full host of facilities, services, and operations. Failure by airports to fix Y2K problems in their facilities means delays, lost baggage,

Y2K *ADDED* RISK FACTOR
Airport Noncompliance

and stranded passengers, not to mention potential safety issues. Translation: trouble for the air transport industry and its profits.

Indeed, airports are a critical but often overlooked weak link in the air transportation chain. Passengers arriving at airports expect to be able to get from the parking garages to their terminals promptly and without incident. They expect that terminal screens will direct them to the proper gates, that their baggage will be handled without error, and that paging and other communications systems will be functional. They expect to be able to embark and disembark relatively on time and not hours later. Merchants expect that their cargo will be loaded and unloaded efficiently. Y2K will change all these expectations. One representative from the American Association of Airport Executive likened Y2K problems to when a major blizzard disrupts air service—but *repeated every day for a month or so.*[37]

What types of problems might occur? As an example, British airport operator BAA conducted some experiments to determine the impact of Y2K on its systems. The Y2K team at BAA turned the clocks forward to the new millennium on a baggage-handling system. The result was disturbing: "[The system] failed to recognize the bags and sent all the bags down the mis-sort chute," admitted BAA's Year 2000 program director.[38]

Another less obvious problem is with auxiliary services at airports. An airport cannot operate, for example, if its alarm systems are off-line, or if its fire trucks can't get out of their garages because the computer has locked them in. Planes obviously can't fly if they have no fuel as a result of airport fuel delivery snafus.

Like the airlines, airports tend to get disproportionately negative coverage from the media when things go awry. You can expect a great deal of airport bashing over Y2K issues in the next year. It turns out that even the most highly touted airports—such as the new Denver International Airport, which serves as a major hub for United Airlines—have serious Y2K problems.

Officials were shocked to learn that DIA, completed in 1995, did not prepare its systems for the new millennium. The Denver airport has identified one hundred systems that could fail as a result of Y2K. Forty of these systems have been deemed "mission-critical," and DIA officials are groaning at the projected $9 million-plus price tag for fixing them[39]—a number nearly certain to rise if other airports' experiences are any indication. (Seattle-Tacoma International airport, for

DIA could be DOA

instance, has projected Y2K costs upward of $30 million.) At DIA these systems include the underground train system, flight and baggage information displays, security and gate access, airport communications boards, and the infamous computerized baggage system, which twice delayed DIA's opening and was the target of critics of DIA's $4.3 billion construction bill. The bad news for airports is that there may not be enough time to implement and test all the fixes: As of the end of April 1998, DIA was still in the assessment phase and had not yet begun repairs and replacements of systems.[40]

The bad news for airlines is that the cost of Y2K will not be foisted upon the taxpayers alone. For example, 1999 airport fees for airlines operating at DIA are going up, in part due to expected Y2K costs. Complained one executive from Frontier Airlines, "Projects like Y2K take money to resolve. I know DIA has a consultant working on this, but $9 million seems huge."[41] We wonder what Frontier is saying about Sea-Tac's projected $30 million fix.

DIA is not alone in its Y2K woes. Hartsfield Atlanta International Airport—which is a hub for Delta Airlines and handles more than 70 million passengers a year—only began to evaluate its 117 at-risk systems in May 1998. Everything from runway lighting to fuel systems at Hartsfield is part of a network of computer systems used by the airport, airline tenants, vendors, and the Federal Aviation Administration. "We're behind where we should be as far as Y2K is concerned," said Hartsfield's information systems manager. Others were not so charitable: "They will not have enough time to do the job right," concluded the managing director of the Information Management Forum's Y2K group. "The question is, will they have enough time to do the job at all?"[42]

Other airports owning up to their problems include the Dallas/Fort Worth International Airport, a hub for American Airlines. A Year 2000 Task Force for the airport determined that fifty-three major systems had to be renovated, including computerized parking transactions and runway and taxiway lighting. The cost of the fixes initially was estimated at $10 million.[43] We bet it goes much higher.

The Air Transport Association is busily conducting reviews of so-called "external" systems at 150 airports around the country. The news is not good. Tom Browne, who heads up the ATA's Y2K program, noted that there are more systems that need to be checked than anyone had expected. Moreover, he found it "alarming" that as of mid-1998, some airports "hadn't even begun Year 2000 work yet."[44] By the end of the third quarter of 1998, the ATA admitted that among the eighty-one airports it surveyed, *35 percent* had done nothing to prepare for Y2K—not even form a plan—and nearly as many were more than three months behind in their existing plans.[45] Part of the problem is money: smaller airports simply can't absorb the financial hit from Y2K, and so the FAA has joined them in asking Congress for additional appropriations. We're afraid it is probably too late to make good use of this money, assuming it is possible.

Even if these airports started their Y2K work today, it would leave little if any time to complete comprehensive testing of their systems.

No time left to test?
As most Y2K experts agree, testing is the most time-consuming component of a typical Y2K compliance plan. A test failure means additional remedial work and further testing. Failure to test all systems in an airport could prove catastrophic, as the Hong Kong airport authorities would tell you. (See chapter 1.)

But even a thorough test of systems cannot prepare an airport for actual operations. When the new, state-of-the-art international airport in Kuala Lumpur, Malaysia, was near completion, its opening was delayed for two months while exhaustive system testing was conducted on its Total Airport Management System.[46] But as in Hong Kong, Malaysian officials were still left unprepared for the magnitude of computer-related foul-ups, which turned the grand opening into a disaster. Computer problems with cargo systems resulted in long waits and tons of spoiled vegetables and fish, and the Malaysia Airlines cargo center ultimately had to stop accepting goods until the problems were resolved. Passengers waited up to four hours to disembark from aircraft and another four for their bags to arrive at the carousels. Airlines complained of losses incurred by the delays.[47]

(One other interesting and revealing tidbit: While public criticism was focused on TAMS for having failed to measure up to its billing, TAMS spokespersons cited problems with smaller subvendors, whose reliability TAMS could not completely control.[48] This supports our earlier point that the success of a Y2K program may depend completely on the compliance status of *vendors*.)

Still, the problems at Kuala Lumpur, which had run some system-wide testing, were not as prolonged as those that plagued Hong Kong, which was under pressure to open the airport and had failed to complete necessary tests. With Y2K, there won't be an option to push back the date. The sad fact is that many airports won't be able to test their systems and—excuse the expression—will be flying by the seat of their pants come January 1, 2000. We may have nationwide airport chaos that will dwarf the disruptions in Hong Kong and Malaysia. The problem may be much worse overseas. This is bad news for air travelers and for the industry, but there is little anyone can do about it now.

As If That News Weren't Bad Enough

Airlines and air courier companies face another potential Y2K disaster that is beyond their power to control. In the introduction to this book, we noted that industries that depend on the government to continue normal operations face an additional, even higher risk from Y2K. The U.S. government operates one-fourth of the computers in the United States, but lags far behind the private sector in key government departments and agencies. It so happens that air transport is entirely at the mercy of the FAA and other government air traffic agencies around the world to be able to route flights safely and on time.

Y2K *ADDED* RISK FACTOR

FAA Noncompliance

Government agencies often lack the business management structures and profit incentives to tackle problems like Y2K, and this is surely the case with the FAA. Airlines and air courier companies can take decisive action with respect to their own internal operations, and though vendors may be slow to respond, at least the industry can exert financial pressures on companies that fail to comply. But with the FAA, airlines can only lobby for accelerated Y2K efforts. The industry has rightly pointed out that it makes no difference how much work is done internally if the air traffic control systems are not ready to let planes fly. In fact, during a meeting with the FAA, airline representatives bluntly warned that "flights could not even get off the ground on January 1, 2000, unless FAA is substantially Year 2000 compliant—and that would be an *economic disaster.*"[49]

Economic disaster?

Most people know the FAA is responsible for air traffic control, without which planes could not take off and land safely at the nation's airports. Indeed, of the mission-critical systems iden-

Forty million flights per year

tified by the FAA, 209 of them are used by 17,000 air traffic controllers to manage over forty million flights annually. The system is made up of thousands of interdependent radars, computers, displays, and telecommunication networks.[50]

But the FAA has many other less visible tasks to perform. It is in charge of certifying airworthiness for new commercial aircraft designs. It is responsible for inspecting and certifying commercial aircraft, repair stations, mechanics, pilots, and aviation industry schools through some 100 flight standards offices. It maintains security in hundreds of airport facilities. It provides current weather conditions to pilots in coordination with the National Weather Service. It even keeps watch over high passenger traffic situations in order to make sure airlines and airports bring in more personnel during busy periods.

The FAA performs all of these tasks through a complex system of interrelated computer networks, many components of which are rela-

1980s Technology

tively antiquated. For example, the FAA's notorious Host Computer System—a set of forty IBM model 3083 mainframes whirring away at the FAA's twenty en route centers—dates back to the early 1980s. Those machines receive data from radars and integrate that data into a usable picture for air traffic controllers.

The FAA maintains a hodgepodge of other computer systems, nearly all of which were specially built for the FAA's use and are therefore not easily replaced. The FAA's flight standards offices are supported by over thirty safety database and analysis systems. The airlines' flight planning systems are hooked up to the FAA's Enhanced Traffic Management System. The Terminal Doppler Weather Radar System uses a network of radars and satellites to detect weather anomalies, alerting aircraft to dangerous weather conditions around airports and providing advanced warnings of changing weather conditions. All of these systems are potentially at risk from Y2K.

The FAA has also acquired a host of new systems scheduled to be operational before the end of 1999. These include a major system called the Standard Terminal Automation Replacement System, which

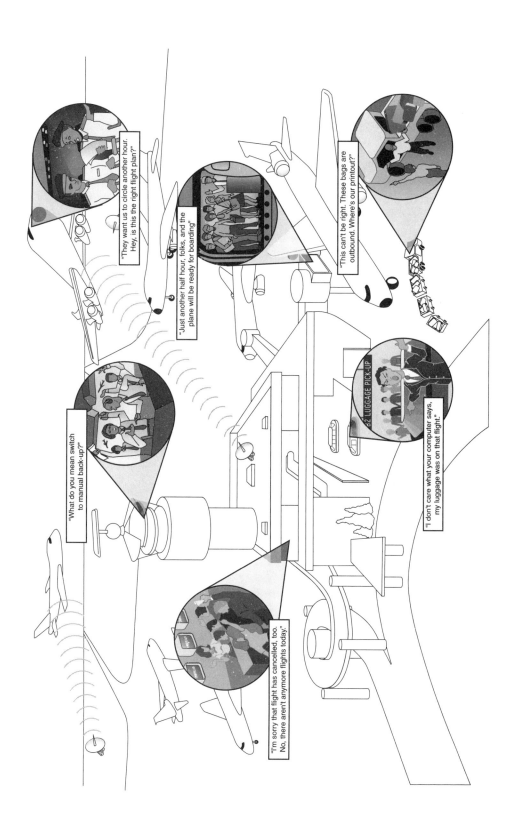

will replace an obsolete air traffic control system, and the Wide Area Augmentation System, which is a system that will use satellites for communication, navigation, and surveillance between air traffic controllers and pilots. There are a total of twenty-three newly purchased but not deployed systems that the FAA has not yet determined to be Y2K-compliant.[51]

With all these systems in place or to be added, the FAA understood that it was at great risk from Y2K. Sure enough, when the FAA began to assess its mission-critical systems, the results were alarming. The FAA's Air Traffic Control line of business initially reported that thirty-four of the one hundred critical systems it had assessed were likely to result in catastrophic failure if not renovated. Other problems were less easily discerned but equally disturbing. For example, FAA teams found a deeply embedded code that issues a date-dependent command to turn on a cooling pump for the en route surveillance radar equipment. If left unfixed, the pump could fail to turn on, and the system would overheat and shut down.[52]

Given the extent of computer dependence and the importance of safe and efficient air transportation, you would expect the FAA to have been one of the leaders among government agencies in Y2K planning, implementation, and testing. After all, the deadline is not movable, and the nation's air transport industry, airports, and air travelers are depending on the FAA to function. Sadly, in studies prepared in 1998, the FAA was among the least prepared of government sectors, according to the General Accounting Office, congressional oversight committees, and internal industry critics. The FAA and the Department of Transportation in general have been targets of intense criticism for having dropped the ball, and this understandably has the airlines and air courier companies highly disturbed.

The FAA is among the least prepared agencies in the government

First, the Good News

The FAA appears to have been given an eleventh hour lucky break. Until July 1998, concern had been mounting that the FAA's core systems—its forty IBM mainframes comprising its Host Computer System—would crash fatally on January 1, 2000. Here's why: It should be no surprise that airlines use different flight plans on weekdays than they do on weekends. The system relies on the date, however, to determine which day of the week it is, then uses that determination to plot different prescheduled flight plans. This is a problem, since January 1, 1900, was a Monday, but January 1, 2000, will be a Saturday. If the system were to reset itself as expected, it would lead to incorrect flight plans and inevitably to delays out of fear of crossed flights.[53] IBM itself had warned in a letter to FAA contractor Lockheed Martin Air Traffic Management that "the appropriate skills and tools do not exist to conduct a complete Year 2000 test assessment" of its Model 3083s, and it urged the FAA to mothball the system.[54]

Under the gun and uncertain whether it could integrate a whole new system in time, the FAA conducted tests on the IBM mainframes to see what would happen at the end of 1999. The FAA technicians concluded (to their relief) that the system would survive the millennium. Why? It turns out that the original IBM programmers *didn't* use a two-digit date to record years. Instead, they used a thirty-two-year internal count, with the first year set to 1975. This means that the system doesn't go back to 1975 and crash until 2007, buying the FAA a lot more time.

An eleventh-hour break

It's going to need it. As the following history reveals, the FAA has a miserable record on Y2K, even compared to other ill-prepared government agencies. Had the IBMs failed the test, it is a near certainty that the FAA would not have made it in time. Now, they have a fighting chance. But we still wouldn't bank on it.

This Tortoise Wouldn't Win Any Races

The Feds prepared a guide for government agencies to tackle the Y2K problem that consisted of five principal phases—awareness, assessment, renovation, validation, and implementation. These phases pretty much entail what they sound like: raise consciousness in your agency, take stock of your problems, fix those problems, test those problems, then put your complete program into place.

Although the FAA had begun to be aware of the issues surrounding Y2K back in 1996, it soon fell far behind other agencies. In early 1997, the FAA had boldly declared to Congress that it would complete assessments by June 1997, renovation by October 1997, and validation by the end of 1998, then spend all of 1999 performing implementation.[55] But by the end of 1997, the FAA hadn't even finished its assessment phase.

This was in large part because the FAA didn't put anyone in charge of overseeing the program. A point person for Y2K programs is considered critical by most experts because of the *Let's form a* necessity of coordinating across numerous computer *committee!* systems, setting standards for conversion and testing, establishing priorities, and reallocating resources. Instead, the FAA set up an "Agency Wide Steering Committee" composed of the representatives from each of the FAA's seven Lines of Business. The steering committee was "responsible for facilitating the development of LOB project plans, documenting Y2K progress through systematic reporting, and providing a forum for the regular exchange of information." Typical committee-speak. It is a small wonder that nothing much got accomplished, though the FAA did manage to put together a website and have a Y2K "Awareness Day."[56]

The FAA didn't find someone for the post of Y2K manager until July 1997. At the same time, the agency also had to contend with a change in administrators. Current FAA Administrator Jane Garvey didn't take office until August 1997. Transportation Inspector General Kenneth Mead admitted during a congressional hearing that the FAA got a "very late start" in addressing the Y2K problem. In fact, Mead confessed, the issue was not addressed "with a sense of urgency" until mid-1997.[57]

"Urgency" appears to be a relative term in the FAA. The FAA program manager appointed in July 1997 did not submit a draft Y2K plan to Administrator Garvey until December 1997. Amazingly, the program manager then promptly *retired.* (We hope it had nothing to do with his confidence in the plan.) This left the FAA again without a person in charge of its Y2K efforts, further delaying the program at a time when delays could be least afforded.

By this time, there were only two years left. If this sounds like plenty of time to you, consider this: The assessment *No room or* phase takes only a fraction of the time that renova-*time for error* tion, testing, and implementation take. You need only look at what the FAA had spent in assessment ($8 million) and what it had expected to spend in renovation, testing, and implementation ($90 million in 1998 and $64 million in 1999) to see that the FAA itself knew that most of the hard work remained undone. That may be why it initially set a target date of November 1999, for completion of its Y2K work—a date that critics charged left little room for slippage.

By way of comparison, take a look at the FAA's record on other technical upgrades and systems integration. When the FAA elected to implement a new system called the Display Channel Complex Rehost, the deployment took two years to complete in just five of its twenty centers. In a report to Congress in August of 1998, the General Accounting Office cited one FAA official who estimated that it took four to six weeks to implement and test a single modification to a computer system.[58] The Y2K problem will   *A dismal* reach across *hundreds* of systems in *all* of the FAA's cen-   *track record* ters. The FAA also has a poor history of managing software upgrades; the General Accounting Office branded the FAA's software acquisition processes "immature" in a report in 1997.[59] The GAO's associate director of transportation, a critic of the FAA's "modernization" program, put it this way:

> Over the past sixteen years, FAA's modernization projects have experienced substantial cost overruns, lengthy schedule delays, and significant performance shortfalls. To illustrate, the centerpiece of that modernization program—the Advanced Automat (AAS)—was restructured in 1994 after estimated costs to develop the system tripled from $2.5 billion to $7 billion and delays in putting significantly less-than-promised system capabilities into operation were expected to run eight years or more over original estimates.[60]

So despite Administrator Garvey's predictions that January 1, 2000, will be "business as usual" for the FAA,[61] given this poor record we simply don't see how there is enough institutional management expertise at the FAA to make it in time.

Playing the Numbers

By the end of 1997, the FAA had finally inventoried most of its systems and made most of their required mission-critical determinations.

In internal reports from November 1997, the FAA initially reported that it had inventoried 619 systems, comprising about 18,000 subsystems and sixty-five million lines of software code. Of these systems, it deemed 329 of them to be mission-critical. By the end of December, FAA had revised this number to 741 systems, 420 of which were mission-critical.[62] The number of mission-critical systems finally leveled off at over 430. But as the GAO pointed out, the designation of mission-critical systems was not enough to complete the assessment phase. FAA still had to determine *what steps* it was going to take with each system—that is, replace it, repair it, retire it, or do nothing. Under this definition of assessment, a paltry eighty-four of the FAA's systems had been completely assessed by the end of 1997, with *over 50 percent* slotted for repair or replacement.

Of the 430 mission-critical systems, 209 are related to air traffic control.[63] These systems and some forty other supporting systems comprise the National Airspace System and contain more than twenty-three million lines of code in fifty computer languages. Without these systems, air traffic controllers would have to fall back on the old-fashioned way of using altitude and time to track aircraft and keep them safely separated. "This would slow down the system while air traffic is either re-routed or deliberately delayed to maintain safety," FAA Administrator Garvey admitted during congressional testimony.[64]

Progress on fixing these systems proceeded slowly. In its quarterly report to the Office of Management and Budget in March 1998, the FAA disclosed that it had successfully renovated just *A long way to go* 10.8 percent of its systems, validated just 8 percent, and completed program work on only 4.7 percent.[65] This caused the General Accounting Office to issue a bleak assessment that "at its present rate, FAA will not make it in time."[66] The FAA later admitted that it would miss its revised March 1999 deadline to remove all Y2K bugs from its system, but it promised to finish by June 1999.[67] By January 1999, however, the FAA had revised its plan *again* to state that it would be ready by September 1999.[68] We hate to break it to the FAA, but they have no more wiggle room left in 1999.

For its part, the FAA is sounding relatively upbeat, despite its poor history and the barrage of criticism it has received. In our view, the

FAA understandably does not want to alarm the public, and this may explain some of the bizarre optimism that seems to prevail, at least in the FAA's public statements. Indeed, both Administrator Garvey and President Bill Clinton's Y2K czar, John Koskinen, appear to understand the importance of public faith in the safety of the air transport system, and both intend to be on cross-country flights at the turnover to underscore their belief.

But deep down, those at the FAA may know what they are up against. "We've got a very short time to finish what's left," said Raymond Long, the head of the FAA's $191 million Y2K effort, though he, too, expresses confidence that the FAA will be ready in time.[69] To her credit, Administrator Garvey recognizes the extent of the problem. In her testimony before a congressional committee, she admitted, "FAA needs to do a better job of managing this problem. We are behind, and that is unacceptable."[70]

The consequences of the FAA missing the deadline would be nothing short of disastrous for airlines and air courier companies. Delays and grounded flights may be preferable to unsafe skies, but this is small comfort to the air transport industry. Even optimistic Administrator Garvey anticipated the likely extent of the problem. When a government oversight committee raised the possibility of as much as a *50 percent drop* in air traffic during the first part of the year 2000, she responded that this was only a "slight exaggeration."[71]

What About the Backup Plan?

Given the fact that the FAA is unlikely to experience "business as usual" at the turn of the millennium, you would expect the agency would have a comprehensive contingency plan to do the best that it can on what systems are functioning. We hate to disappoint, but here's what the National Air Traffic Controllers Association has to say about the FAA backup plan:

> Briefly stated, upon conclusion of a review of contingency plans considered completed by the agency thus far, along with a thorough review of the guides, directives, and orders utilized in their development, NATCA concludes: These plans as produced provide *no realistic levels of operational readiness* . . . [and] represent

an administrative gesture at best. . . . The contingency plans put forth are convoluted and vague in an Air Traffic operational sense and are *nearly worthless.*[72]

Not exactly a ringing endorsement of the contingency plan.

And If All That Isn't Enough to Depress Air Transport Executives . . .   Even if by some miracle air traffic is not seriously impacted in the United States, air traffic control operations overseas are even more likely than the FAA to be crippled. For all our criticism of the FAA and our government's response to the Y2K crisis, the United States and certain Western nations are far ahead of other nations in Y2K preparedness. Of particular concern are the developing nations of Asia and Latin America, where advances in technology and integration into the world economy have often outstripped those nations' abilities to adapt and reform their government institutions to properly manage change or crises.

Y2K *ADDED* RISK FACTOR

Noncompliance Overseas

Earlier in this chapter, we mentioned that at least one airline—KLM Royal Dutch—was preparing a list of no-fly zones in preparation for possible safety concerns in foreign destinations. "KLM is ready to fly, but in order to do that you have to cross borders and go to airports. Air traffic control is out of our hands," said KLM's chief information officer.[73]

Officials at the Department of Transportation concurred. Deputy Secretary of Transportation Mortimer Downey commented that there are some countries that he wouldn't fly to after the turn of the millennium because of safety issues raised by Y2K. "There are parts of the world where air traffic control is rudimentary and awareness of this issue is almost nonexistent," said Downey. "For this reason, the DOT and the State Department are already looking into whether it may be necessary to bar U.S. air traffic to these countries until standards are met."[74]

If there are significant flight reductions to destinations in Asia, Latin America, and other developing regions as a result of unresolved Y2K problems, this will negatively affect airlines that count on passengers who fly to and from such regions. In addition, if, as we predict, there is a general worsening of the economic situation in such areas, passenger and cargo bookings will continue their downward trend.

Airline and Air Courier Stocks Could Nosedive

In this section, we discuss and make recommendations about specific airline and air courier companies. In general, we don't like air transport's overall outlook under Y2K. It is possible, however, to make some distinctions among the airlines, primarily based on the extent of their global operations, which carry

Y2K Stock Watch

the highest level of risk of Y2K disruptions. We rate the companies as either an "avoid" or an "underweight." For convenience, we have included a summary of our recommendations in chapter 10.

International Air Couriers Will Be Hit Hard

At the extreme, certain air courier companies, such as Federal Express (whose parent company, FDX Corporation, is traded under the symbol FDX), face worldwide risk. (Well-known competitor DHL is also at risk, but it is not publicly traded.) Tellingly, Merrill Lynch—in an otherwise optimistic global Y2K assessment—singled out FedEx as facing an increased risk from Y2K on account of the global nature of its business, despite protests by FedEx that its internal operations were not as complex as those of the airlines. FedEx's solution? If a foreign airport lacks an upgraded computer system, FedEx says it will merely *bypass* it. "The key is understanding, knowing what a particular country is doing," FedEx's Y2K director stated.[75] But how many countries can the carrier blacklist before investors start blacklisting the stock? After all, FedEx derives a substantial percentage of its revenue from its International Priority, International Express Freight, and Airport-to-Airport services. These lines of business made up around one-quarter of its total revenue for the fiscal year ending May 1998.[76]

Rival Airborne Express (symbol: ABF), which is the third largest domestic carrier after FedEx and UPS, reassures customers and investors on its website that its Y2K programs are well-developed, having begun remedial work back in 1995, and will be complete far ahead of the turn of the millennium.[77] But there is little that Airborne Express can do to change the fact that it also serves over two hundred countries and derives around 13 percent of its revenue from overseas operations, which will be hard hit by Y2K. We recommend underweighting this stock.

Other less well-known air couriers also face disaster from the breakdown of international air transport systems under Y2K. BAX Global (formerly Burlington Air Express, now traded under its parent company Pittston BAX Group; symbol: PZX) operates global freight transportation and logistics management, including international supply chain management services. BAX Global is also aware of its daunting Y2K problems, including a total of more than twenty million lines of code worldwide to review.[78] But even if it manages to get its arms around its own Y2K problems, it still must be concerned that its global operations include over five hundred stations in more than one hundred countries.

Another potential victim is AirNet Systems (symbol: ANS). Never heard of them? They're the folks who provide time-sensitive shipments for the banking sector and other U.S. industries, as well as providing aviation fuel sales and some ground services. The good news for AirNet is that they operate nationally, not internationally, so their exposure is not as pronounced.

More vulnerable is Atlas Air (symbol: CGO), which specializes in airport-to-airport transportation services and whose clients are most of the major passenger airlines, serving more than sixty cities in thirty-eight countries. Remember the cargo nightmares that took place during the openings of the new Hong Kong and Kuala Lumpur airports? Yes, this is the kind of company that would be burned worst by these types of disasters. Atlas's own description of its business, which would once have sounded appealing and forward thinking, reveals the extent of its risk under Y2K:

Globalization of the world market, relaxation of international trade barriers, and the search for cost-effective operations and low-cost labor has resulted in the transfer of manufacturing capabilities abroad, particularly to the export-driver countries of the Pacific Rim. *The increasingly time sensitive nature and shorter product life cycles, coupled with just-in-time inventory needs, have resulted in the rising demand for on-time delivery, with air transport the means by which to meet this need. Industry trends and supply and demand clearly favor Atlas.*[79]

But under Y2K, they don't. Industry trends that once favored companies staking their business on just-in-time deliveries and other time-sensitive operations are totally reversed under Y2K. For Atlas's sake (and other courier companies mentioned above), we hope the rest of the world's air traffic doesn't discover next year that it depends entirely on computers to keep operations running smoothly.

U.S. Airlines With Serious International Exposure

United Airlines (symbol: UAL), the world's largest carrier, derived 20.4 percent of its operating revenue and 21.7 percent of its operating income from its Pacific flights in 1997.[80] United has hubs in London and Tokyo, in addition to its four U.S. hubs in Chicago, Denver, Washington, D.C., and San Francisco. Its 500-some-odd jets fly to a whopping 150 destinations worldwide in the United States and twenty-nine other countries, and it has code-sharing partnerships with German Lufthansa and other world airlines. United may well be in for earnings shocks if it has to scale back worldwide operations while the Y2K bug is fixed in foreign air traffic systems.

Another potential casualty of the worldwide Y2K phenomenon is Northwest Airlines (symbol: NWAC), the fourth largest airline in the United States. Northwest does a huge portion of its business with Asia, having begun its Asia focus as early as 1947 with its "Great Circle" route service to Tokyo, Seoul, Shanghai, and Manila. Now, it has more than 130 nonstop flights between the United States and Asia each week.[81] All told, with its global alliance partner, KLM, Northwest serves 400 destinations in over eighty countries. It is one of the world's foremost cargo carriers (cargo makes up about 8 percent of its revenues) and has a strong stake in the WORLDSPAN computer reservation system. We think Northwest—which suffered a downturn during the Asian Economic Crisis on top of its labor troubles in 1998—will have a rough ride through the Y2K crisis as a result of its dependence on Asian routes.

The fifth largest U.S. carrier, Continental Airlines (symbol: CAIB), also faces potential catastrophe from Y2K. In addition to its 120 U.S. destinations, Continental serves over seventy cities overseas on four other continents, including several airports in Latin America and Asia, where we expect significant Y2K disruptions. With over 2,300 daily departures and some forty million passengers in 1997, the company boasted, "Continental aircraft are in the air around-the-clock, around-the-world."[82] This is precisely why Y2K-minded investors should be concerned.

Another U.S. carrier at significant risk is Delta Airlines (symbol: DAL), which handles the largest number of international passengers and does a significant portion of its business with Latin America, with modest exposure in Asia. Delta serves forty-six cities in thirty-one foreign countries, in addition to its primary business in forty-two of the fifty states. Its international seating capacity accounts for around 24 percent of its total capacity.[83] Along with Trans World Airlines and Northwest, it is a significant stakeholder in the WORLDSPAN computer reservation system. While not as much attention has been focused on the state of air traffic control systems and airports in Latin America, our prediction is that significant problems will arise that will hamper Delta's operations in that part of the world, given the general lack of action by foreign governments to address the issue.[84]

Other Major U.S. Airlines Will Fare Somewhat Better

Not all major U.S. airlines are in the same bind. We're predicting that at least one major U.S. airline with international exposure—U.S. Airways (symbol: U)—will fare better under Y2K than those discussed above. USAir is the sixth largest U.S. carrier, but it operates flights predominantly in North America and in Western Europe—places that are considered ahead of the curve on air traffic systems Y2K compliance.

Similarly, while TWA (symbol: TWA) operates globally, serving eighty-nine cities on four continents, the destinations are primarily in North America and Europe, with a few in the Middle East and Africa and no flights to South America or Asia, where the trouble is likely to be worst. Its 186 aircraft make about 825 flights a day—a comparatively low number—meaning that serious delays may not result in as many cancelled flights.

Another well-known carrier is Alaska Airlines (symbol: ALK), owned by the Alaska Air Group, which also owns regional carrier Horizon Air. Alaska operates primarily in the Pacific Northwest, with only a few flights to Mexico and to Russia. Apart from its busy hubs in Seattle and Portland, its destinations tend to include lower-traffic airports, which might have more flexibility in slowing down operations through the Y2K crisis.

Shareholder-adored Southwest Airlines (symbol: LUV), which has posted a profit every year for the last twenty-five years, will fare better than its international competitors because all of its 2,300 daily flights are within the United States. One caveat, however: Southwest prides itself on ticketless travel and its proprietary reservation system, which had better be in perfect shape come the turn of the millennium.

Popular America West Airlines (symbol: AWA), which operates out of hubs in Phoenix, Las Vegas, and Columbus, is also relatively better off than larger carriers with broader international exposure. Apart from seven tourist destinations in Mexico and its service to Vancouver, America West operates entirely within the United States. In our view, its fortunes under Y2K pretty much depend on how well the FAA, local airports, and vendors tackle the problem.

U.S. Regional Airlines

Regional U.S. airlines will tend to fare comparatively better than the airlines with international or broad U.S. exposure. While we still think they should be underweighted in a portfolio, given the danger to the entire sector, if you want to hold some airline stocks, these regional operators are preferable to the major carriers.

One of the largest regional airline is Comair (symbol: COMR) which operates mostly as a Delta Connection carrier. Comair offers almost 700 flights a day from its hub in Cincinnati, moving over five million passengers a year. Luckily for Comair, all of its destinations are to eighty cities in the United States and Canada—apart from its regular flights to the Bahamas—so there is little exposure to Y2K problems outside of those of the FAA and North American airports. Still, the region served by Comair includes around 75 percent of the U.S. population, and Comair will be hard pressed to see that its ninety-two aircraft can keep up a demanding schedule in the face of likely Y2K delays.

Other regional carriers that will do comparatively better under Y2K than their larger national and international brethren include:

- Atlantic Coast Airlines (symbol: ACAI), which flies in nineteen U.S. states on the East Coast and operates as a part of United Express under agreement with United Airlines;
- Mesa Air Group (symbol: MESA), which derives most of its sales from code-sharing contracts with America West and USAir;

- AirTran (symbol: AAIR), which was formed from the merger of the notorious ValuJet (of the Everglades crash in 1996) and Airways Corporation, and which operates no-frills, short-haul flights, primarily along the Eastern seaboard and in the Midwest;
- Mesaba Airlines (symbol: MAIR), which serves as an affiliate of Northwest Airlines through reservation code-sharing and provides flights to ninety-one cities in the United States and Canada; and
- SkyWest Airlines (symbol: SKYW), with 600 daily flights to fifty cities in a dozen western states through code-sharing with United, Delta Connection, and Continental Connection.

Foreign Airlines

Airlines based outside of the United States are often listed on U.S. stock exchanges. These airlines are typically large international carriers that derive a significant percentage of their revenues from operations in foreign countries whose air traffic control systems and airport operations are at significant risk from Y2K. For example, Air Canada, Canada's largest airline, trades on the NASDAQ (symbol: ACNAF) and boasts of serving over 545 destinations around the world.

British Airways trades on the NYSE under the ticker symbol BAB. British Airways has pursued a strategy of global partnerships with other major carriers, such as Qantas and American Airlines, as well as franchises with smaller airlines, so that its total global service goals can be met. British Airways boasts that through its global alliances, it serves 492 destinations in ninety-nine countries, with some 7,000 daily departures.[85] This sounds great from a marketing standpoint, unless you are worried about Y2K. The company has estimated its worldwide Y2K costs to be around £100 million,[86] but again, the true threat comes from the lack of preparedness at all of the airports around the world where its airplanes need to take off and land.

Japan Airlines (symbol: JAPNY) has a hefty load of international services, including a 25 percent stake in international air courier DHL, which, though not publicly traded, is unlikely to escape the Y2K crisis unscathed. Japan Airlines carries over 30 million passengers annually and has code-sharing and computer reservation system sharing with American Airlines.

Industry giant KLM Royal Dutch Airlines (symbol: KLM) is truly a global airline with global Y2K exposure. KLM services 164 destinations in seventy-five countries on six continents. It has a code-sharing partnership with Northwest Airlines (another high-flyer at risk from the bug) and other agreements that raise its total service to more than 400 cities worldwide. Like Northwest, it is heavily dependent on its cargo sales, which are the type of services that will suffer dramatically if Y2K shuts down airports.

Specialty Airlines

Some publicly air carriers offer unique services, such as charter planes. The largest such charter airline is Amtran (symbol: AMTR), based out of Indianapolis. Amtran operates tour group charters to vacation destinations, mostly in the U.S., Europe, and Latin America. In our view, charter airlines face fewer Y2K consequences, provided they get their internal systems into compliance. This is because, unlike other airlines which operate full schedules, charter airlines have greater flexibility in their scheduling and aren't as vulnerable to airport or air traffic related delays. If a charter flight is delayed, it won't necessarily impact on other charter flight operations.

Another specialty airline is Midwest Express Airlines (symbol: MEH) which offers nonstop service to destinations in the Midwest and Canada that larger low-fare airlines can't economically service. Like Amtran, Midwest Express is not likely to suffer as much under the Y2K crisis, in this case because the total amount of traffic at its destination cities is comparatively lower and less likely to be snarled.

Concluding Thoughts

Our discussion on airlines and air courier companies isn't intended as a criticism of the industry, though the same can't be said for the FAA. The fact is, the industry is up against enormous odds when it comes to Y2K. Could it make it through the crisis? Maybe. If there is any industry that has shown it can weather crises big and small, it is air transportation. But our job is to tell you why we think air transport is going to have a tough time licking Y2K, and why their stocks probably will take a beating.

One final telling signal: the insurance industry has begun to hint that airlines might not be able to obtain insurance against Y2K-related failures. If the insurers go so far as to deny coverage for Year 2000 problems, this could ground airlines altogether, according to Y2K experts from the Gartner Group.[87] Insurers in general are already busy lobbying state legislatures to allow them to exempt Y2K-related claims from standard coverage, arguing that the danger is avoidable and is well-known to business.

Some insurers have already curtailed certain types of travel insurance coverage. While accident and medical coverage will most likely be covered, British insurance companies already have begun to add disclaimers to their policies stating that they will not settle claims for cancellations, disruptions, delays, and lost baggage.[88] We expect U.S. insurers will not be far behind, once they take a look at the breadth and magnitude of the Y2K problem in the airline industry. Could the insurance companies know something the airlines don't? If the insurance industry isn't prepared to bet on air travel to come through during the Y2K crisis, investors also should take their money elsewhere as well.

THREE

CRITICAL CONDITION: THE HEALTH CARE INDUSTRY AND Y2K

If tonight when the clock struck midnight the calendar flipped to December 31, 1999, large portions of the health care system would fail.

—Senator Bob Bennett, chairman of the Special Senate Committe on the Year 2000 Technology Problem

Nowhere are the stakes of Year 2000 failure as high as in a hospital.

—John Koskinen, chairman of the President's Council on Year 2000 Conversion

Where health care is concerned, there is no Y2K problem too small to overlook. Malfunctioning elevators may be a nuisance to the average office worker, but they could be deadly to someone on his way to the emergency room. For a bank's customers, improper date calculations could mean an extra visit or two to clear things up, but for a hospital's patients it could mean a life-threatening misdiagnosis. Problems with phone lines and pager systems could snarl commerce, but they spell utter chaos for surgeons on call twenty-four hours a day.

In some ways, the health care industry is similar to the airline industry. Hospitals, nursing homes, and other services operate around the clock, every day of the year. We put our trust and our lives in the hands of the professionals of the industry, making both of the industries relatively high-profile targets for media and public scrutiny. Correct and complete data is critical to the continued, proper functioning of services. And government plays a critical role in the overall system.

But unlike airlines, which can always ground flights in the event of serious Y2K disruptions, hospitals don't have the luxury of delaying vital services while computer or systems problems are sorted out. While Y2K probably won't cause planes to drop out of the sky, it is quite possible that it *will* cause serious lapses in the quality of patient care, even to the point of unnecessary injury or death—raising the specter of legal liability. If this sounds extreme, don't just take our word for it: The British government released a study warning that there would be between 600 and 1,500 deaths in the United Kingdom as a result of Y2K failures in health care services.[1] A more recent survey of health care providers by Rx2000 Solutions Institute, a non-profit organization assisting the health care industry through the Y2K crisis, found that 94 percent of respondents foresaw "significant potential" for unnecessary deaths.[2] And the Association of American Medical Colleges has urged hospitals to deal with Y2K soon or face "potentially disastrous ramifications for patient care."[3]

Y2K failures mean "significant potential" for unnecessary deaths

While airlines rely on the government to manage air traffic so that their operations run on time, the health care industry's financial backbone is the Medicare system, which pays for around *half* of medical services in the U.S. today. Government experts already have begun to warn that problems with processing of Medicare payments—and they are legion—would mean financial ruin for many health care providers.

In this chapter, we'll explore the health care industry's vulnerability to Y2K and show why investors should pay attention. Most of us are not used to thinking of hospitals and health care companies as businesses that also need to watch their earnings and share prices, but in fact a lot of money is at stake in health care equities. By some accounts, the industry makes up a full one-seventh of the U.S. economy.[4] While many of the nation's 6,000 hospitals, 30,000 nursing homes, and countless physician practices are privately owned or not-for-profit, industry consolidation has seen the rise of large, publicly traded health care corporations. Small investors worried about Y2K should underweigh, stay clear of, or even short these health care companies until the crisis has passed.

When Do They Sleep?

We all know that emergency room doctors and other health care professionals enjoy much less quality shut-eye than the rest of us. That's because they can't control when emergencies will arise that require their services. In this sense, the health care industry is even more time sensitive than the airlines. While both industries operate around the clock,

Y2K RISK FACTOR
Time Sensitivity

every day of the year, hospitals can't always predict when they will be in a crunch. This means communications have to be 100 percent reliable—especially the critical pager networks that doctors rely on when on call. It means computer systems and equipment have to operate as expected, or lives could be lost. Supplies with limited shelf-life or rare prescription medications need to be available on request. Inventory and other computer records have to be accurate; patients can't always afford to wait while a critical machine, blood test result, or patient record is tracked down.

All these time-sensitive operations make the health care industry particularly vulnerable to Y2K. In the previous chapter, we discussed how the principal unwelcome consequence of Y2K will be *delay*. For health care providers, especially in emergency care, significant delays resulting from Y2K are simply unacceptable. If the Y2K problem is ultimately perceived as life threatening, it will fundamentally change the way hospitals operate during the first part of the year 2000.

How will Y2K delays impact the health care industry's bottom line? One factor will be an increase in the number of lawsuits. If what should be routine surgeries start to go terribly wrong because of unnecessary delays, the floodgates would open to litigation, and hospitals would spend much of their time and money defending their Y2K compliance programs in the courts. Malpractice insurance will become more costly, and perhaps even unavailable for

Gauge the insurance companies

Y2K-related incidents. In fact, insurance companies have been quietly busy protecting their interests in light of Y2K: As of mid-1998, forty-six states had given permission to the insurance industry to deny Y2K-related claims.[5] Later in this chapter, we'll break down the types of Y2K-related medical failures that could lead to crushing legal liability for health care providers.

There are other costs associated with expected delays which fall generally into the category of business contingencies. In anticipation of the crisis, hospitals will stock up on inventories, particularly perishable items and critical medications. Hospitals will also pay staff to work longer or extra shifts to ensure there are enough hands for when systems may need to switch to manual operations. (So concerned is one rural hospital in Texas that it is taking the extraordinary step at the stroke of midnight, December 31, 1999, of posting a health care worker at the bedside of every patient—armed with medical equipment and a flashlight.)[6] Many hospitals are planning to postpone the scheduling of profitable elective surgeries until after the crisis is under control in order to ensure that enough hospital resources are available to handle emergency cases. And as the extent of unrecoverable contingency costs becomes clearer, you can expect some health care firms to issue earnings warnings and to experience significant falls in their stock prices.

Comatose Compliance Plans

Given the high risk that Y2K poses to health care firms, you would expect that the industry would be a leader in Y2K preparedness.

Y2K RISK FACTOR

Lack of Y2K Preparedness

Unfortunately, the health care sector is among the least ready of all. It was slower than other sectors to recognize the danger posed by Y2K. Surveys have found that as of mid-1998, while 80 percent of hospitals were looking at the Y2K problem, only *30 percent* had any formal plan to deal with it. In addition, a worrisome *90 percent* of physicians were taking *no action whatsoever* in their offices, where computerized records are often kept.[7] This despite the fact that 65 percent of respondents to an Rx2000 Solutions Institute survey had already experienced Y2K-related failures in their health care organizations.[8]

Those familiar with the extent of the work required to tackle the Y2K problem in hospitals were not optimistic. "If they are only starting work on the problem this year, I'm afraid it's too late," commented the chief operating officer for Inova Fairfax Hospital in Falls Church, Virginia. That hospital had begun its Y2K work as early as

1995.[9] "Health care in general is probably behind the curve," said an officer of the Oklahoma Hospital Association. "Hospitals must do everything possible to be compliant. But there are so many unknowns. Many people are talking in 'what ifs.' "[10]

Health care firms have only recently started to come out of their comas. By mid-1998, they finally had recognized Y2K as their number one information technology priority. Fretted one IT spokesperson for Oakland, California-based Kaiser Per- *No money for* manente, "Next year, we're worried that we won't have *anything else* any money to do anything else."[11] Added Kaiser's national project manager for information technology, "No one has ever dealt with a problem of this magnitude before."[12]

According to a study by market researcher Gartner Group, Inc., which surveyed 341 integrated health care firms, Year 2000 compliance work is the runaway priority for Integrated Delivery Systems,[13] which coordinate primary care and specialty physician services with hospital outpatient and inpatient services. Gartner estimated that health care firms will spend an average of $4.8 million on Y2K fixes and testing. But Gartner also projected that each will face an additional average $10 to $20 million once legal fees, contingency plans, business continuity expenses, and project management costs are taken into account.[14]

According to Gartner, these higher costs are due to the fact that health care delivery systems didn't even have Y2K on their radar maps in 1997, when there was still time to bring all devices and systems into compliance. Due to their late *87 percent* start and their "totally inadequate funding," Gartner pre- *failure rate?* dicts that 87 percent of those surveyed will experience system failures related to Y2K.[15] Other broad surveys back up these statistics. According to Cap Gemini America, a leading IT service company, among large U.S. corporations major health care providers rank lowest in Y2K preparedness.[16] As one Senate watchdog remarked, "If there isn't more action, I'm afraid this Y2K problem could have this nation's health care system on a respirator come January 2000."[17]

One of the problems in the industry is that it is extremely fragmented, without significant cross-communication and cooperation. There are no "Big 3" or "Big 6" companies as there are in the automotive and telecommunications sectors. As a result, there have been a lot of duplicative efforts and little information sharing within or among competitors and payers, and even less with industry vendors, as discussed later in this chapter. There is also little, if any, consensus within the industry as to how best to tackle the Y2K problem. This disparity is apparent in the difference in testing procedures across different health care groups—from aggressive system-wide testing to complete reliance on vendor assurances. Further, government has been of limited assistance in coordinating and disseminating critical information. The result of the disorganization and lack of leadership is a dangerously late start for the industry in addressing the problem, widespread underestimation of the cost and time required, and an increase in overall expenses and risk-exposure from Y2K.

Disaster Mode

Some hospitals have expressed concern that they will be under the kinds of pressures indicative of natural disasters, when normal operations are disrupted and nothing can be completely counted on. The good news is that most hospital workers are trained for crisis situations. "As an industry we continuously have to be prepared for disasters," said the vice president of corporate service at Exempla Healthcare. "We have to deal with backup plans and emergency situations every day, and the Year 2000 problem is no different."[18]

No different? Well, not quite. Compare Y2K to an earthquake. An earthquake might disrupt power, might cause a sudden increase in the number of emergency patients, and might make transportation of critical medical supplies difficult or impossible. The hospital facility itself might be unsafe to work in, and hospitals would resort to temporary triage centers. The medical staff would be in "disaster mode," and would take precautions and measures accordingly. Under Y2K, however, the "crisis" would be quite different. Things might appear on the surface to be perfectly normal. But then, the machines stage a quiet revolution. Patient records disappear. Blood by-products are lost in the supply chain. Devices from imaging equipment to medical cameras provide faulty output. Are hospitals prepared for this kind of crisis? How do you prepare for a bug that you can't always see but that could strike anywhere in the system?

Auto Rx

Modern health care providers use an array of computer systems and software to streamline their patient services. When a patient needs hospitalization, a typical process[19] might be as follows:

Y2K RISK FACTOR
Automation

- The patient's doctor schedules a hospital admission date from an office computer and includes specific medical orders.

- The same computer interfaces electronically with the patient's insurance company to process and settle coverage and claims.

- The hospital computer automatically generates and sends a letter informing the patient which tests will be performed.

- The tests themselves use devices and interface with software that will process and electronically transmit data into the hospital's clinical data system.

- The hospital's scheduling computer designates a time for the surgery, surgical suite location, and staffing for the operation, as well as any medical needs.

- These staffing, scheduling, and inventory requirements are electronically forwarded to the proper departments where they are confirmed.

- During the operation, the patient relies on complex devices such as monitors, anesthetic machines, and infusion pumps, all of which use embedded chips to function properly.

- After the operation, the patient's meals, medications, and other post-surgery services are scheduled by the hospital computers.

- The patient is automatically sent a bill for the procedure and hospital stay, which is also processed with the patient's insurance company.

This simple example demonstrates that hospitals and other health services, like other modern businesses, have become quite dependent on computers to run complex operations and to manage the flow of business. It also refutes those who argue that the health care industry won't be deeply affected by Y2K because doctors are still in the "technological stone age." Even if many doctors still keep handwritten records and patient charts in manila folders, there are a lot of places where software has replaced people in order to improve services and lower costs. For example, the American Medical Assocation, in a survey conducted in 1998, found that some 90 percent of U.S. doctors use computers in their practices, and 40 percent have logged in their patients' medical histories. This is understandable, indeed probably necessary, due to the increasingly complex demands of managed care, where information sharing requires data interchange on referrals, prescriptions, and insurance claims.[20]

The example also helps show how many points there are in the system where things could go wrong from Y2K-related glitches. Software errors could cause the whole patient sched-

No appointments today, or tomorrow . . .

uling system to crash long before the patient even gets to the hospital or testing lab. In fact, this has already occurred with one system in Pennsylvania that is used to schedule appointments for three local hospitals and seventy-five local clinics. As early as 1997, when the system was asked to accept patient appointments past the year 2000, the entire system shut down.[21]

Y2K glitches could result in the corruption or unavailability of crucial information such as known reactions to prescription medications. The pharmacy subsystem itself, which uses information such as a patient's age in its calculations, could prescribe the wrong dosage of a drug, with disastrous consequences.[22] Or the system could try to subtract a patient's age from "00" and arrive at a negative number, resulting in a complete shutdown. Lamented a spokesperson for Mercy Healthcare in Sacramento, "There is no rhyme or reason as to which time or date will come out of a system."[23]

A pharmacy itself may have its inventory tied into a Y2K-affected internal clock and might fail to reorder medication, leading to inadequate stocks. Warns Frederick Kohun, a Y2K expert at the Robert Morris College in Pennsylvania, "If I were someone on a life-sustaining prescription, I would stock up before the end of the year."

Kohun further observed that insurance companies "are beginning to break down their own policies and rules on this, knowing who will be liable—them—if somebody dies because they cannot get their drugs. They are starting to allow people to stockpile."[24] Kohun's warnings were given an added sense of urgency when the clocks turned over to 1999 and some 100,000 enrollees with Blue Cross-Blue Shield were denied their prescription authorizations due to a programming glitch. (Officials at PCS Health Systems, which manages the drug benefit plan, state that the date problem was unrelated to Y2K, but it may be a prelude of what we can expect.)[25]

The same British study that predicted hundreds of Y2K-related deaths in the U.K. laid out a scenario that pointed not to primary life-sustaining devices as the chief culprits, but rather to faulty computerized medical records or emergency systems, which could lead to lost or bad data on diagnoses, medical histories, and treatments.[26] Dr. Kenneth Kizer, Veterans Affairs undersecretary of health, is worried about precisely this type of problem: "[A] patient could get the lab results of the patient who preceded or succeeded him or her, with potentially adverse consequences."[27]

These examples help show why many health care providers are spending most of their efforts fixing problems in their care delivery operations, perhaps to the detriment of problems that will result in hospital billings, insurer interfaces, and other financial software systems. Given limited time and resources, this prioritization is understandable, and perhaps is even indicative of how providers also consider themselves public servants first and businesses next. This may be comforting to patients, but it won't go far to alleviate investor concerns.

My Problem Is Your Problem

In our earlier examples in chapter 1 of the United Parcel Service strike and the Galaxy IV satellite pager network failure, the health care industry was in both situations one of the hardest hit industries. As we showed, the UPS strike affected JIT operations, on which hospitals largely depend. The pager outage in some cases left doctors with no options but to be physically present at hospitals during the entire time that the network was down. These examples demonstrate how modern health care has grown dependent on the seamless operation of other systems and businesses. Hospitals today, like other industries, have been able to capitalize on the efficiencies and technical advances of others in order

Y2K RISK FACTOR
Interdependence

to better serve the public. But when other sectors experience break-downs, hospitals feel the pressure disproportionately.

Hospitals depend on an array of other health care services and sup-pliers in order to provide comprehensive patient care. Ambulance and other emergency services are often independently operated and could experience delays from dispatch errors and other system glitches. The nation's blood supply could face distribution problems. Linen and food services are often outsourced and could be disrupted. The list of poten-tial breakdowns in support services and supplies is alarmingly long.

One ominous possibility is a shortage of key drugs in 2000. Critical pharmaceutical products are often manufactured by a few key com-panies with their own set of Y2K problems. For example, according to one Y2K expert in the health care sector, 70 percent of the world's insulin supply comes from one manufacturer based in Holland and could be at risk if normal supply channels are disrupted.[28]

Hospitals also rely on around-the-clock, uninterrupted operations by power, water, telephone, and transportation companies. Spot out-ages or delays, which of course affect all sectors, are particularly wor-risome for health care providers, whose patients' lives are at stake.

The interdependence of the health care industry is also clear when you look at the level of interaction between providers and others in the payment process alone. Later in this chapter we devote separate sections to the gargantuan Y2K problems in the Medicare and Medic-aid systems. But besides the government, health care companies inter-act constantly with insurance companies, claims processors, banks, and third-party payers. All of these systems must be compliant in order for data exchange to occur properly.

Deeply Embedded Problems

One obvious preparation that hospitals must undertake is the thor-ough evaluation of all electronic medical devices. Hospitals are espe-cially vulnerable to failures in embedded chips—the microprocessors that contain "burned-in" software, as opposed to the standard programmable software code associated with computers. A microchip is actually a "mini-computer" that con-trols a device's operation. Chips lurk in all kinds of equipment, and

Y2K *ADDED* RISK FACTOR
Noncompliant Medical Devices

date-dependent ones could cause devices to shut down or begin to process incorrect data on January 1, 2000.

The embedded chip problem is a significant worldwide threat. Estimates put the number of embedded systems in existence between ten and twenty-five billion. Between two-tenths to 1 percent of these systems use current dates to perform calculations or to operate. These chips are considered subject to failure due to Y2K, putting the number of at-risk embedded systems somewhere between 20 and 250 million.[29] Within the health care sector, the potential failure rate may be substantially higher: an ongoing survey of medical devices by Catholic Healthcare West reveals a failure rate of *20 percent.*[30]

In some ways, the Y2K problem with embedded chips is easier to deal with than that of noncompliant software. A device is often simpler to identify as noncompliant than is a bug-filled software program with millions of lines of code. With hospitals, some have taken the low-tech yet effective approach of tagging devices that have been inspected and certified as Y2K ready. "We want our patients to see that we are working on this problem," said a director of Columbia HCA's information systems. "When they ask if a machine will work at midnight, I want a nurse to be able to turn that machine around and show them that it was checked on this date and that date and that it will work."[31] In addition, Y2K fixes for embedded microchips don't always require the hiring of programmers familiar with old computer languages such as COBOL. When vendors are cooperative, it may be just a matter of a quick fix, replacement part, or work-around plan.

In other ways, however, the Y2K embedded chip problem is more vexing than bad software code. Some devices may appear to be working properly but run afoul later in unexpected ways. Devices that appear identical might contain different kinds of chips, some that are date-dependent and some not.[32] Nontechnical staff on walk-through inspections may overlook critical equipment that they assumed had no need for date calculations. "The hardest part will be finding out which systems have these hidden embedded chips," admitted an information systems specialist at Integris Health System, where some 40 percent of the equipment is thought to be affected.[33] A noncompliant device, even if successfully identified, will often either have to be upgraded with a new microprocessor or replaced. This could be very expensive in the case of specialized instrumentation or equipment.

Hospitals got an early scare in January 1999 when the FDA

announced that fifteen medical devices made by seven different manufacturers actually failed to make the transition to 1999 successfully. These included one model of Hewlett-Packard defibrillators, which are used to stabilize a patient's heartbeat. The model in question would display the wrong date—1985—and might store and print incorrect dates if not adjusted before 1999.[34] Another device with problems was the ironically named Millennia 3500 multiparameter patient monitor, made by Invivo, which would experience record-keeping problems if the display clocks were reset during the year's turnover.[35] While the problems reported did not pose immediate health risks, they "created a potential for confusion and incorrect records," according to the FDA.[36]

When the Chips Are Down

Manufacturers and health care end users of devices at least agree on one thing: Many crucial medical devices are at risk of "hard crashes" occurring within their embedded systems. In a midsummer 1998 tour of a Washington, D.C.-area hospital, aides to Senator Christopher Dodd found that nearly 35 percent of medical devices would fail if the millennium were upon the hospital at that time.[37] The list of potential device failures and potential consequences is enough to make anyone think twice about checking into a hospital soon after the turn of the millennium. Rx2000 Solutions reports that its members have experienced serious problems, including reported glitches with hemistry analyzers, hematology analyzers, coagulation profilers, and immuno-assay analyzers.[38] We can't tell you precisely what each of these pieces of equipment does, but we are sure that we wouldn't want them failing us if we were patients in a hospital, and they are obvious lightning rods for plaintiffs' attorneys.

There are already serious problems in devices

More familiar equipment at risk from Y2K includes CAT scanners, MRIs, dialysis machines, and mechanical ventilators.[39] One blood gas analyzer brought before the Senate committee has been trying to reboot itself for three-and-a-half months.[40]

Another alarming example cited during Senate testimony was that of a radiation emitter. This is a device typically used to treat cancer patients. To function correctly, the system needs to perform current date calculations, including the age of the radioactive isotope and the date of the patient's last visit. The consequences of a miscalculation are serious, since a patient could get the wrong dosage of radiation.[41] Of course, in the world of Y2K, such machines—and they cost a pretty penny—might as well be junk metal if they are not checked, fixed, and tested.

Another example is an infusion pump, which measures drops of medication as they are given intravenously. Problems with the embedded chip in such a pump could result in real-time miscalculations and wrong dosage of medication. One provider in Minnesota, Allina Health Services, has had trouble confirming with its vendor whether its some 800 infusion pumps will be compliant: "At a certain point, we will begin to eliminate those infusion pumps from our inventory if we don't get any vendor information about them," said Allina's vice president of risk and insurance services.[42]

While in some cases the risk is an outright failure of medical devices—the nightmare scenario of flat lines on patient monitors or the above example of radiation overdoses for patients—in most cases, medical devices with noncompliant chips will continue to operate but will give faulty date readings, possibly resulting in incorrect patient diagnoses. For example, defibrillators and portable EKG readers have failed in tests to print the date of patient treatments, meaning doctors will have to hand-write the date or remember to manually program each device.[43] While this might seem like a small thing to ask, remember that doctors are used to relying on machines to keep these kind of date records, and getting practitioners to do things the old-fashioned way may not be easy or prudent from the standpoint of malpractice exposure.

Another important point is that medical devices that are otherwise unaffected by Y2K may be hooked up to software programs that are affected. Take the case of pacemakers, which industry defenders often point to as being safe and not date sensitive. A software program that is date-dependent may fail to properly convert pacemaker telemetry data or calculate its rate response.[44] Thus, doctors and hospitals will have to make sure that their pacemaker *programming* machines are Y2K compliant, even if the pacemaker itself is not at risk.[45] Another frightening example cited was an intensive care monitor, which would accurately read a patient's heart rhythms (and therefore seem perfectly compliant), but, due to a Y2K problem, would fail to sound an alarm if the heartbeat became irregular.[46] Hospitals that fail to conduct thorough tests wouldn't know about this problem until after it was too late.

The risk of medical device failures has serious legal consequences for health care providers. In the world of medical malpractice, lawyers will look for evidence of *negligence* by doctors and hospitals. They will argue that Y2K was a preventable problem that should have been eliminated in plenty of time. The kinds of breaches of the duty of professional care, along with examples of nightmare Y2K equipment failures, were laid out by the Rx2000 Solutions Institute as a warning to health care providers:

- Failure to treat. A physician fails to perform a caesarian section in time. The diagnostic equipment went down due to a Y2K glitch in its date-coded microchip, and the doctor failed to detect fetal distress, resulting in brain damage to the infant.

- Failure to diagnose. A physician examines a patient complaining of chest pains. Because his diagnostic equipment fails, the doctor unwittingly releases the patient, who then dies a few hours later from a heart attack.

- Failure to monitor. A nurse fails to observe weakening vital signs on a patient because the monitor provides inaccurate data, causing the patient to suffer respiratory arrest.

- Failure to administer medication. A physician administers too much, too little, or the wrong medication, which injures or kills the patient, because the equipment the physician relied upon did not yield accurate data.

- Failure to administer anesthesia. A nurse anesthetist administers too little anesthesia—or worse still, a fatal dose of anesthesia when the anesthetic equipment in the operating room provides incorrect date-sensitive data.

- Failure to promulgate appropriate policies and procedures. A hospital's staff lacks sufficient awareness of Y2K and its manifestations, or was not trained in detection techniques or treatment of the patient in the event equipment fails, and consequently makes repeated errors in patient care.

The Rx2000 Solutions Institute concludes:

All of these examples highlight exposures arising out of Millennium Bug infections caused by the products which rely on date-coded microchips. Hospital directors and officers have an obligation to ensure that functioning medical equipment has been acquired to provide the care offered by the institution, and that it has been adequately maintained. If the directors and officers have not taken appropriate steps to treat the Year 2000 Virus [sic] in these and other hosts in the hospital environment, they will be held personally liable for breaching the duty of due care if patients are harmed because of biomedical equipment that has been fatally infected with the Millennium Bug.[47]

The irony of the Y2K medical device crisis has not been lost on the industry. As one trustee for the American Medical Association observed, high-tech medical devices and advances in technology have been responsible for major improvements in medical treatment during the twentieth century. But these same devices and technologies now pose significant risks for patients at the end of the century.[48]

Left to Their Own Devices? The Struggle With Medical Device Vendors

In hospitals, the situation is particularly thorny because there are so many medical devices made by so many different vendors. According to the Food and Drug Administration, there are over 100,000 different kinds of medical devices divided into some 1,700 different categories.[49] Of course, many of these devices are not electronic, and among those that are, a smaller percentage contain embedded chips. Such devices include, for example, infusion pumps, pacemakers, and ventilators. Among these devices, however, only a few rely on the current date to operate. For instance, experts agree that pacemaker devices are not at risk from Y2K because they do not need to know the date in order to stimulate the heart. The problem stems, however, from the unknown number of devices that could still fail. Columbia HCA, the nation's largest hospital operator, with over 300 hospitals, is spending over $60 million to assess, and where necessary fix, over 400,000 of its devices.[50]

One company, 400,000 devices

Many hospitals unfortunately took the early position that vendors of medical devices ultimately would provide certification data on their equipment. "There's some equipment that we'll be able to test, but on much of it we'll have to take our vendor's certification that it's year 2000 compliant as gospel," admitted a director at Robert Wood Johnson University Hospital at Hamilton, New Jersey.[51] Others echoed that sentiment. The chief information officer of Capital Health Systems said brightly in early 1998, "We're in the process of contacting our vendors and having them put in writing what equipment they sold us has embedded-chip systems that are year 2000 compliant and which ones are not."[52]

Sadly, vendors have been proven hard to pin down on Y2K compliance information. Today, few hospitals would expect vendors to put such information in writing. A substantial number of vendors are not at all cooperative. Fearing legal liability, they are unwilling or hesitant to certify their equipment as Y2K compliant. Some refuse to respond, and others flat out lie. In some circumstances, according to industry spokespersons, manufacturers may be reluctant to respond until they have a "patch" to repair their systems and prevent users from purchasing from other manufacturers.[53] Other smaller vendors have either gone out of business or left no forwarding address.[54]

The FDA has originally estimated, perhaps too conservatively, that of the 16,000-some medical device manufacturers, around 2,700 of them make products that could be affected by Y2K. Even though the FDA had requested reports on safety and repair plans from these manufacturers, only around 500 of them had responded by mid-1998.[55] As of November 1998, according to one publisher of a medical device newsletter, out of a pool of 4,150 manufacturers of potentially at-risk devices, the FDA had identified over 500 companies that had not offered any information on their Year 2000 readiness.[56]

The Veterans Administration complained of similar noncooperation from its vendors. As of mid-1998, there were still some 233 vendors who had not even responded to the VA's repeated requests for basic Y2K compliance information.[57] And among the medical device vendors that did respond, many of the responses were virtually worthless.[58] Other Y2K crusaders were met with similar inaction. In September 1998, Senator Dodd told Congress that he had identified approximately 1,180 medical device companies that still had not released adequate year 2000 information.[59]

Congressional spokespersons and physician groups have criticized the FDA for not doing more to get the vendors to own up to the problem. The FDA had an opportunity (which it promptly blew) in June 1997 to take a hard line on the issue. At that time, the FDA issued a letter to medical device manufacturers that was intended to "remind" them that some of their equipment "may experience problems" due to Y2K. This letter, however, had absolutely no teeth. It simply wound up "recommending" conducting hazard and safety analyses with respect to existing equipment, and if problems were detected, to take "appropriate steps" to "assist customers who have purchased such devices."[60]

FDA speaking softly, but no big stick

The FDA and the Department of Health and Human Services finally started to take a tougher stand in early 1998. In a letter sent in January 1998 to the same health care device manufacturers, the FDA had changed its lackadaisical tune, noting that the Y2K bug in medical device chips "could pose potentially serious health and safety consequences." The FDA intended to publish data on compliance on its website and to do "targeted follow-up regarding nonrespondents."[61]

But by this time, the lawyers for the health care manufacturers already had beaten the FDA to the punch. The Health Industry Manufacturers Association, a group whose members make 90 percent of all medical devices, took the position that while Y2K is a significant problem, keeping track of which companies' devices could fail is tricky, and companies are best approached on a "case-by-case" basis.[62] HIMA also asserted that the FDA "has no legal authority" to require device makers to submit Y2K information on their products for publication on its Internet site.[63] Sadly, they are probably correct: The FDA lacks authority to force companies to publicize problems *before* they occur— which in the Y2K crisis would be far too late.

The medical device industry's hard-line stance has irked many. The chairman of the Senate's Special Committee on the Year 2000 Technology Problem, Senator Bob Bennett of Utah, has threatened to publish the names of vendors that don't reveal product assessments to end users. "I get very, very impatient with people who hide behind lawyers," Bennett declared.[64]

Are the device manufacturers hiding behind their lawyers?

His vice-chair on the committee, Senator Dodd, agreed, calling HIMA's position "arrogant" and saying he was "deeply disturbed by the fact that instead of taking steps to deal with this problem, the medical-device industry as a whole seems to be exacerbating the problem by refusing to provide information either to the FDA, which regulates device safety, or even to the hospitals and clinics which use the devices every day."[65] Stung by the criticism, HIMA later agreed to urge its members to cooperate with the FDA.

The result of these competing legal, economic, and regulatory interests is that hospitals and the public are left with significant doubts about the status of important medical devices. In 1998, this has led some in the industry to call for immediate government intervention. Said one spokesperson for the American Hospital Association, "We need the federal government to exercise its authority in this area— now. We need the federal government to create an atmosphere in which everyone involved in the health care field will view the full and timely disclosure of Year 2000 computer problems not only as diligent and prudent behavior—the right thing to do—but also as mandatory conduct."[66]

But given the impasse and the government's inaction, the medical community knows it must take proactive steps itself. The AHA has issued a written warning that hospitals and doctors may be liable for incidents resulting from Y2K noncompliance. Hospitals now understand that they must test every device, even if the vendor claims compliance.[67] As we show below, this is a costly, time-consuming, and, in some cases, impossible task with serious consequences in terms of legal liability and financial exposure.

Anteing Up

In addition to the threat of massive legal exposure, the cost of upgrading, replacing, or retiring these defective systems cannot be understated. This includes the current costs of Y2K assessment, implementation, and testing. Then there is the cost of replacing defective equipment. The industry itself has calculated that 3 percent of noncompliant devices cannot be fixed[68] (though others would place this percentage considerably higher). As one Y2K consultant observed, many diagnostic medical devices that must be retired have outlived their depreciation, and the capital required to replace them is significant. One health care company, according to the consultant, is

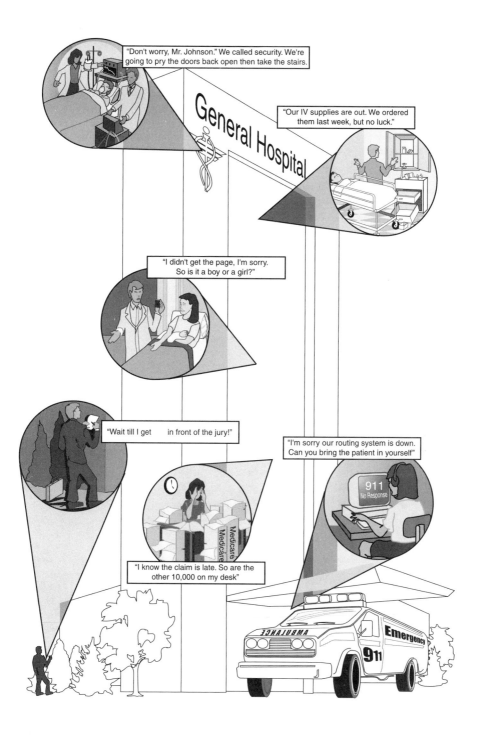

wrestling with $1 billion in such costs.[69] Hospitals must decide whether to eat the high cost of replacement or diminish the quality and range of health services available while devices are left idle.

There are also the less visible opportunity costs. Money spent on Y2K is *nearly* pure maintenance. It has no appreciable payback in terms of greater efficiency or better machinery. This money could otherwise have been spent on information technology projects such as clinical information systems, which would ultimately reflect back positively on the bottom line. Equipment that must be retired or shelved while awaiting replacement can't be used, so fees can't be generated from them. Add to the mixture the financial exposure from liability and business contingency costs resulting from systems that are not made compliant in time. All these factors could lead to significant earnings shocks for the health care industry in the coming quarters.

Medicrash? The Health Care Financing Administration's Y2K Crisis

Over forty million Americans currently receive some sort of Medicare benefits. There are some seventy claims processing centers with seventy-eight different payment systems dealing with over 1.7 million providers nationwide. The system processes some seventeen million transactions per week, for a total of *800 million* claims each year. This amounts to payments of hundreds of billions of dollars annually and forms the backbone of health care industry.

Y2K *ADDED* RISK FACTOR
Government Systems
Noncompliant

The size and scope of Y2K problems within the Medicare system are as large as the system itself. A full 98 percent of inpatient hospital and Medicare Part A claims (covering institutional care) and 85 percent of physician and other Medicare Part B claims (covering physician, supplier, and other outpatient services) are handled electronically, making Medicare the most automated health payer system in the country.

50 million lines of code and counting

Given these figures, it is not surprising that the Health Care Financing Administration—the government entity in charge of processing and paying Medicare claims—has its hands full with the Y2K crisis.

According to the HCFA, some fifty million lines of internal and external code need to be renovated.[70] In addition, the HCFA must depend on its local Medicare contractors—the insurance companies that process claims for the HCFA—to bring their systems into compliance. Each of these Medicare contractors must work with health care providers to make sure the upgraded systems properly interface. It is a monumental task, and one that has the Y2K experts and watchdogs worried.

A breakdown in the Medicare and Medicaid payment system would be nothing short of catastrophic for health care providers. As we mentioned earlier, currently these payments account for around *half* of the revenues hospitals need to operate. "If that much revenue were to be suddenly cut off, hospitals could not survive, and patient care could be jeopardized," said a spokesperson for the American Hospital Association.[71] The industry already faces acute cash flow problems and operates on thin margins. A meltdown in the Medicare system would no doubt cause widespread health provider business failures and send investors running for cover.

Medicare Health Check

Unfortunately, the chances of an incomplete Y2K fix for the Medicare system are high. Since many people aren't familiar with exactly how Medicare payments work, what follows is a simple outline of the Medicare payment process. This will help show how vulnerable the payment network is to Y2K failure, and how most of the problem is beyond the power of the health providers to control.

Step 1: After a patient covered under Medicare receives treatment, the health care provider submits a claim to a local Medicare contractor.

Step 2: "Front end" systems at the local Medicare contractor collect, format, and edit the claim.

Step 3: Six standard systems at each Medicare contractor validate and screen claims data, eliminating duplicates, checking for fraud and abuse, assigning rates, and computing any patient liability.

Step 4: HCFA-supplied software gives standard provider codes, service groupings, payment rates, and fee schedules to the Medicare contractor. A main database for Medicare information—such as entitlement, eligibility, deductibles, and payment limits—is accessed and updated.

Step 5: "Back end" Medicare contractor systems issue payments, settle provider reports, coordinate with other insurers, maintain data files, and undertake rate reviews and payment adjustments.

Each of these steps represents a potential Y2K problem area. For example, submissions by health care providers at Step 1 are almost all done electronically. Problems could originate with the hospital's computer or the hospital's billing agent's computer. Medicare contractors must have Y2K compliant computers that can interface with all hospitals in the system. The HCFA must also make sure its systems are up to par so that it can access and use the data of its contractors.

Date calculations abound in the payment process because eligibility is defined by the beneciary's age (often calculated by taking today's date and subtracting the date of birth). We could see countless of cases of denied claims by otherwise eligible beneficiaries. In addition, we could see ineligible claims sail through, with the system so exposed to fraud on every level.

With so many potential problem areas and with so much at stake, the HCFA should have been on top of its Y2K program long ago. Sadly, however, the HCFA and the entire Department of Health and Human Services is way behind most other government departments and agencies. In 1997, the General Accounting Office issued a highly critical report on the state of the HCFA's Y2K program. Among the problems it cited were the following:

- The HCFA had not required its Medicare contractors to submit their Y2K plans for approval.
- The HCFA did not have specific legal agreements with Medicare contractors stating how or when the Y2K problem would be corrected.
- No critical areas of Y2K responsibilities had been identified; although HCFA's regional offices in part oversee Medicare contractors' efforts, their specific Y2K responsibilities had not been defined, nor had any guidance been given on how to monitor or evaluate their performance.

- The HCFA had not completed a review of Medicare contractors' claims processing systems, nor had it required contractors to prepare an assessment of the severity of potential Year 2000 problems.

- There was no plan for independent validation of Medicare contractors' strategies or test plans.

- While contractors were asked to identify their system interfaces, the HCFA had no plans for approving their approaches to addressing interface and data exchange issues.

- There were no contingency plans addressing business continuity issues; the HCFA was instead relying on the Medicare contractors to complete the work, but the Medicare contractors were also found to be lacking contingency plans, believing this to be the HCFA's responsibility.

- The HCFA had not considered the severity of a breakdown of the system on health providers—how many would not get paid, or would be paid late or in incorrect amounts.[72]

Because of these deficiencies, the Department of Health and Human Services received a D grade from the chairman of the House Subcommittee on Government Management, Information and Technology.[73] And in its report to Congress in September of 1998, the GAO reiterated its earlier concerns, stating that the HCFA was "severely behind schedule." The GAO added, "It is highly unlikely that all of the Medicare systems will be compliant in time to ensure the delivery of uninterrupted benefits and services into the year 2000."[74]

Here We Go Again

How did the HCFA fall so far behind and do so poor a job? The simple answer is *mismanagement*. In 1994, the HCFA had a grand idea: Solve the agency's multitude of computer problems (including Y2K) by changing over to a brand new system called the Medicare Transaction System. This system would have unified all of the systems and reduced out the redundant or outmoded ones, at a price tag of *one billion dollars*.

But the program never got off the ground. Congressional investigators pointed to delays, poor management, and serious cost overruns. The HCFA was criticized for charging into MTS before a plan was even developed to guide the process—kind of like building a house without first getting an architect to provide a plan.[75] What's worse, the HCFA had been attempting to upgrade to MTS while solving its existing Y2K problems—a strategy it later conceded was impossible—with the result that neither program succeeded. In 1997, MTS was axed by the Clinton administration, and the HCFA has been playing Y2K catch-up ever since.

Contractors that were preparing to switch to MTS had figured on bringing systems into Y2K compliance in tandem with the MTS transition. When MTS was dropped, the contractors had to go back to their old systems and plan to bring them into compliance, thus wasting precious information technology time and resources.

To make matters worse, just as with the FAA, in the fall of 1997 there was a change at the top of the HCFA. A new administrator, Nancy-Ann Min de Parle, was brought over from federal health programs at the Office of Management and Budget to head up the HCFA. From day one, she had to clear her desk of nearly every other HCFA program and focus on Y2K. "I think the turning point was, for me, when I got here and realized that not much had been done at all. And I was terrified, frankly, about the prospect of how much had to be done," de Parle told the *Washington Post*.[76] One early nightmare: de Parle learned that her staff had overlooked *twenty million* lines of computer code that had to be reviewed.

Passing the Bug: The HCFA and Medicare Contractors

In fairness, Medicare's Y2K crisis management is also hampered by the restraints placed on the HCFA with respect to Medicare contractors. The law requires that the HCFA only contract for services with insurance companies, rather than more technology-savvy transaction processing firms or IT firms. In addition, the HCFA is required by law to reimburse Medicare contractors for all allowable costs, and therefore it can't exert any financial pressure (e.g., the threat of withholding payments) on its contractors to bring their systems into Y2K compliance. The only thing the HCFA can do is threaten to cancel contracts based on breach of obligations by the contractor, or to keep noncompliant contractors out of new Medicare lines of business.

Will the HCFA be able to kick out noncompliant contractors from the system? Not likely. When the HCFA has canceled contracts with Medicare contractors in the past, it has taken *six to nine months* to transfer the workload to another contractor.[77] Thus, if a substantial number of Medicare contractors are not Y2K ready, the HCFA will either have to ask them to process the paperwork by hand or go through the arduous and time consuming process of transferring workloads. In either case, health providers will suffer the consequences of billions of dollars of unreimbursed claims.

When the HCFA has tried to get tough with its contractors, it has been met with resistance. The largest contractor by far is Blue Cross-Blue Shield, which processes 85 percent of Part A and 66 percent of Part B claims nationwide. When the HCFA proposed an amendment to its contracts making full Y2K compliance mandatory by December 31, 1998, Blue *Political hot potato* Cross-Blue Shield balked at the notion of "full compliance," noting that its own systems were dependent on the compliance of other vendors, which it could not force into compliance by a certain date. Blue Cross-Blue Shield also rejected the HCFA's call for certification of contractors' vendor compliance, saying this would pose an "unacceptable level of liability." When the HCFA prudently proposed that noncompliant participants be prevented from entering into other Medicare contracts such as new managed care contracts, Blue Cross-Blue Shield retorted that it found "no statutory basis for unilaterally debarring plans with Medicare contracts from participating in other Medicare programs . . . based on noncompliance of Medicare contractors."[78]

This buck-passing (or should we say "bug" passing?) recalls the infighting between the FDA and health industry device manufacturers discussed earlier. But while the lawyers are busy denying responsibility and covering their clients' legal behinds, the clock continues to tick on toward January 1, 2000. And while the circumstances may make the HCFA less blameworthy for Medicare's current Y2K crisis, it does nothing to alleviate the concerns of health care providers left holding empty wallets.

The lack of authority by the HCFA to force contractors to fix the Y2K problem may help explain the Medicare contractors' relatively slow response and alarming current status. By June 1998, only 75 percent of Medicare contractors had completed the *assessment* phase of their Y2K fix programs. As you recall, this is the second phase after awareness, and it is among the least time consuming. This means that a full 25 percent didn't even know how bad their problems were.

By January 1999, the situation looked somewhat better, with most contractors into the testing phase of their remediation process, and with the HCFA reporting "completed" fixes on some 95 percent of its own systems. But some ominous signs remain. At least one contractor that maintains software for seven other contractors has reported it is behind in its Y2K fixes. This contractor alone could paralyze around 15 percent of Medicare claims, not accounting for spillover effects from bad data in the system.[79]

No matter how the overall Y2K remediation process with the HCFA goes from here, it is already clear that health care providers will face some pain from the HCFA's struggle to quash the bug. The HCFA has already told Congress that it will miss several statutory deadlines under the balanced-budget agreement because of Y2K problems, including one provision that would have reduced what elderly patients must pay for hospital outpatient services.[80] The Balanced Budget Act had also mandated a new Medicare payment system that was to go into effect January 1, 2000. Because of the HCFA's workload with Y2K, the introduction of the new payment system has been pushed back until April 1, 2000, and health care providers already are out those extra allocated funds.

What About Plan B?

The HCFA's chief information officer has admitted, "We also know there is a possibility that, try as we might, some systems may not be fully compliant in time. Therefore, we are requiring the [operating divisions] to develop contingency plans that permit business continuity in the event of system failure." These plans include rerouting claims in the event of failures in some Medicare contractors' or providers' systems, assuming that it is clear that a failure has occurred. The HCFA must develop contingency plans for the 275 critical business functions and transactions that underpin the Medicare system. Its staff has estimated the number of backup plans needed at fifty to sixty.[81]

In the meantime, exactly what kind of contingency plans are already in place? None, apparently. Administrator de Parle made the following amazing statement to a Congressional committee:

If we do not fix all information systems that might have Year 2000 problems, enrollment systems might not function, beneficiaries could be denied services because providers may not be able to confirm eligibility, and providers could have cash flow problems because of delayed payments. *Processing paper claims by hand is one contingency if we fail.* Given the nearly one billion Medicare claims we process each year, it is a possibility that strongly motivates us to succeed." (Emphasis added.)[82]

Processing claims by hand? They can't be serious. Currently, Medicare processes the equivalent of twenty-seven million pages of paper daily.[83] If the average person working eight hours a day could handle ten pages an hour, the HCFA would still have to hire over 300,000 people to get the job done. And if the HCFA is concerned about duplication and erroneous data in its computer systems, just imagine what the system would face with all those mistake-prone humans shuffling the paperwork around.

A much better solution, and one supported by the American Hospital Association, is for Congress to authorize the use of interim Medicare payments to health care providers based on past payment levels. The HCFA has also considered this contingency, but has warned that it would also be a "considerable endeavor." Investors will have to wait and see whether Congress steps in to save Medicare in time.

As If That Weren't Bad Enough, There's Medicaid

The government's health care Y2K problems do not end with Medicare. There's also the Medicaid program, which is a jointly funded insurance program of the federal government and the states. Medicaid, begun in 1965, was a brainchild of President Lyndon Johnson's "Great Society" program. It provides coverage to about thirty-six million low-income and needy people, including children, the elderly, people with disabilities, and those eligible for federal income assistance. Medicaid covers services including hospital, physician, and nursing home care in all fifty states. In some states, other services are covered, including prescription drugs, hospice care, and personal care services.

Medicaid is the largest insurer of long-term care for Americans, paying over 50 percent of all nursing home costs. It is also the largest program providing health-related services to America's poorest, and it serves to keep several health care firms' coffers full. In 1995, Medicaid expenditures came to $152 billion, of which the states paid $66 billion and the federal government picked up the rest. (The figures are somewhat higher now, but were not available.) For some states, Medicaid takes up a huge percentage of the budget. For example, in 1995, California spent around 20 percent of its total state budget on Medicaid.[84]

Within broad federal guidelines, the states by and large operate the Medicaid program, setting eligibility standards, the scope of services, the rate of payment, and how the program is administered. Medicaid programs vary from state to state. Each state therefore has its own computer systems with its own set of code problems arising from Y2K. Because eligibility is often dependent upon age, date-based calculations abound in the system. And unfortunately, the more local you go with respect to the government, the more the Y2K problem seems to go unaddressed. While the federal government gets low marks for its Y2K efforts to date, some states, counties, and municipalities are so unprepared as to be beyond help. (For a more detailed criticism of local governments' Y2K programs, see chapter 8.)

Indeed, a study by the General Accounting Office in late 1998 of state Medicaid programs revealed that only *16 percent* of systems were on track for completion. The failure to remediate *Only 16 percent* systems, the report predicted, could "result in bil*of state systems* lions of dollars in benefit payments not being deliv*are on track* ered." Joel Willemssen, who supervises the GAO on computer operations in government agencies, called the study results "fairly discouraging."[85]

The HCFA indeed is worried about how Y2K could impact the nation's health care system by disrupting the Medicaid program. While the HCFA's Y2K program covers only its own systems and, to some extent, those of its contractor carriers and intermediaries, the HCFA also knows that failure by the states to address their systems could impact health care for the very poorest of beneficiaries and result in huge economic losses for providers seeking payments. In March 1998, the HFCA sent a letter to all state Medicaid directors informing them about the HCFA's own Y2K strategy. However, in that letter, the question of data exchanges between Medicare and state Medicaid systems was left unaddressed; the HCFA promised to contact state agencies "in the near future" to determine formats and compliance dates.[86]

Without a national, coordinated effort, Medicaid faces a grim future under the Y2K crisis. At least with Medicare, there is a possible way out of the crisis, through prompt Congressional action, that would preserve current provider payments so hospitals would not face cash crunches. With Medicaid, however, it is unlikely that every state will be willing or able to prepare such contingencies.

So, Which Health Care Companies Are at Risk?

Because health care is such a huge section of the U.S. economy, it is not surprising that there are hundreds of publicly traded health care companies out there, including hospital companies, long-term care providers, physician practice groups, third-party payers, managed care companies, and specialty care providers. **Y2K Stock Watch** There are also hundreds of companies associated with health services, such as pharmaceutical companies, medical device manufacturers, testing and clinical labs, and the like.

Our focus in this chapter has been on the actual providers of health care rather than those that provide ancillary services and products. But are all health care providers equally at risk from Y2K? There is no simple and tidy answer to this question. But from the preceding discussion, a few simple generalizations can be made. First, health care providers that deal with life-threatening or serious illness and injury are at risk due to the need for just-in-time operations and the threat of malpractice lawsuits. Second, providers that regularly utilize at-risk medical devices are at greater risk of being affected by the consequences of Y2K and will have to expend substantial time and money to fix the problem. Finally, providers that depend on Medicare and Medicaid reimbursements for their sales revenues may be in for a nasty cash-flow surprise should those systems crash and cause delays in payment. Using these general criteria, we can make a few observations about many of the largest publicly traded health care providers.

Hospitals on the Front Lines

Hospital stocks are probably the most exposed of all the health care companies to the Y2K menace. Take Columbia/HCA (symbol: COL), by far the largest of the hospital chains. Columbia/HCA owns over

300 hospitals and around 140 outpatient surgery centers and has annual revenues approaching $20 billion. As we mentioned earlier, Columbia/HCA needs to check over 400,000 devices in its hospitals and may incur significant replacement costs or face future litigation.

While it is easy to appreciate that Columbia/HCA will have its hands full at its hundreds of hospital facilities, what most people don't realize is that Columbia/HCA derives over one-third of its revenues from Medicare, and another 6 percent from Medicaid.[87] In short, up to 40 percent of Columbia/HCA's revenue stream could be at risk from Y2K if the government doesn't get its act together.

The second largest hospital chain, Tenet Healthcare Corporation (symbol: THC), which owns more than 120 hospitals in eighteen states, reported that it intended to spend in the neighborhood of $73 million to rid its systems and equipment of Y2K problems.[88] Tenet also gets over one-third of its money from the federal government through Medicare, though it did not list this as a risk to operations in its Y2K disclosures to the Security and Exchange Commission.[89] And number three Universal Health Services (symbol: UHS) gets around *50 percent* of its revenue from the government's Medicare and Medicaid programs, yet in its 1997 annual report it also does not mention this as a possible problem in dealing with the Y2K threat.[90]

Smaller hospitals appear to be no less dependent upon to government money. For the six-month period ending June 30, 1998, federal Medicare and state Medicaid programs accounted for over two-thirds of total hospital days at Province Healthcare Company (symbol: PRHC), which operates hospitals in rural areas in seven states.[91] Similarly, Health Management Associates, Inc. (symbol: HMA), which operates more than thirty hospitals, primarily in the Southeast, derives around two-thirds of its payments from Medicare and Medicaid.[92]

Surgery centers may also be at some risk. AmSurg Corp (symbol: AMSG) owns majority interests in thirty-nine surgery centers, as wells as has majority stakes in two physician practice groups. The company derived about 37 percent of its 1997 net revenues from government health care programs, including Medicare and Medicaid.[93]

Long-Term Care Facilities

Certain long-term care facilities face increased risk from Y2K due to the nature of their operations. If the care facility offers a full array of health care services, including respiratory monitoring, diagnostic services, post-acute care and the like, it may have hundreds of at-risk medical devices that need to be checked and fixed or replaced. On the other hand, if the facility is more of an assisted or independent living center, the number of at-risk devices may be comparably low.

More important, however, companies that care for the elderly are often especially dependent on federal Medicare reimbursements. This of course depends on whether the care facilities have large numbers of Medicare recipients as patients. For example, the largest nursing home operator, Beverly Enterprises (symbol: BEV), lined up 52 percent of its sales from Medicare and Medicaid programs in fiscal year 1997.[94] This was in part due to Beverly's involvement in transitional hospital (post-acute care) operations, but also in part due to its market, which includes many middle- to lower-income elderly residents in its nursing homes and rehabilitation centers.

The number two provider, Mariner Post-Acute Network (symbol: MPN), operates 430 post-acute nursing and assisted living centers in forty-two states. It also derived a whopping *58 percent* of its average inpatient daily census from Medicaid programs, according to its 1996 annual report (the most recent available). (Mariner curiously did not disclose its Medicare revenue, but instead lumped it together with its private payor revenues; we assume the Medicare amount is also substantial).[95]

Other long-term care providers are at serious risk should Medicare and Medicaid payments be delayed or miscalculated. Integrated Health Services (symbol: IHS), which operates over 300 nursing homes in addition to its home nursing and other services, derived over 62 percent of its revenue from Medicare and Medicaid in the six months ending June 30, 1998.[96] HCR Manor Care (symbol: HCR), Sun Healthcare Group (symbol: SHG), Genesis Health Ventures (symbol: GHV), and Assisted Living Concepts (symbol: ALF) all obtained over 50 percent of their revenue from Medicare and Medicaid in 1997.[97]

But leading the pack in government dependency are Vencor, Inc. (symbol: VC), which owns hospitals, nursing facilities, and assisted living communities, and National HealthCare Corp. (symbol: NHC), which operates 110 long-term health care centers and thirty-three home health care programs. Each of these companies had Medicare and Medicaid pick up the bill for an astonishing *71 percent* of their 1997 sales.[98]

On the other hand, companies like Grand Court Lifestyles (symbol: GCLI), Balanced Care Corporation (symbol: BAL), and Brookdale Living Communities (symbol: BLCI) appear less at risk from Y2K. The services they offer—meals, housekeeping, dressing, bathing, transportation, and rehabilitation—are not as dependent on medical devices for success. Further, these companies target middle- and upper-class seniors who tend to pay with private dollars, so they are not as dependent on the government to maintain the functioning of the Medicare system.

Physician Practices

Most physician practices are small, local groups that are not publicly traded. Some physician practices, however, have been acquired by major corporations and lumped together under one roof, to be operated by a "physician practice management" company. Examples include industry giants MedPartners (symbol: MDM), PhyCor (symbol: PHYC), and ProMedCo (symbol: PMCO), all of which face an uncertain future under Y2K. While the computer systems internal to such physician practice management companies can probably be debugged in time, the systems and medical devices used by affiliated physician practices may prove problematic, or other third party problems could affect doctor profitability. For example, physicians might face cash problems from unreimbursed Medicare claims, be exposed to malpractice suits because of faulty patient data or machinery, or be unable to efficiently schedule patient visits and keep good records. If the problem were widespread, it could impact quickly on the parent/ management company.

Health Care Plans

When people picture health care in the United States, large health plan companies such as HMOs (Hospital Management Organizations), PPOs (Preferred Provider Organizations), and managed care providers come to mind. Firms such as Aetna, Humana, United HealthCare, and PacificCare face enormous internal Y2K fixes of computer systems. They must also work with providers to make sure medical devices are working properly, or risk being named in the flood of likely lawsuits from aggrieved patients.

But compared to the providers, the immediate risk to plan providers from Y2K appears to be somewhat lower. Remember that these firms make their money primarily from premium payments, so they operate very much like an insurance company as well as a health care company. These premiums include so-called Medicare risk payments from the government (called Medicare+choice since passage of the 1997 budget). These payments are fixed monthly fees based on the number of Medicare enrollees in the plan, rather than Medicare reimbursements discussed earlier. We are not as concerned that these payments will be snarled during Y2K, so the cash flow problem isn't as acute as for the hospitals and long-term care providers.

Concluding Thoughts

Because of the health care industry's inherent nature—its just-in-time operations, its automated processes and at-risk medical devices, and its interdependencies—we are bearish on the sector through the Y2K crisis. Add to that the fact that health care appears to lag in Y2K preparedness generally, and you have a powerful argument to stay clear of health care stocks. We think particular concern is appropriate for the providers—those on the front lines who own at-risk facilities and who are dependent on the continued functioning of Medicare and Medicaid. A complete list of our recommendations is set out in chapter 10.

FOUR

WILL Y2K LEAVE INVESTOR-OWNED UTILITIES IN THE DARK?

A massive power failure might be an exciting premise for a movie,
but it is certainly not an exciting proposal for our nation's future.

—Elizabeth Moler, acting secretary of energy[1]

I am certain that not all Y2K problems have been identified, fixed,
and tested, nor will they be in the time remaining.

—Michael Gent, president of the North American
Electric Reliability Council[2]

Of all the Y2K nightmare scenarios, the most dreaded is an extended nationwide blackout, which doomsayers predict would lead to widespread looting and people in the North freezing to death in the winter of the year 2000. Let us start by saying we think this is highly unlikely. If we truly thought it was going to happen, there would be no need for this book, because markets would simply shut down, industry would grind to a complete halt, and your portfolio (along with everyone else's) would be history. But just because most of the lights will stay on in the United States doesn't mean Y2K won't shake up the financial picture in the utilities industry.

As with the health care sector, most people aren't used to thinking about the electric power industry as a business. In the past, investments in the utilities sector were considered appropriate for "widows and orphans funds"—as safe, conservative, and dependable as the electricity that the power companies provided. But investors familiar with the industry know that deregulation has brought sweeping changes to the way electric power is produced and distributed in the United States, as well as to the way investor-owned utility (IOU) equities should be viewed. Y2K will have significant implications for the business of making electric energy, and astute investors can reap the rewards.

Investors should keep in mind that these days electric utilities are run much like other large businesses, that is, utilities are concerned with maintaining and operating their internal systems, making a product, and selling that product. Large utilities' operations typically are divided into a few basic parts: internal operations, power generation, and power transmission/distribution. In internal operations, you'll find accounts payable and receivable, customer service, information services, and the like. Power generation can be likened to manufacturing, but instead of producing widgets, the utilities' product is electric power. And power transmission and distribution simply means getting the product to market, which in this case means routing it from the generating facility to the substations to the customer.

Y2K system failures don't necessarily result in power outages. For example, a Y2K-related failure at a generating facility would not mean the lights go out for that utility's customers. A utility whose generators are down can still buy electricity from another utility, package it as its own, and transmit it along normal channels. This sets utilities apart from other "manufacturers" and lessens the potential *initial* disruptive impact of Y2K failures of power generating systems.

A Y2K-related breakdown in the *power transmission* operations, by contrast, would have immediate repercussions. No transmission capacity would mean no power to customers. As we explain later in this chapter, power transmission is the aspect of utilities' operations that is most vulnerable to immediate Y2K failures, due to the interconnectivity and interdependence of the nation's power companies.

Most Y2K experts, government oversight groups, and utilities themselves have focused on the limited question of short-term electric *reliability*—whether electric power will continue to flow normally after the turn of the millennium. Not surprisingly, then, most of the industry's attention has been on maintaining the opera-

They worry about reliability. We worry about profitability.

tional integrity of transmission lines in the national power grid, often at the expense of fixing other systems. For example, Conectiv, a utility in the Northeast, had 90 percent of its inventorying and assessment of distribution systems done by the third quarter of 1998, but *none* of the inventory of its power generation systems.[3] While reliability is certainly most important to the public, it is not the question with which *investors* should be most concerned. In our view, Y2K poses significant risks to electric utility earnings and has longer-term implications for IOU *profitability*.

In this chapter, you'll see that the electric utility industry exhibits many of the same high-Y2K-risk characteristics we have seen with the airlines and the health care companies. Utilities operate a full-time service; they are under intense public scrutiny; they are increasingly dependent on automation; they are highly interdependent on each other and on their suppliers; they have critical weak points and bottlenecks in their operations; they depend heavily on government agencies and cooperatives for delivery of their product; and they must place safety and continuity of service over profits. It all adds up to a risky business for electric IOUs.

Shock Around the Clock

Like the hospitals and airlines, electric utilities provide round-the-clock service, 365 days a year. Power outages or shortages are

Y2K RISK FACTOR
Time Sensitivity

common occurrences, particularly when the weather is to blame, but customers can't and won't tolerate long delays in restoring service. With deregulation steamrolling across the country, utilities that develop the reputation for unreliable service will be the dogs of the marketplace.

While there are seasonal peaks in demand, utilities do not have the option of trimming back services or taking operations off-line while facilities are tested and Y2K problems sorted out. The scary truth is, the actual state of Y2K readiness among electric utilities may not become totally clear until clocks turn over on January 1, 2000—a real stroke of midnight test. And large utilities often have to coordinate their Y2K testing with prescheduled shutdowns, which sometimes puts their testing programs perilously close to the end of 1999. As a spokesperson of the North American Reliability Council (NERC) put it, "You just can't say, 'I'm sorry, folks, but no electricity for August 11, we're going to be testing our system so everything's off.' It just doesn't work that way."[4]

The product made by the utilities—electricity—can also be thought of as the ultimate just-in-time manufactured good. Unlike other products, electricity can't be stored in large quantities in economically efficient ways. Yet electricity has to be available to customers at the flick of a switch, even when the manufacturer may be hundreds of miles away or in another state. There isn't room for transmission delays in the electric power business. And when the power goes down, electric utilities can't make up for lost revenue by providing additional electricity later on.

By now, you have many examples of the devastating effects of business systems failures on JIT operations. It is not surprising, then, that the electric utilities have devoted most of their Y2K efforts to systems that ensure reliable, uninterrupted electric power to customers. This, of course, has to be their top priority, much as airlines must address flight safety first, and health care providers have to put patient care above profits. As we discuss later in this chapter, the IOUs have done a commendable job ensuring that the lights stay on after January 1, 2000, and for the most part they probably will. But for reasons beyond the control of many utilities, a long shadow may be cast by Y2K over IOU profitability and share prices.

The World Is Watching

Major investor-owned utilities know that the electric power industry is ground zero for Y2K critics and the concerned public. Almost every IOU has staff dedicated to Y2K programs and, perhaps more importantly, to spin control and public relations. Utilities have received thousands of inquiries from customers who worry that they will have to buy generators and arm themselves against looters. While these types of concerns are mostly based on unfounded reports and hype, utilities cannot pretend that the public is not nervous.

Y2K RISK FACTOR
Public Confidence

In the past, local politicians have singled out regional power companies as a favored punching bag, especially in the days before consumers had much choice in providers. There are signs that similar political hay is being made over the Y2K threat. For example, in Wisconsin, local politicians have promised that the National Guard will be on alert at the turn of the millennium in case of widespread power outages. While we can criticize our civic leaders for fanning the flames of public anxiety over Y2K, investors have to factor in the reality of lack of public confidence and the possibility of herd mentality.

So while the industry is going all-out to educate the masses about the reliability of the national power grid, it would only take a few highly publicized blackouts or shortages for consumers to worry about their own situation, and for investors to think twice about keeping their money in the traditionally conservative utility sector. If the cost of Y2K fixes begins to materially affect IOU profitability, investors could be in for earnings shocks in this normally stable field. Unfortunately, as with other high-profile stocks, the possibility of rapid investor flight may be self-fulfilling; while we don't advocate panic selling, when it starts to occur investors certainly shouldn't try to swim upstream.

I'm Sorry, Dave, I Can't Do That

The website of San Diego Gas and Electric contains an excellent multitimedia tour of that utility's facilities. One of the featured stops on the tour is in the "Control Room." We're sure that SDG&E's intention was to comfort viewers when it said this about its systems:

Y2K RISK FACTOR
Automation

> Recent improvements in technology have made the power plant work better. Many of the knobs, dials, and switches of the past have been replaced by computers. Computers are more compact and don't need people always watching them. Some parts of the power plant in South Bay are still controlled by hand, whereas other parts are controlled completely by computer. A good example of efficiency is Unit Four at South Bay and Unit Three at Encina. They both use a computer to control all the work the turbine does. The workers in the control rooms can keep track of

everything the plant is doing, either with a computer or by hand. In fact, the entire power plant can be run by seven or eight employees.[5]

Read in the context of Y2K, however, this otherwise upbeat description is downright scary. The level of automation at SDG&E is indicative of other modern electric utilities. Not surprisingly, as utilities have had to become leaner and more competitive in the face of deregulation and market pricing, downsizing expensive error-prone humans has been a top priority.

Computers in Internal IOU Business Systems

If you ask average electric power customers where a utility might have a computer problem with Y2K, the top answer would probably be, "In the billing department." Utilities rely on date calculations to determine total electric power usage by each customer over a certain period of time. Dates are also important for the calculation of overdue accounts and for sending notices of delinquency. If noncompliant computer software is not upgraded, customers could be sent erroneous charges or, worse yet, even have their records deleted from the system.

A less well-known fact is that devices as simple as a meter reader might also fail. Gone are the days when meter reading was done completely by pen and clipboard. Today, a meter reading is often entered into a handheld device that stores the infor- *Even meter* mation alongside the customer record. The reading is *readers could* later downloaded at a computer station. Some manufac- *go haywire* turers have already warned utilities that their handheld readers and upload/download stations won't work past January 1, 2000, and will have to be replaced.[6]

In addition to billing and meter reading, payroll has to be met, vendors and suppliers must be paid, the plant must be maintained, parts must be ordered, financial plans must be drafted, and so on. Like other large companies, big electric utilities use computers to conduct complex transactions, procure supplies, store customer information, and maintain all of their internal records. Y2K threatens these systems as it does every other date-dependent computer system around the world. But utilities are also cash-intensive companies, and their bond ratings will depend on how well financial risk organizations such as the SEC, Moody's, and Barron's view their Y2K information system preparations.[7]

Our research indicates that most large investor-owned utilities aren't sparing efforts in fixing their software programs to ensure that they send out correct bills, keep good customer records, and maintain their internal business systems. These fixes are a nuisance and could be costly, but they are manageable for well-organized companies. Said one Year 2000 coordinator for the Kissimmee Utilities Board in Florida, "If something went wrong with our business software, there's nothing potentially catastrophic that could happen like it could with our embedded systems,"[8]

Y2K Threat to Generation and Transmission

Electric utilities are indeed faced with an enormous problem of embedded chips. Throughout generating plants, equipment contains embedded microprocessors—sometimes dozens on a single circuit board. According to Jim Fortune, operations manager for the Y2K embedded systems program at the Electric Power Research Institute, in a typical fossil fuel–powered generating plant there may be several *thousand* embedded devices. "In a power plant, you get these things buried inside equipment," he notes. "It is a daunting task to account for everything there is. And you have to understand what role it plays."[9]

To get a glimpse of the extent of the problem, let's take a basic look at how electricity gets made and delivered. Electricity goes through five general steps before it gets to your residence or business:

1. A generator in a power plant makes the electricity. Usually, generators are coal-, oil-, or gas-fired, but there are of course alternative sources of power, like water, wind, and geothermal, and there are some 107 nuclear generators still operating.

2. The raw volts go from the generator to a transformer, which controls and changes the electricity, often to a much higher number of volts.

3. The transformer sends the electricity to a switchyard, where it gets divided and routed.

4. The switchyard sends the electricity to a local substation, where it is reduced to a low voltage for customer use in thousands of homes and businesses.

5. A distribution system consisting of primary and secondary lines (overhead or underground) as well as more transformers and switching equipment ultimately delivers the electricity to your home.

Where do computers and chips figure in? Many utilities use a digital control system to operate a generating station—the kind of "computer" that SDG&E was talking about on its website tour. DCSs decrease the need for warm bodies to monitor the status of the power station. The problem is, these DCSs sometimes contain microprocessors that

DCS: The "brains" of generating stations

are date-dependent and could fail as a result of Y2K in the same way a date-dependent computer software program could. A failure in a DCS would be akin to severing the "brain" from the "body" of a utility and could cause the whole facility to go off-line.

In addition to DCSs, facilities use digital processors in a variety of other control and protection devices, some of which are highly time-sensitive. For example, in one facility in the United Kingdom, testing for Y2K problems revealed systems failure in the generator temperature control system, which is used to make sure things don't overheat. When the clocks were turned forward to December 31, 1999, the system crashed at twenty seconds past midnight, shutting down the generator. Apparently, the program controlling the valve for generator cooling couldn't accept 00 as a number over which to integrate (kind of like how you can't divide by zero), and it went into fail-safe mode, tripping (shutting down) the whole system.[10]

Utilities also need to be concerned about Y2K problems in their power transmission systems. Power produced by a utility is typically routed using complex computer systems, which are located in 200 or so "bulk electric control centers" around the country. The systems are commonly referred to as Energy Management Systems

EMS: The "nervous system" of the power grid

and are used to control breakers, manage power generation schedules, provide against voltage, current, and frequency irregularities, and compensate for line breaks. Due to the sophistication required to meet the shifting demands for power around the United States, these EMSs typically use microprocessors and software programs to operate and manage the supply of electric power, rather than have people make all these decisions.

At any given time, some 10 to 20 percent of the EMSs are in automatic mode, overseeing electricity loads and regulating grid frequencies.[11] While most EMS operations are not date-dependent, in the field of "energy scheduling" there are numerous date-dependent calculations in built-in chips and software used to monitor, dispatch, and control power. These processing systems thus remain highly vulnerable to Y2K failures, and utilities must assess, fix, and test all noncompliant EMS systems.

Substations also contain control equipment—such as circuit breakers, disconnect switches, and transformers—which could be affected by Y2K. These substations need to be able to communicate with central control centers. Substations contain critical protection relays that must be able to act quickly to isolate a problem before it spreads. While many of these relays are electromechanical (and therefore "low-tech" and not at risk), some newer ones are digital and need to be checked for Y2K compliance. A relay that fails to operate when it should could mean permanent damage to lines or facilities.

To manage electrical transmission systems, utilities often use software known as Supervisory Control and Data Acquisition, which is a complicated sensing system typically made up of millions of lines of computer code. SCADA systems are used to send information on the state of the isolated parts of the grid back to the master system. One examination of a SCADA program at Silicon Valley Power revealed some 100,000 cases of date-related calculations.[12] This puts SCADA systems at risk, because if they miscalculate the date, they could miscalculate the time through a simple addition or subtraction error. Facilities that use SCADA software are being forced to expend significant resources to find and fix Y2K glitches.

SCADA: The "eyes" of the system

Some experts have pointed out that failures in EMSs and SCADA systems don't necessarily mean the lights will go off. These systems tend to provide supervisory and management support. Most of the time they aren't needed at all, and in some regions of the country utilities get by without them.[13] But to investors, failures by utilities to fix Y2K problems in these systems means significantly increased labor costs when problems do occur, since the supervisory work they once performed quite efficiently and cheaply now must be done by humans.

Whew! We promised to cut down on the tech-talk, and the last few pages probably have you scratching your head wondering what this means for the average electricity user. But before we get to that, we need to talk about something even more worrisome.

Gridlock

Electrical power in North America is distributed across three major, largely independent interconnections. The largest of these, the Eastern Interconnection, handles the eastern two-thirds of the continent. The Western Interconnection covers the western one-third. A third, smaller interconnection connects up most of the state of Texas. The interconnections may

Y2K RISK FACTOR
Interdependence

meet somewhere in Nebraska, but they do not tie together synchronously, so outages in one typically do not result in outages in the others.[14]

However, a highly connected and interdependent network exists within each interconnection. Disruptions at one point could potentially cause a cascade failure effect, and the strength of the interconnection may only be as great as the weakest link in the system. As the North American Reliability Council noted,

> [The] NERC's concern is that all electric utilities with a direct reliability impact on North American electrical interconnections must address the Y2K problem in a coordinated manner. This concern is due to the high degree of interdependence of electric systems within an electrical interconnection. One unprepared system has the potential to adversely impact the operation of the rest of the interconnection.[15]

Usually, a cascade failure doesn't happen, because even if one or more facilities go down, there is enough surplus electricity in the grid to compensate. The threat from Y2K is from *simultaneous* stresses on the system from *multiple* facilities. This makes planning somewhat more problematic than, say, for a natural disaster like a hurricane, where the outages can be predicted. One example is a failure of electrical "protection systems" in substations. Newer model protection systems are often digitally controlled and thus at possible risk from Y2K. Because relays could be designed upon the same faulty model, a "common mode failure" (meaning the same kind of failure in the same kind of device) would result in simultaneous and widespread substation facility failures, leading to a regional blackout.[16]

Concern over "common mode failures"

The problem is compounded by the sheer number of power companies connected to the grid. You may only be familiar with the utility company that sends you your monthly bills. In fact, the billing company in many cases isn't the actual producer of the electricity, nor is it always responsible for transmitting electric power within your region. By the time electric power reaches your home, it typically has passed through many different companies' lines, switches, and meters. The electric power business is now crowded with companies with varying operations. With further deregulation, the field will only get more crowded in coming years. The figure may surprise readers, but there are now *thousands* of companies that provide and/or distribute power in the United States. Some of these companies will be ready for Y2K, but many will not be.

There are over 200 investor-owned utilities operating in the United States. Other utilities are owned and operated by the government or by end users, and include over 900 so-called cooperatives, over 1,800 municipal systems, some seventy-five public power districts, and over 100 state or federal projects. In addition, there are over 4,000 "nonutility generators." These include so-called cogenerators (which are facilities that produce electrical power and heat, usually for industry or commercial users), certain small power producers, and independent power producers. Finally, there are some 400 "power marketers" who buy, sell, and swap power generated by the utilities and nonutility generators.[17]

More players, more problems

All of these companies form a network of generators, buyers, distributors, and sellers of electricity. Viewed simply (and at risk of oversimplification) about 6,000 power plants, half a million miles of high-voltage power lines, and around 112,000 substations[18] form what is called the *national grid*. Along the grid, electricity gets bought and sold very much like a commodity. Power generated in one region can be purchased and sent hundreds of miles away to be distributed within a different region. In fact, this practice is quite common and is used to make up for peaks and troughs in supply in different areas. This has cleared the path for deregulation in many regions and market-based pricing throughout the electric power business.

But these interconnections mean that if Y2K can strike one of them, it can strike them all indirectly. Outages in one region may have immediate consequences for other neighboring parts of the grid, and widespread outages could bring down *The danger of* even the most prepared of utilities. This is the threat to *cascade failure* the grid that so worries industry critics. "Having an interconnected system really makes for more efficient use of our natural resources and keeps the cost down," said a spokeswoman for Bonneville Power Administration, which oversees the power grid in the Pacific Northwest, "but it means when something goes wrong, it can cascade through the system."[19]

In other words, even large IOUs that otherwise have their act together could be in for a shock. For example, Northern States Power Company, based in Minnesota, began working on the Y2K problem in 1995—a relatively early start. It had a realistic view of the extent of the problem, identified some thirty million lines of code that it had to go through, and owned up to the daunting number of embedded systems that were at risk. It has over 150 people working on Y2K, has budgeted over $20 million for the task, and looks to have its internal systems compliant well before the turn of the millennium.[20] But in May 1998, the Minnesota Department of Public Service conducted a year 2000 survey that included nearly 200 electric companies. The survey revealed that only around half of the respondents had established a year 2000 team, and nearly two-thirds had no detailed Y2K plan.[21] Their lack of preparation could rain on Northern States' Y2K parade when distribution system failures clog up the grid.

Another example is industry giant Southern Company of Atlanta, which began working on Y2K long before the nation woke up to the threat. Southern has allocated $85.6 million to its Y2K program and is long into its testing phase, with particular attention to its control systems at its power plants.[22] But Southern Company's primary concern is with smaller, city-owned utilities that could crash the grid and make all of Southern's efforts for naught.[23] As the NERC warns, "An individual electric utility that invests tens of millions of dollars in solving Y2K problems could be affected in a major way by an outage initiated in neighboring systems that have not been as diligent."

This phenomenon is reflected across all regions of the country. While the Public Service Company of Oklahoma (Tulsa's electric company) began its Y2K work back in 1996 and is going to spend all of 1999 running tests, only 143 out of more than 500 other regional utility companies reported having any kind of Y2K plan at all, according to the Oklahoma Corporations Commission.[24] PacifiCorp, which services seven western states, is spending some $30 million on its Y2K compliance and is confident that power outages will be no worse than during a major storm.

At the same time, it is hastily developing contingency plans, because it worries its partners in the electrical delivery end will fail to prepare adequately.[25] Duquesne Light and Allegheny Energy, serving over two million customers in Pennsylvania and four other states, have been working on the Y2K problem for five years and expect to be ready for the millennium. When asked where their concerns lie, they focus on the smaller regional utilities to which they are linked.[26]

We're From the Government, and We're Here to Help

Before you feel that computers run everything in the electric utility business, here's another less than comforting fact: The government runs a lot of it, too. It should come as little surprise that hundreds of small electric power distribution companies, many of which are owned by municipalities or other governmental or quasi-governmental entities, lag the rest of the industry in Y2K preparedness. Most such distribution companies typically don't own their own generating facilities or transmission lines, and are instead solely in the business of distributing power to customers within their respective regions. These distributors generally have taken a less aggressive and sometimes cavalier attitude toward Y2K, in part because they sense the Y2K problem to be less critical from the electricity distribution side, but in part because, well, they're the government.

An informal survey by industry guru Rick Cowles, who has

authored a book on Y2K and the utility industry, showed that investor-owned utilities in general have a head start over government-owned entities.[27] A formal statewide survey by the Texas Public Utility Commission in early 1998 backs up this claim. The Texas PUC sent a questionnaire to 176 electric utility companies, including investor-owned utilities, distribution cooperatives, and municipally owned utilities, along with other smaller generators and independent operators.

The IOUs surveyed provide power to around 85 percent of Texas's consumers. All of the IOUs surveyed reported having a detailed Y2K plan with significant resources and staff working on the problem. Most had management level Y2K teams heading up various projects. All had completed some amount of repair and testing—one as high as 60 percent of its identified systems—and all planned to complete repair and testing programs in 1999. In short, the picture was about as rosy as could be expected.

The survey results among the distribution co-ops were less encouraging. The Texas co-ops service around 1.3 million power meters. Some three-quarters of co-ops contacted responded to the survey. About one-fourth of respondents had not begun a Y2K plan at all, and more than half had only informal, unwritten plans. Most efforts focused on billing systems. Ominously, most intended to rely on third-party vendors to handle Y2K problems.

The most disturbing results from the survey were among the municipally owned utilities. Like the Texas co-ops, the MOUs seldom operate their own generating or transmission facilities. Rather, they maintain distribution lines and metering-related equipment. The Texas MOUs serve some three million customers through around 1.3 million meters. In part because the Texas PUC doesn't have regulatory authority over the MOUs, only around ten out of the seventy-five MOUs that were sent surveys even bothered to respond. These ten fortunately included the two largest, based in San Antonio and Austin, which reported completion rates of 50 and 40 percent, respectively. Of the rest, only one had a written plan, one had an unwritten plan, three had not yet developed their plans, and three *did not intend to address the issue.*

We predict problems among municipal utilities

Some experts point out that distribution systems usually use electromechanical or analog controls and are therefore not very susceptible to Y2K. Analog equipment is favored for the monitoring of voltage, current, and frequency, and has no need to know what year it is. But distributors of power still have to worry about digital meter readers, software billing systems, and any digital chips in their distribution equipment. The NERC warns that distribution equipment outside of substations may be at risk, including reclosers, capacitors, voltage regulators, and special monitoring devices.[28] In our view, no matter how low-tech a company may perceive its operations to be, most still rely on computer systems and equipment containing microchips to conduct basic operations. Small government-owned electric companies that take *no action* with respect to Y2K may be in for quite a shock at the turn of the millennium.

Failure to address the problem could result in area outages, especially in smaller communities. If the problem were widespread enough, it could impact the profits of large IOUs, which sell their power to these distributors or license them to sell it on the IOUs' behalves. In other words, if the co-ops and MOUs can't distribute power to customers, can't get proper meter readings, and can't send out and collect on their bills, they won't be in much of a position to be dealing in electric power with the larger utilities.

Up the Stream Without a Paddle

Unfortunately for the electric utilities, they are not only interdependent with one another, they also depend critically on the continued functioning of other sectors' business systems, computers, and daily operations. For example, most people wouldn't expect that the electric companies are counting on the phone companies to keep communications up and running. But as far as the electric utilities are concerned, the telecommunications companies also had better not drop the ball during the critical period after midnight, December 31, 1999. Warns the NERC:

> If the control centers are the "brains" of the electrical grids, communications systems are the "nervous system." Telecommunications is the single most important area in which the electric systems depend on another industry. . . . The dependency of elec-

tric supply and delivery systems on external service providers is a crucial factor in successful performance during Y2K transition periods.[29]

The humor in this (if anything can be funny about Y2K) is that other industries are busy laying the principal risk of operations failure at the doorstep of the utilities, observing that without power nothing is going to operate as usual. As the NERC further noted, "It is somewhat ironic that initial contacts with the communications industry indicate that they feel they will be Y2K ready—if the lights stay on. From the electric industry perspective, the feeling is reciprocal."

A far greater risk to the long-term health of electric utilities, however, is posed by the possibility of failure of the fuel supply—the coal and oil deliveries that so many utilities depend on to function. Disruptions in the supply of fossil fuels will drive up costs and drive down earnings for IOUs in much the same way jet fuel shortages could crimp airline profits. Later in this chapter, we devote an entire section to this thorny and potentially disastrous problem, which has been given scant attention, even by the likes of the NERC.

Finally, utilities are also saddled with interdependence on local governments, perhaps the worst of partners in the fight against Y2K. We have already seen how local cooperatives and municipally owned electric distributors account for a sizable portion of the electrical delivery capacity in the United States. As we discuss later in our section on Y2K and nuclear power, local governments also are responsible for emergency services and local transportation systems, which must be fully operational in order for utilities to operate nuclear facilities in compliance with federal safety regulations.

Current Events: The Status of the Industry

So where does the industry stand in Y2K preparedness? Generally speaking, most Y2K *software* efforts appear to be under control at the major investor-owned utilities. At Pacific Gas and Electric, software that runs billing, energy management, and SCADA systems were all on schedule to be fixed and tested by the end of 1998.[30] Other utilities have expressed similar confidence that their computers will perform as usual.

Y2K Readiness in IOUs

But the picture for embedded chips is less rosy. For example, PG&E had only completed its inventory of embedded systems in mid-1998, but the Y2K status of those systems still hadn't been fully assessed to determine which were at risk and which were most critical. Utilities seeking to replace or repair defective chips encounter some of the same kinds of problems from their equipment vendors as hospitals face from medical device manufacturers, though they have fewer vendors to contact. Vendors can be difficult to track down, nonresponsive, or worried about their own liability. Utilities getting late starts replacing their equipment may find themselves bottom fishing from among the supply of replacement parts and equipment, as utilities around the world scramble to purchase the same embedded chip components.

The depth of the embedded chip problem in the utility industry has made some Y2K watchers nervous. In the middle of 1998, the Senate Special Committee on the Year 2000 Technology Problem held hearings on the state of readiness of the utility industry. At that time, Senator Bob Bennett's office had conducted an informal survey of ten of the largest U.S. utilities, representing broad regional diversity. The results from that survey were rather alarming: Out of the ten, only two had completed assessment of their systems, none could give assurances that its vendors and suppliers would be compliant, and none had completed contingency plans.[31] Senator Bennett's informal survey was backed up by a comprehensive survey of large American corporations by Cap Gemini America, which ranked utilities as among the least prepared of industrial sectors. Utilities were tied with the transportation sector near the bottom of the list, with only health care lagging further behind.[32]

Utility readiness questioned

Those in the government in charge of keeping tabs on the state of the industry (namely the Federal Energy Regulatory Commission) conceded that "any failure to fully understand the seriousness of the issues must be regarded as a significant problem." They had to admit that as late as June 1998, "the state of year 2000 readiness of the utility industry is not yet fully known."[33] Many utilities, once confident of their ability to lick the bug, are now inexplicably less forthcoming and assuring. For example, utilities in Pennsylvania stated during public hearings in 1997 that they anticipated few vital computer problems that could not be fixed before the turn of the millennium. But in a follow-up survey by the state's Public Utility Commission in April 1998, only 21 percent of electric companies responded, prompting an alarmed Pennsylvania PUC to order an independent investigation.[34] Pennsylvania regulators perhaps have the toughest stand in the country: Comply by March 1999 or face a $1,000-per-day fine.

PUC regulators in Maine also faced a stony silence from state utilities after it sent out a questionnaire on Y2K readiness in June 1998. Of the 257 utilities queried, only 112 responded, prompting the Maine PUC to follow the lead of neighboring Connecticut and New Hampshire and open a formal inquiry in September 1998.[35]

In addition, the industry is in the middle of a massive restructuring resulting from deregulation, where retail and wholesale competition for electricity promises only to get more intensive. Utilities have devoted many of their managerial and technical resources to cutting costs, increasing market share, and completing reorganization.[36] Y2K is an unwelcome additional burden with no visible payback in increased productivity or competitiveness. Some utilities have been reluctant to address the issue head on in the face of the market pressures of deregulation. Another by-product of deregulation is the rush by many larger utilities to divest themselves of unprofitable generating plants and focus on power transmission, distribution, and marketing. This divestiture unfortunately may result in less attention being paid to Y2K problems in facilities that are on the auction block.

Y2K problems complicated by deregulation

Further, the lack of legal clarity with respect to Y2K liability has left many industries, including large utilities, worried about the repercussions of technical information sharing, due diligence, and even trade libel.[37] IOUs that willingly disclose their Y2K problems to others may find those same disclosures as exhibit one in a shareholder derivative suit or a defamation suit filed by an aggrieved vendor.

On the other hand, the industry has several positive things going for it, including a well-organized and coordinated remediation program headed by the NERC, a transmission system that is largely not chip-dependent or date-dependent, and a distributed electric power supply network that can compensate for local shortages. Even Y2K Paul Revere Senator Bennett has now expressed confidence that the national grid will stay up and operating.[38] As we discuss below, a large part of the credit for the industry's preparedness belongs to the NERC and its Y2K program.

Industry Optimism

The NERC is confident that the major utilities will not drop the ball, and that the juice will still flow after 01/01/2000. In its public statements, the NERC has declared that "most electric utilities have established Y2K programs and invested substantial personnel and technical resources in identifying and resolving Y2K problems."[39] As the NERC stated in its critical September 1998 status report on the industry:

> Recent reports in the news media and on the Internet regarding anticipated widespread electricity outages are unsubstantiated. In an industry that meets record peak demands during heat waves and quickly restores service to millions of customers who lost power due to a hurricane or earthquake, preparing for and dealing with operating risks is an ingrained part of the business.[40]

Follow up reports published by the NERC downplay the threat of Y2K blackouts even more, predicting only "minimal impact" and "nuisance" type problems in electrical production

NERC: Y2K not a threat to reliability

and distribution. Still, at a news conference called to announce the findings, the head of the NERC's Y2K program refused to provide any total assurances: "No one will stand up here and give you . . . a guarantee," he said. "There's just enough uncertainty."[41]

The NERC does back up its optimistic statements credibly. It has in place a three-part Y2K program that provides for regular progress reports to the Department of Energy on the state of the industry, the coordination of contingency plans across the sector, and a master checklist to assist program participants with Y2K compliance of common equipment and systems, as well as advice on best practices.[42] In our opinion, such a program places utilities in a better position than health care companies, which lack central coordination, and air transport companies, which are hampered rather than assisted by the FAA as a regulating body.

The NERC has been conducting an ongoing and extensive survey on the Y2K readiness of the utility industry. The survey includes more than 75 percent of the electric supply and delivery organizations in North America, as well as about two-thirds of the distribution entities. The results from the third quarter of 1998 were fairly encouraging. Taking the respondents to the survey as a whole, an average of 87 percent of inventory, 65 percent of assessment, and 28 percent of remediation and testing had been completed across the sector. By November 1998, some 45 percent of systems among survey participants had been fixed and tested. The average forecasted completion date for remediation and testing was June 1999.[43]

"We don't feel there are any types of failures that will jeopardize our ability to provide electricity to our customers," said Gerry Cauley, Y2K project manager for the NERC at the first Y2K summit called by the Clinton administration's Y2K council. "A properly tested and repaired unit at the component level does not have a problem that would prevent it from operating."[44]

The survey did point out, however, that there are some entities that lag far behind, having completed less than 10 percent of their *inventory* phase. In addition, some 500 distribution companies have not joined in the NERC program, and of those that did sign on, 35 percent still had no written Y2K project plan as of December 1998. Faced with these challenges, the NERC has admitted to a "huge coordination problem in the distribution area."[45]

Still, the industry is fortunate to have organizations like the North American Electric Reliability Council, which is dedicated to coordinating industry efforts to prevent system failure. Indeed, the NERC was formed in the wake of the 1965 nationwide blackout in order to prevent such events in the future. The NERC is currently advising utilities to take concrete measures to reduce their exposure to Y2K when it strikes. Some examples of these precautions include reducing the planned level of electricity exchanges between utilities during the crisis, putting into service all available transmission facilities, revving up additional generating facilities, and mixing in older generating units that use analog rather than digital controls. The NERC has also suggested increased staffing at control centers, substations, and generating stations during critical periods.[46] Some utilities, such as Detroit

Edison, have already notified employees that there will be no vacations around the turn of the millennium.[47]

From a technical standpoint, Y2K may have a smaller effect than most had earlier predicted. For example, some utilities have reported that the embedded chip problem is less serious than experts originally feared. According to the NERC, electric utility systems consist "mainly of wires and metal devices" such that "[m]ost equipment is electromechanical, meaning there is less dependence on digital controls." The NERC further notes that "even when tests have been completed on digitally controlled devices . . . those tests have indicated there are very few date-interpretation problems that affect the ability to operate electric systems."[48] In other words, say the experts, most systems in power plants are not time-dependent at all, and even the chips in those systems don't really care what year it is. In addition, many plants are operated by experienced technicians who can adjust operations manually to maintain reliable electrical output. Ironically, the ability of these operators to intervene manually may decrease the more sophisticated and digitized the generating facility is.

Date-dependent chips are rare in utilities, say the experts

Even if there are a few such failures and regional outages, most experts do not expect them to last long. Once the source of the power outage is isolated, power can be routed around the problem or the automatic trip can be manually overridden.

Wait—manually overridden? Isn't this too much to expect in our computer-addicted society? Didn't we say manual operations were pretty much a thing of the past? Well, as utilities rightly point out, they are in the business of manual overrides all the time. The difference here will be that there may be many times the number of switches to check, meaning that power could be out longer than, say, in a bad storm. The good news is, the electric utilities have time to prepare for the possibility and will have people ready and waiting to switch the system over to manual. At the Edison Electric Institute, another nonprofit industry watch group, they are optimistic that any problems will be short-lived. Noted a senior vice president at the EEI:

Manual operations are possible

U.S. electric supply and delivery systems are not heavily reliant on computers and electronic controls. Those operations that do rely on computer systems can be manually operated in emergencies—and often are during power outages arising from storms or mechanical problems. Electric companies plan for the unexpected every day: windstorms, snow and ice, heat waves, downed trees and power lines, or equipment failures. We are accustomed to dealing with unplanned events. While Y2K is a unique occurrence, it is a planned event.[49]

In short, manual operations *are* a realistic contingency in the case of utilities, as opposed to the situation with the FAA or the Medicare system discussed in earlier chapters. This is why we share the belief that nationwide blackouts lasting weeks just aren't credible and aren't based on solid facts. As we explain later, more likely scenarios include regional power shortages that cause spikes in local electricity prices and fundamental fuel supply problems that leave long-lasting financial scars on certain utilities.

What the EEI and others in the industry *haven't* focused on are the long-term repercussions of having to *keep* things in manual mode. Remember that when the system is switched over to manual, this may temporarily resolve the problem of date-dependent computer chips crashing the system, but it introduces *additional costs* of having extra personnel keep watch over the generating stations, substations, and power lines. It is entirely possible that the utilities could handle the days and weeks after the new year and keep power going. But they can't stay in manual mode forever without hiring more people or paying to fix faulty systems.

Manual operations are also pricey

This again is the big difference between *reliability* and *profitability*. While customers can be fairly confident that electric reliability is not going to be the issue, investors shouldn't mistake this for a green light for profitability. The nagging question investors are left with is this: How long can the electric utilities afford *not* to depend on computer controls of generation and transmission systems? The alternative is to hire workers to do the jobs the computers used to do. But can the electric utilities turn back the clock on automation and still post good earnings?

Fueling the Problem

We have other serious concerns that further temper any optimistic outlooks for large IOUs. First, electric utilities are critically dependent on reliable supplies of fuel in order to make their product. In the case of fossil fuels (specifically coal and oil), massive disruptions in the supply chain mean operational and financial disaster for most utilities. Even moderate disruptions—or the *threat* of disruptions—could have an impact on operations and profits as utilities scramble to stock up on supply.

Y2K *ADDED* RISK FACTOR
Fuel Supplier Noncompliance

Coal and Oil Supplies at Risk

In chapter 2, we outlined some of the Y2K problems that oil suppliers face in their refineries, pipelines, and computer systems. These same types of problems, compounded by problems in the nation's transportation infrastructure, could significantly impact the critical fossil fuel supply for utilities. As we noted earlier with respect to the oil supply, a significant percentage will be coming from overseas, where Y2K problems continue to go largely unaddressed. But even if the fuel suppliers can manage to get their product out of the refineries, they still have to depend on rail cars and tankers to ship the fuel to the utilities.

Most utilities rely on the nation's railways to provide fossil fuel to power their generators. According to the Association of American Railroads, railroads transport 65 percent of the coal used by utilities to provide some 60 percent of the nation's electricity needs.[50] However, Y2K infects major systems at railroads just as it does other transportation sectors. Indeed, the Y2K situation among major U.S. railroads is troubling enough that John Koskinen, Clinton's Y2K czar who normally toes the "we're all going to be fine" line, gave an uncharacteristically pessimistic assessment of them: "We are deeply concerned about the railroads," he admitted. *"We have no indication that they are going to make it."*[51]

Naturally, railroads need to inventory, assess, remediate, and test their mainframe and PC systems and client-server systems.

A more dangerous situation, however, exists with railroad Electronic Data Interchange systems, which are now commonly used by the railroads to communicate and interface automatically with customers, vendors, other transportation-related companies and financial institutions. A still larger unknown lies with *vendor supplied* software and embedded chips. Union Pacific warns ominously of a threat we have heard voiced in other industries:

> The Year 2000 date problem exists within software products and systems provided by vendors and software embedded within purchased equipment. Vendor-supplied software and hardware is used widely throughout Union Pacific. The full impact of the Year 2000 issue will not be determined until each supplier of software, hardware, and equipment has responded to a formal request concerning Year 2000 compliance.[52]

A further consideration is also one we have heard before, but with respect to the airlines. In their system priorities, railroads need to put the issue of safety above all else. This means that when there is a possibility of an accident occurring because of a faulty switch, failed monitoring device, or malfunctioning maintenance scheduler, the railroad must err on the side of caution and reduce or halt service.

The exact status of the major railroads' Y2K efforts is less than clear. Some operators appear outwardly confident, but their timelines leave some room for doubt. Burlington Northern Santa Fe, for example, boasts that it began its Y2K program in 1997, but expects its testing to be complete as late as *October 1999,* sparing little room for slippage.[53] Norfolk Southern, which has slated $25 million for its Y2K fixes, began its program in 1995 and has combed 18,000 programs and twenty million lines of code. Still, laments Norfolk Southern's top technology man, "You get into potential problems anywhere you have a chip. . . . It could be in a machine in the mechanical department, it could be in the dispatching system or it could be in the elevator. . . . We have chips out the ears, they're everywhere."[54] And as he rightly points out, "What about our vendors? . . . If you can't get diesel fuel, the railroad's in trouble."[55]

According to one Y2K industry analyst, most utilities that use fossil fuels have between one and three weeks of reserve fuel storage available, allowing for only minor disruptions in the fuel supply.[56] In this sense, utilities have taken advantage of a highly sophisticated and interdependent supply chain that permits them to conduct just-in-time operations and keep fossil fuel inventories low. The problem is that the railroads that typically deliver fuel to the utilities have to be operating effectively, or there will be electrical power shortages from utilities being unable to power their turbines. In addition, if there is a shortage of fossil fuels, the price of such fuels will rise, putting pressure on utilities' earnings. We predict large utilities will undertake contingency plans that provide for an increase in their fossil fuel inventories—a "just in case" rather than "just in time" switch that could impact the near-term bottom lines of investor-owned utilities.

To our surprise and dismay, the threat from a disruption of the fuel supply is barely being addressed by the NERC and other industry watch groups. In its eighty-eight-page September 1998 status report, this is all NERC had to say about the fuel supply:

> Fuel supply is a critical part of the power production chain and needs to be considered in the Y2K effort. The importance of the dependence on fuel supplies from other entities cannot be overstated. The Federal Energy Regulatory Commission is coordinating a similar effort to NERC's in the natural gas industry to assure the readiness of natural gas supply systems. Coal and oil delivery systems are equally important. Because of these dependencies, the Y2K efforts in the electric industry must be closely coordinated with these related industries.[57]

For a problem that "cannot be overstated," this one has been given relatively low billing, not only by the NERC but by other organization and industry spokespersons. Do the utilities have

Are the experts overlooking the biggest problem?

a handle on this problem in terms of contingency planning, or are they simply expecting things will not go terribly wrong? Our outlook is that as large utilities ready their own systems, more attention will be paid to the minefield of problems presented by other companies' systems, particularly with respect to the fuel supply. As the situation becomes more clear and IOUs start to stock up, you can expect industry analyst downgrades and earnings warnings for IOUs heavily dependent on coal and oil.

One final thought: We are somewhat more optimistic toward electric utilities that fire their generators with natural gas, which faces fewer and more manageable delivery issues than do oil and coal. We are positively bullish on IOUs that generate a significant portion of their power from hydroelectric and alternative sources, since fuel delivery is not a big issue. Electric utilities that can continue to produce low-cost, reliable energy will be able to bundle and sell that energy to IOUs that are stumbling and scrambling about for fuel.

Things Aren't All Aglow

Even more worrisome to the financial health of IOUs is the very real threat of shutdowns of nuclear power plants, which provide certain IOUs with substantial amounts and sometimes the majority of their electric generating capacity. The nuclear power industry represents a microcosm of all the things that Y2K tends to plague. If, as we predict, a sizable percentage of generators must spend a good deal of time off-line while Y2K issues are sorted out, this will have a very noticeable impact on certain IOU bottom lines.

Y2K *ADDED* RISK FACTOR

Nuclear Generator Noncompliance

Y2K presents unique challenges to the nuclear power industry. The principal reason is one we've heard before: nuclear power plants (like airlines, hospitals, and railroads) must make operational safety—that is, the risk of death or injury from an accident—their highest priority. After the Three Mile Island incident in 1979, regulations were implemented so that *any* circumstances that could adversely affect plant safety must be reviewed as soon as they are discovered, and any changes to design or equipment have to pass regulatory muster. This means that if there is the slightest chance that a system failure could result in an accident, then regulators—and operators—will err on the side of caution and shut down facilities to work out the problem.

This is not to say that the chances of a Y2K failure in a nuclear power plant are higher than in any other plant. Indeed, they are usually substantially lower, since many of the systems at U.S. plants are still analog in nature and do not contain embedded systems. The Y2K problem still exists, however, and should not be understated. According to the Nuclear Regulatory Commission, licensees (that is, nuclear facility operators licensed by the U.S. government) rely upon software to schedule maintenance and technical specification surveillance, programmable logic controllers and off-the-shelf software and hardware, DCSs such as a feedwater control or valve control, digital systems for collecting operating data, and digital systems to monitor postaccident plant conditions. These systems may be date-dependent, and may need to be fixed, replaced, or taken out of service. In a June 1998 letter to all nuclear licensees, the NRC listed specific systems that could be affected by Y2K. These included:

- material control and accounting safeguards
- physical protection safeguards
- safety parameter display system computers
- emergency response systems
- radiation monitoring systems
- dosimeters and readers

In addition, the NRC warned of Y2K threats to systems typically found in other generating facilities, such as communications, computer security, plant process, inventory control, engineering programs, surveillance and maintenance tracking, plant process control, and document control.[58] The problem with these systems in a *nuclear* facility, however, is that if one of these ancillary systems goes down, the whole generating system might have to be shut down. In other words, while most utilities can be Y2K-ready and go into operation even with some systems questionable, nuclear facilities must be Y2K-*perfect* to maintain normal operations.

Similarly, problems with outside communications and transportation systems could result in shutdowns of nuclear generators. For example, during a particularly nasty flood in *No 911? No* Nebraska, the Cooper Nuclear Station had to be shut *nuclear power.* down, not because the plant itself was flooded, but because emergency response teams wouldn't have been able to respond to a nuclear emergency had one occurred.[59] Unfortunately, emergency response services are usually managed by local governments, which are generally *far* behind other sectors in Y2K preparation. A host of other external circumstances could similarly cause plant shutdowns, including failures of local communication systems, water pumping facilities, transportation grids, or even other electric utilities. For example, nuclear power reactors usually use two independent sources of off-site power to operate their reactors. The systems are designed to shut down if a loss of all power occurs.[60] Thus, a spot outage in a region might result in nuclear generator facility shutdowns (thus, ironically, compounding the shortage of power) because electric power can't get to the reactor site.

The NRC claims that by mid-1998 it had not received any notice from any licensee that any Y2K problem existed in any "safety related initiation and actuation system." We're not sure if we should be concerned or relieved. It is hard to conceive that *no* safety systems in nuclear power plants contain embedded chips or date-dependent software that need to be updated. To us, it is more likely that existing problems may not yet have been discovered or acknowledged. Experience from other nations may be illuminating: In Sweden, date-related failures in tests of feedwater systems have prompted that country to warn of shutdowns of nuclear facilities in the first part of the year 2000.[61]

But even giving the licensees the benefit of the doubt, the NRC has still acknowledged that "some problems have been identified in computer-based systems that, while nonsafety-related, are nonetheless important." It went on to note that "[s]uch systems, primarily databases and data collection processes necessary to satisfy license conditions, technical specifications, and NRC regulations that are date driven, may need to be modified for Year 2000 compliance."

Why is this statement important? After all, what is the danger from having a few problems occur in your database or data collection processes, right? In the case of nuclear power, it is everything. To explain this, we have to venture into the murky world of nuclear power regulation.[62]

The regulations are very strict and include a mandate for exhaustive management of what are called unreviewed safety questions. Within a nuclear plant, if you've got a condition that is a potential threat to safety and that has shut the plant down, it must be reviewed and analyzed before the plant can go back on line.

The real threat to nuclear power plant operability

Now, it is not uncommon for a routine event to cause a nuclear power plant to shut down, or trip. Normally when this happens, an "event recorder" (usually a computer of some kind) keeps track of what went

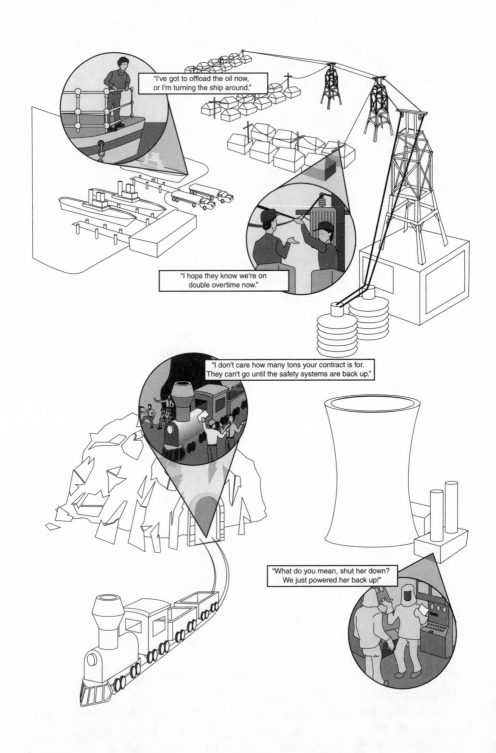

wrong. Things are happening much too quickly for mere humans to both get control of the plant and do the analysis of what went wrong at the same time. The event logger lets managers go back and look at what went wrong and reconstruct the event later. But if Y2K knocks out the event logger or gives it bad data, the event can't be reconstructed properly, and you have an unresolved safety question. Result: Keep the plant shut down.

There are hundreds of possible Y2K scenarios that could force a generator off-line or keep it off-line. Noting that it was unlikely all systems would be fixed and verified in time, the NRC has asked its licensees to develop contingency plans for Y2K failures.[63] In our opinion, these contingency plans will more likely than not result in temporary shutdowns of operations in a few if not many nuclear power plants.

Nuclear Reactions: The NRC Steps Up Its Y2K Program

Investors should know that the NRC is now carefully monitoring its licensees' compliance programs and will *force* shutdowns in questionable cases. In June 1998, the NRC sent a letter to all its licensees demanding a written response within ninety days stating how each planned to address the Y2K problem.[64] During a Global Year 2000 Action Day conference held in August 1998, the deputy director of the NRC warned that whole plants "might have to be shut down" until they complete their Year 2000 remediation programs.[65] By July 1999, the NRC will require written statements from each licensee confirming that each is or will be Y2K-compliant by the year 2000. If a facility does not give full assurances of compliance, the NRC could well view the facility as being in an unanalyzed status, and pursuant to federal regulations, require a shutdown. The NRC also intends to conduct inspections of facilities to assess Y2K preparedness, making shutdowns even more likely.[66]

Investors should also note that preemptive shutdowns might occur as early as mid-1999, when written statements from the licensees are due. If this occurs, or is even threatened, utilities that depend on nuclear power to produce a substantial portion of their energy may feel the economic pinch much sooner than the turn of the millennium. Investors should therefore consider adjusting their portfolios in anticipation of possible action by the NRC.

It's too bad the NRC didn't take a harder stance much earlier. The NRC appeared decidedly laid-back when it first raised the issue of Y2K with its licensees and certificate holders in December 1996. In Information Notice 96-70, entitled "Year 2000 Effect on Computer System Software," the NRC staff simply described the potential computer systems and software problems that could result from Y2K. The NRC did nothing more than *encourage* licensees to examine their systems before the year 2000 and *suggest* that they look into appropriate actions such as examining and evaluating their systems for Y2K vulnerabilities. But now, realizing the extent of the issue, the NRC appears prepared to put absolute safety ahead of all other considerations.

No Nukes Is Good Nukes

With the high possibility that nuclear power facilities will shut down in the early part of the year 2000, it is important to remember that not all utilities are as heavily dependent on nuclear power as others. In fact, the distribution is markedly regional in nature. Of the over 100 nuclear facilities in the United States, a disproportionate number are located on or near the Eastern Seaboard. Thus, while nuclear power accounts for around 20 percent of the total electrical output in the United States, the Eastern half of the country derives nearly 40 percent of its power from nuclear plants.

While there is no way to predict with certainty how large an impact Y2K will have, investors should keep in mind that the *risk* of shutdowns is substantially higher than if Y2K did not exist. In our view, the risk is high enough for us to recommend *avoiding* investor-owned utilities that depend heavily on nuclear energy to make electrical power.

How the IOUs Pan Out

If your portfolio contains any investments in electric utilities, our basic advice is to reduce your exposure. If any utilities in which you own stock are highly dependent on nuclear power, consider selling some or all of your interest. We

Y2K Stock Watch

have researched the leading IOUs, including electric utilities and diversified utilities with electric generating capacity, and our findings are summarized below.

The largest utility in terms of market capitalization is Duke Energy Corporation (symbol: DUK), which is also the largest gas and electric utility by revenues. Duke has about two million customers in North Carolina and South Carolina, and operates, through its subsidiaries, dozens of generating plants using coal, gas, hydroelectric, and nuclear power.[67] Duke is roundly acknowledged as among the utilities that have made the most progress on Y2K in its systems. On the other hand, while it is diversified across many energy sector industries, its three nuclear plants (Oconee, Catawba, and McGuire, each with two units), eight coal-fired stations, and over 70,000 miles of distribution lines nevertheless make Duke a high risk in our view.

PG&E Corporation (symbol: PCG) rings in at the number two spot behind Duke. Through its subsidiary, Pacific Gas & Electric, the utility services 4.5 million electric customers and 3.7 million gas customers. It is busy divesting itself of power generating plants and focusing on marketing in California, while acquiring power plants in New England through another of its subsidiaries. PG&E gets most of its power (46 percent) from purchases, so it is susceptible to hikes in prices resulting from a supply crisis under Y2K. A full 20 percent comes from its nuclear power plant at Diablo Canyon (a two-unit facility). We recommend holding little to none of this stock through the Y2K crisis.

Another giant is Southern Company (symbol: SO), which serves 3.7 million customers in four southeastern states, and whose stock is one of the most widely held in America. Southern Company owns five subsidiary regulated utilities and operates 278 coal, oil, gas, nuclear, and hydroelectric plants, producing more electricity than any other company in the United States.[68] Southern should be *underweighted* by risk-adverse investors.

Texas Utilities Company (symbol: TXU) is the holding company for TU Electric, which operates twenty-four plants, making it that state's largest utility, with some three million customers. Even though nineteen of those plants use natural gas, TU Electric derives 37 percent of its energy needs from coal, 16 percent from its nuclear facility, and another 16 percent from other producers.[69] This mix doesn't bode well under Y2K.

Consolidated Edison, Inc. (symbol: ED) is the parent company of Consolidated Edison Company of New York, which provides electricity to three million people in New York City. The vast majority of its revenues come from its electric operations. Con Edison is better off than most major utilities, with nearly 60 percent coming from natural gas and renewable resources. Only around 8 percent comes from nuclear power.

FPL Group (symbol: FPL) rounds out our list of electric utilities with market caps over $10 billion. FPL is based in Florida and provides service to 3.6 million customers. FPL derives around one-quarter of its energy from coal and oil, another quarter from its nuclear operations at the St. Lucie and Turkey Point plants, and another 20 percent from purchases. We would *avoid* FPL altogether.

Among the scores of other IOUs, here are some that we are particularly worried about: Rochester Gas and Electric (symbol: RGS) (very high nuclear energy dependence); Unicom Corporation (symbol: UCM) (a unit of Commonwealth Edison, which, despite having a decent and well-funded Y2K program, obtains over 50 percent of its power from nuclear sources); Niagara Mohawk Power Corporation (symbol: NMK) (high percentage of purchased power and nuclear dependence); Entergy Corporation (symbol: ETR) (operates five nuclear power facilities); Carolina Power and Light Company (symbol: CPL) (fuel sources are around one-third nuclear and over half coal); PP&L Resources, Inc. (symbol: PPL) (27 percent from nuclear and 44 percent from coal); Northern States Power Company (symbol: NSP) (31 percent from nuclear and 47 percent from coal); PECO Energy Company (high nuclear power exposure, despite strong Y2K program) (symbol: PE); Dominion Resources (symbol: D) (operates four nuclear power units); First Energy Corp. (symbol: FE) (one-quarter from nuclear power, and most of the rest from coal); Pinnacle West Capital Corporation (symbol: PNW) (holding company for Arizona Public Service, which operates the largest nuclear power facility in the United States); SCANA Corporation (symbol: SCG) (24 percent from nuclear, and almost all the rest from coal).

We have some concerns over other major electric utilities as well, particularly those with high dependence on coal and oil or purchased power, instead of gas or renewable sources. These include DPL Inc. (symbol: DPL) (derives 99 percent of its electric output from coal); American Electric Power Company, Inc. (symbol: AEP) (mostly coal-fired generation, with one nuclear plant); DTE Energy Company (symbol: DTE) (75 percent fossil fuel—mostly coal—with 11 percent nuclear); Pacific Corp (symbol: PPW) (around 85 percent coal-fired production); Energy East Corporation (symbol: NEG) (around 85 percent from coal-fired production); Florida Progress Corporation (symbol: FPC) (26 percent purchased power, 39 percent from coal and 12 percent from oil); TECO Energy, Inc. (symbol: TE) (almost all energy production coal-fired); Allegheny Energy (88 percent coal-fired); NIPSCO Industries, Inc. (symbol: NI) (heavy coal dependence); Central and South West Corporation (symbol: CSR) (41 percent from coal, 7 percent nuclear, 7 percent purchases); Mid-American Energy Holdings Company (symbol: MEC) (65 percent coal and 18 percent nuclear dependence); Puget Sound Energy, Inc. (symbol: PSD) (high dependence on purchases of energy); LG&E Energy Corp. (symbol: LGE) (uses primarily coal-fired generators); Conectiv (symbol: CIV) (38 percent coal, 24 percent purchased power, and 9 percent each of nuclear power and oil-fired generators); and Western Resources, Inc. (symbol: WR) (62 percent from coal and 10 percent from nuclear power).

Some U.S. electric utilities operate extensively overseas, usually by building generators and selling the energy to foreign governments or customers. Our concern is that the infrastructure problems in the developing world will make electrical production and delivery even more problematic, and that general global economic problems resulting from Y2K will depress earnings from such operations. Companies to avoid include CMS Energy Corporation (symbol: CMS), which on top of its base operations in Michigan has interests in over thirty power plants in over twenty foreign countries, making it the largest independent power developer in the world. Another stock to stay clear of is AES Corporation (symbol: AES), which has interest in more than 100 plants around the world.

Concluding Thoughts

For the risk-adverse investor, the utilities are a minefield to avoid until the risk from Y2K is past. Because of the large number of publicly traded utilities, we have only listed the large market caps in chapter 10. If you are invested in a utility that we have not listed, we recommend you inquire how it is preparing for Y2K, whether it distributes its power directly or sells it to power distributors such as MOUs or other government-owned utilities, what contingencies it has prepared in the event of a fuel supply disruption, and how much, if any, of its power is derived from nuclear facilities. If you don't hear back, or you don't like the answers based on what you have read here, we think you would be wise to put your money elsewhere.

FIVE

DON'T BANK ON IT: HOW Y2K COULD IMPACT BANK EQUITIES

The stakes are enormous, actually, nothing less than the preservation of a safe and sound financial system that can continue to operate in an orderly manner when the clock rolls over at midnight on New Year's Eve.

—Federal Reserve Governor Edward Kelley, Jr.

A common public fear is that, come January 1, 2000, Y2K will cause banks to foul up depositor records by the millions, creating chaos in interbank transactions and panic runs on the banks. We don't say this kind of complete meltdown is impossible. It is, however, highly unlikely.

A more probable scenario is less the stuff of Hollywood movies but still cause for concern in the banking sector. As the end of 1999 approaches, there could be increasing scrutiny of a small but nonetheless important percentage of banks that have been unable to complete their Y2K adjustments. A large discrepancy between U.S. and foreign bank Y2K preparedness will also become evident. The public could realize that the whole barrel of apples could spoil from a few bug-eaten ones. Instead of bank runs, we predict a gradual sea change in depositor mentality and a steady pattern of "practical" withdrawals. This in turn would lead banks to undertake expensive contingencies with respect to their reserves.

If you're like most investors, you have two basic questions: Is my money safe in the bank? and Should I own any bank stocks? The simple answers are yes and maybe not.

If left unfixed, Y2K would certainly devastate banks. Banks rank among the most computer-dependent of all sectors, and nearly all of those computers rely on accurate dates to perform their calculations. Banks are the first to admit they simply couldn't function at all without computers. Millions of transactions worth more than $1 trillion are handled on a daily basis by the electronic systems that connect up a truly global financial network. Maintaining an orderly volume of transactions with reliable data is critical to the success of the industry. Y2K problems, even comparatively small ones, could slow or halt electronic bank transfers at crucial junctures.

Also worrisome and unpredictable are the interdependencies banks must consider in fashioning their Y2K remediation programs. Think of all the daily interactions a bank has with other banks, businesses, and individual customers. Banks could get hit with problems upstream, downstream, and cross-stream. In fact, the whole financial stream could just dry up. A Y2K "multiple detonation effect" would quickly envelop banks in a cloud of uncertainty as business failures—particularly among ill-prepared small businesses and in overseas markets—impact heavily on commercial lenders.

On the other hand, the banks are roundly viewed as the best prepared companies when it comes to the Y2K crisis. Banks were among the first to raise awareness of the Y2K problem. They got an early start in inventorying and assessing systems, and most banks are far into the testing phase. Industry coordination and information sharing has reduced duplicative efforts, at least in the United States. And banks are accustomed to managing large information technology projects, working with each other's systems, and dealing with regulators.

These competing considerations leave investors with more questions than answers—a condition we hope to remedy. In this chapter, we'll take a closer look at the banking sector. We'll walk through our familiar list of at-risk industry characteristics to show why Y2K spells trouble for banks. We'll provide an overview of how electronic commerce is conducted among banks and see where the industry stands in its Y2K defense plans. You'll see why bigger is not necessarily better when it comes to Y2K. The chapter concludes with our picks for which bank stocks to dump and which ones to lighten up on in your portfolio.

For Banks, Time *Is* Money

Remember the old joke about "bankers' hours"? Well, the big banks today are a far cry from the 9:00 to 4:00 stuffy institutions of years past. With the transition to eletronic data interchange and global banking, major banks conduct transactions around the clock. When it's midnight in New York, it is high noon in Hong Kong, where traders on the Hang Seng Stock Exchange depend

Y2K RISK FACTOR

Time Sensitivity

on U.S. money center banks to confirm and settle transactions. Some of the larger banks even have offices in Asia, Europe, and every other continent, so the sun never really sets for these banks.

For banks, time is perhaps the most important business consideration. Time determines how much money a bank will make on an interest-bearing loan. Time defines a bank's obligations to its CD depositors. While you as a customer might not care if the bank gets to use your money for one day or ten, for the bank this is a critical question, and when extrapolated over all its customers, it can mean the difference between profitability and insolvency.

Of course, given the importance of *time* to banks, Y2K is a big, fat albatross slung on their shoulders. Y2K could slow down how quickly banks process transactions, or even halt those transactions altogether. Remember that Y2K infects and distorts *time-based calculations*. Interest could get figured

Time figures into every bank transaction

backward, deducted from customers' savings accounts, or improperly added to bank loans. Thirty-year mortgages could show up as having expired decades ago.[1] Bank credit cards with expiration dates past 1999 could freeze up systems. Whole customer records could vanish.

In fact, it's really hard to think of an industry more dependent on the accuracy of the *date* than the banking industry. This fact has not been lost on banks, however, and probably explains the relatively early start of their Y2K programs, the high prioritization of Y2K in the industry, and the massive amounts of money they are throwing at the problem.

Wait, You Want to Withdraw *How Much?*

Like the airlines, banks are at the mercy of public confidence in their ability to provide a reliable service. It has been over sixty years since a depositors' run on the banks has been on the minds of the Federal Reserve. The establishment of the Federal Deposit Insurance Corporation pretty much made keeping money in the bank a risk-free affair, at least for the vast majority of people with under $100,000 in deposits. As we discuss below, however, the government may not have the right tools and mechanisms to deal with the kind of loss of depositor confidence Y2K could bring about.

Y2K RISK FACTOR
Public Confidence

Square Pegs, Round Holes

It is important to consider that the FDIC was established primarily to ease fears of the public in the event of *outright* bank failures. Depositors wouldn't need to run to the bank and withdraw their money before the bank failed, since they could always turn to the government later. This essentially prevented the *rumor* of a bank failure from becoming self-fulfilling. However, Y2K presents banks and regulators with a very different problem. Bank customers looking at the year 2000 aren't so much concerned that their banks will *fail*—even though it is likely that, ultimately, some will. Rather, depositors have a real and valid concern that, for some unknown period of time, they will be unable *to have access* to their money.

What this means is that the FDIC—the foundation of our banking regulatory safeguards—may not be at all well-suited to deal with Y2K. After all, neither the FDIC, nor any other government agency for that matter, is prepared to hand out $1,000 in cash to any depositor who can't get to his or her account in the first months of the new millennium. The danger, then, is not of bank runs on failing banks, but of a slow bank *bleed* as prudent depositors quietly begin to withdraw billions of dollars in the latter part of 1999.

Perhaps as an indication of its inability to do much to stave off this type of "run," the FDIC has distributed 3.5 million copies of a Y2K awareness brochure to banks, hoping they will stuff them into customer statements. Whether this strategy will work remains to be seen; it certainly has the potential for backfiring as depositors start to focus in 1999 on the question of Y2K and their bank accounts.

A Fractional Problem

The possibility of a bank "bleed" raises a troubling possibility. Our banking system is set up on a *fractional reserve* basis. That is, banks need only keep a small percentage of their deposits in reserve to meet depositors' withdrawals, and they can loan out or invest the remainder. Once upon a time, these fractional reserve requirements were meant to ensure the safety of deposits and the financial soundness of the banks. Today, the fractional reserve requirements are mostly helpful to the Fed because they provide a stable, predictable demand for reserves and increase the Fed's control over short-term interest rates.[3] Banks hold these required reserves either in vault cash or in required reserve account balances with various regional reserve banks. Some banks hold "excess reserves" with the Fed, but the cost to them is high because these reserves earn no interest.

The fractional reserve theory works, and banks make money from the opportunity to use *your* money, so long as there are not sudden withdrawals of money in excess of the amount on reserve. The danger of a Y2K bank bleed is that *Banks will have to* there will be increased pressure on bank reserves, *shore up reserves* and banks will be forced to borrow money from the Fed to cover depositors and shore up their own reserves. This means less money available to the bank to lend out and more costs associated with keeping additional reserves. This in turn would put pressure on near-term earnings for banks. If the risk becomes serious enough, banks will take the precaution of building up their *excess* reserves with the Fed. Of course, they hate to do this, since this is money that could have been working for the bank rather than sitting idle. Indeed, assuming the bank has to pay interest to depositors on money it receives, turning around and putting that money in reserves is a *net loss* for the bank. Still, stockpiling excess reserves is preferable to running out of money to give to anxious depositors.

Keep the Cash Rolling

The Federal Reserve is keenly aware that there may be a "just in case" Y2K mentality developing among depositors, and it has begun to take some advance measures. In mid-1998, the Fed took the unprecedented precaution of deciding to print more money—$50 billion more—to be stored in government vaults in preparation for a possible cash crunch at the end of 1999.[4] This amount is in addition to the some $460 billion in cash currently in circulation in the United States and abroad. According to Clyde Farnsworth, the director of Federal Reserve Bank operations and payments systems, the extra $50 billion is "purely a precautionary measure." The Fed basically wanted "to be able to meet increased demand from commercial banks should private consumers request more currency."[5]

$50 billion more just in case

How much extra demand for cash is the Fed expecting? The Fed estimated in 1998 that some seventy million American households could withdraw $450 apiece in order to pay for necessities such as food and gas during the millennial changeover. Using these figures, the country will need at least $31 billion more cash in circulation.[6]

Y2K experts applaud the move. The extra $50 billion will be "a more than comfortable safety margin," according to the Gartner Group of Stamford, Connecticut.[7] This is good news for the Fed, but not much of a comfort to banks and their earnings. If the money is withdrawn as expected, this is another $50 billion that is out of the hands of banks and in the hands of their depositors. This also means that reserves are expected to be depleted by at least that amount, so banks may have to shift even more money away from working loans to nonworking reserves.

Getting a Read on Depositors

Precautionary measures by the Fed may be well warranted. In a survey conducted in mid-1998 by *CIO Magazine,* the following question was asked of 643 randomly selected U.S. residents:

> What changes, if any, do you plan to make with your finances if it becomes apparent in mid-1999 that companies will not solve this [Y2K] problem by January 1, 2000?

More than half of the respondents stated that if the Y2K problem was not solved by mid-1999, they would "move their money around." *A full quarter said they would take their money out of the banks until the problem was past.*[8] A poll of chief information officers of large companies raised similar disturbing concerns, when 38 percent said they would withdraw all of their money prior to the new millennium.[9] Overseas the fear factor also has to be taken seriously. A straw poll conducted in London in July 1998 indicated that *seven out of ten* people familiar with Y2K will withdraw *some or all* of their money from banks on the eve of the new century.[10]

Banks will certainly bear the brunt of whatever Y2K fears may develop among the public. As early as mid-1998, Wells Fargo reported fielding 200 to 300 hundred Y2K-related calls a month, and First Union Corp decided to set up a Y2K hotline.[11] Banks may come to dread public panic more than the threat of Y2K itself. Figures vary, but some experts point out that it would take less than 4 percent of people taking their money out of banks for the situation to be considered a serious bank crisis.[12]

Banks have understandably turned their collective attention toward educating consumers and clients about the safety of bank systems, and they are busily reassuring depositors that there is no need for people to withdraw money. We doubt this message will be totally effective. Banks are not in the best position to be the heralds of Y2K optimism. The more banks go to great lengths to reassure customers, the more customers are likely to worry that there really *is* something to this Y2K thing. It's like your local hospital telling you that all of their medical devices will work perfectly, and you can go ahead and schedule that surgery. Or the airlines telling you, "All of the problems are fixed. Book your New Year's flight today."

Banks have recently become more aggressive in their tactics and have started fighting fear with fear. Some banks are warning customers that massive withdrawals of money are even more dangerous than Y2K because of the risk of theft, fire, and scams. "It would be inordinately foolish for anybody to come into the institution and withdraw every penny and walk down the street and take the risk of getting mugged," warned Brian Smith, of the America's Community Bankers trade association.[13] Others echoed similar scary warnings. "Criminals have their own Y2K contingency plans and senior citizens are particularly vulnerable," noted Consumer Bankers Association Vice President Fritz Elmendorf. In our view, this sort of fear-mongering is not always constructive to a reasoned discussion on the dangers of Y2K, but it is a good indication of how worried banks are.

If, as we predict, the media has a field day with Y2K as the clock ticks down, we will see a steady stream of bank withdrawals, which could accelerate into hemorrhaging by December 1999. As this possibility looms larger, the Fed will have to come up with new mechanisms and safeguards for banks or risk serious pressures on the reserve system.

Trying Doing That With Pen and Paper

Computers handle virtually every aspect of financial institutions' business operations. In the days before computers, cash, gold, and property defined a bank's ability to lend. Today, according to the Federal Reserve, around 90 percent of bank assets are electronic entries in databases.[14]

Y2K RISK FACTOR
Automation

With respect to a bank's customers, we all know that computers are used at banks to accept and invest deposits, process loans, transfer funds, track accounts, and issue credit cards, among their many functions. For retail bank customers, computers are used to process point-of-sale transactions such as debit purchases and credit card transactions through suppliers such as Visa, Master-Card, and American Express. Corporate bank customers depend on computers for electronic data interchange, wire transfers, and letters of credit.

Banks also use computers to negotiate with automated trading systems for financial markets, perform regulatory reporting, manage customer service systems, and maintain internal systems such as accounting and payroll. Bank computers connect to and interface with outside electronic systems such as the CHIPS and SWIFT automated payment services, correspondent systems with other banks, and clearinghouses, electronic transfer centers, credit card merchants, credit reporting centers, and benefits transfer systems.[15] As the Bank of Japan bleakly put it:

If computer disruptions materialize, the adverse effects on financial institutions will be substantial because financial institutions
rely heavily on computers, for example host computers for the
main accounting systems and information systems, and decentralized systems (i.e., LAN and personal computers). If a financial institution fails to achieve Year 2000 readiness, it may not be
able to confirm or manage settlement dates or transaction data,
calculate interest rates or carry out accounting procedures, which
could be a potential threat to its fundamental business of taking
deposits, extending credit, and carrying out settlements.[16]

In such a computerized industry, Y2K is a true sword of Damocles,
and the thread holding that sword over bankers' heads is awfully
thin. Unlike manufacturing or other sectors, banking cannot afford
errors—even small ones—in its date calculations. Federal Reserve
Governor Edward Kelley put the matter succinctly: "If the problem
doesn't get fixed ahead of time, a bank . . . may find itself unable to
depend on the information provided by its general ledger including
its funding position and the account balances of its depositors and
trading customers. Obviously, a bank's inability to understand and
manage its funding and liquidity positions could have disastrous consequences for the organization, its customers, and its counterparties."[17]

"Ninety eight percent correct is not going to cut it," admitted one
group executive vice president at Bank of America.[18] But even a 2
percent problem might be optimistic. *Large-scale errors*
in the processing of electronic fund transfers and   *2 percent margin*
other transactions are possible given the complexity   *for error?*
of the system and the sheer dollar value of the funds
being transferred. A bank whose systems are unable to recognize or
interface correctly with national or international automated payment
centers and clearinghouses will quickly find itself shut out of the flow
of electronic transfers and will be crippled immediately, often beyond
rescue.

In testimony before a Senate subcommittee, an executive from
BankBoston, which is widely regarded as having the best Y2K program among the big banks, was quite candid about the kinds of problems his bank would have faced had it done nothing. He testified:

- "We would not have been able to mature our customers' certificates of deposits in the year 2000 and beyond;

- our negotiable collateral system would have lost expiration dates and review dates on collateral used to secure loans in the event of loan default;

- the system processing a daily volume of $800 million of controlled disbursements for our corporate customers would have been inoperable for ten days while the problem was corrected in January 2000, resulting in massive overdrafts to the bank; and,

- our precious metals business would have been inoperable for up to two weeks while systems changes were being made to correct erroneous date processing."[19]

The extent of the computer problem makes it clear why BankBoston and other U.S. banks are spending *billions of dollars* to squash the Y2K bug.

Let's take a typical customer at a bank. This customer might have a savings account, a checking account, a car loan, a home mortgage, and a credit card with the bank. The bank's computers need to be able to calculate interest on the savings account deposit, settlement dates on the checking account, balances and amortization schedules on the car and home loans, and interest on the credit card balance. Errors in date calculations arising from Y2K could result in skipped billing, overpayment or underpayment of interest, or, in severe cases, total loss or corruption of a customer's computer records.

These types of mistakes could be costly. They could result in loss of consumer confidence, expose the bank to financial liability, and, if widespread, paralyze the institution. Understandably, banks want to get their arms around this problem quickly.

One of the problems, however, is that many if not most banks rely on *outside* vendors for their critical data processing. According to the FDIC, "Over 90 percent of all FDIC-insured institutions receive data processing support from an independent party external to the bank or have purchased their financial software applications (such as deposit and loan information systems) from a vendor."[20] This means that Y2K-fix programs across the U.S. banking sector are going to be competing for the time and services of

90 percent of institutions use outside vendors

a limited number of programmers, thus driving up costs as the millennium draws nearer. It also means that the banks will be at the mercy of the schedules of these vendors, despite their best efforts to fix their computer systems.

My Money Is Your Money: Bank Interdependencies

There are some 13,000 commercial banks in the United States. The number of interbank transactions occurring daily is itself enough to depress even the most optimistic of those working to eradicate Y2K from bank computer systems. A small percentage of noncompliant systems—or a

Y2K RISK FACTOR
Interdependence

few bugs left in the ones thought to be compliant—is enough to cause the whole system to crash. As one major bank warns:

> There is a possible systemic risk if one financial institution or one of those payment and settlement systems fails to achieve Year 2000 readiness. Banks and securities companies are mutually connected through various payment and settlement systems for settlement of transactions. If a financial institution fails to achieve Year 2000 readiness, the computer disruption could be passed on to other ones through their interdependence in financial transactions and settlement. If a computer failure due to a lack of Year 2000 readiness materializes in a settlement system, not only financial institutions but also end users or customers will be affected because they may not be able to withdraw or transfer funds through cash dispenser and ATM networks.[21]

One example of bank interconnectedness is the Belgium-based SWIFT system, which provides an automated payment service to banks. (SWIFT stands for the Society for Worldwide Interbank Financial Telecommunications.) SWIFT has 6,000 members (mostly banks) that use its services. The global network carried more than 800 million payment messages in 1997, with roughly $2 trillion in messages a day. SWIFT is confident that its system won't crash, but it can't say the same of its participants' computers: "If a member's system is not compatible with 2000, it will not mess up our

800 million payment messages per year

network," explained one SWIFT spokesman. "It will just mean that the message *cannot be processed* at either the transmitting or receiving end."[22]

In other words, if Bank A (payor's bank) wants to pay Bank B (beneficiary's bank), it usually routes the payment message through a service like SWIFT, sometimes with the help of a correspondent bank (Bank C). The data containing the payment instructions has to pass through at least three and sometimes four or more systems before settlement. All of these systems must be Y2K-compliant, or the transaction will fail or be corrupted.

We doubt that a given failed transaction can be processed efficiently by hand, since if there is a problem in the system it probably indicates thousands or even millions of other failed transactions. This means the transaction has to be undone while the problems are sorted out; the money will stay with Bank A, and the beneficiary will be left waiting for Bank B to say the money has arrived.

Worse still would be a *corrupted* transaction, for example, where Bank A's computers confirm that payment has been made correctly, but Bank B's or Bank C's computers show that it hasn't, or that only a portion has been paid, or even that too much has been credited. It is easy to see how this type of problem, compounded over millions of transactions, could quickly shut down the whole network.

Sure, Blame the Little Guys

Most experts have been warning that a significant danger to intrabank transactions arises from *smaller* banks that lacked the resources to upgrade their systems and that developed their Y2K programs much later than the big banks. Asked about small and mid-sized banks' Y2K problems, the vice president of the New York Federal Reserve admitted candidly, "Some just won't be open for business on January 3, 2000."[23]

Some small banks not expected to open for business

Small and mid-sized banks also depend on outside vendors for most of their programming. There is a very real danger that these vendors simply will not be able to service all of these smaller banks in the few months remaining. This will leave government regulators with a tough choice: Shut down or force mergers on all the noncom-

pliant banks (and risk spooking depositors) or keep them in the
system and hope they don't bring down the big banks.

The Money Wheel

Of course, interbank networking and dependency is only part of the
picture. Banks also interact with other kinds of financial institutions
on a regular basis. The chairman of the Joint Year 2000 Council, Federal Reserve Bank of New York Vice President Ernest Patrikis, provided a good example in his testimony before the House Banking and
Financial Services Committee. He asked the panel to consider just the
daily activities of a U.S.-based *mutual fund* holding stocks and bonds,
including some in foreign jurisdictions. He noted that the mutual fund
would execute trades through its relationships with securities dealers, which might themselves use brokers and dealers. These parties
would all depend on real-time price and trade quotations from financial information services.

The mutual fund would also maintain relationships with "global
custodians" (e.g., banks) for its recordkeeping, administration, and
trade settlements. These custodians would operate a network of sub-
custodians around the world. Settlement would occur at a "domestic
securities depository" such as the Fedwire National Book-Entry
System in the United States, and additional clearing firms would be
used to round out the trade clearance and settlement process. Payment
would involve correspondent banks using "domestic wholesale payment systems" such as the Clearing House Interbank Payment System
(CHIPS), and cross-border payments might route through SWIFT to
advise and confirm payments. Failure at any one of these points
would mean that the trade could not settle properly. Corrupt data
along the path could mean errors in recordkeeping for the bank, which
basically is a recipe for lawsuits, regulatory shutdown, or insolvency.

Oh, So Now It's the *Customers'* Fault

Outside the complex world of intrafinancial institution transactions,
banks face more generic problems. Banks are highly dependent on
their customers, particularly those commercial customers (sometimes
referred to as "counterparties") to which banks have loaned lots of

money. After all, a bank makes money by lending money at higher interest rates than it pays to "borrow" it from depositors. This works fine as long as borrowers can make their payments. When they can't, that entry in the asset column becomes a plain old loss. Unfortunately for banks, dependence on their commercial borrowers is the one Y2K factor over which they have the *least* amount of control, yet it is the single biggest wild card for banks.

The commercial loan wild card

In some parts of the world, there is only a hair-thin line separating companies that can repay loans from those that can't. The banking crisis in Japan, kept from getting worse only through a government bailout of hundreds of billions of dollars, is essentially a crisis of borrowers that can't repay loans and bankers who made the mistake of lending to them. Y2K fix-it costs alone might be too much for companies teetering on the edge; Y2K disruptions will likely send those same companies plummeting over. This is *very* bad news for large international banks. Just the increased risk of bad loans to businesses failing during the Y2K crisis means banks need to keep greater loan-loss reserves.

Citibank is so concerned that it has sent out questionnaires to customers to learn how they are approaching Y2K remediation programs, what the costs of the fixes will be, and what expected timetables are. The goal is to get a comprehensive picture of client credit risks.[24] An analyst from Credit Suisse First Boston Corp. puts that risk fairly high—at ten to fifteen basis points—based on a survey of bank managers. This could add up to loan losses of $5 billion—an amount equal to a half year's earnings growth.[25] At least one bank—Amsouth Bancorp—has already set up a special reserve fund to cover potential loan losses from borrowers whose systems fail due to Y2K.[26]

The bottom line is that bank interdependencies—with one another, with other financial institutions, and with customers—mean that the risk of Y2K failures runs high among banks. As Deputy Treasury Secretary Lawrence Summers stated in testimony to Congress:

> All financial firms are potentially at risk. Even those entities which act responsibly to renovate their own systems can still be harmed, because of the intertwined nature of the financial system. A failure by a counterpart, supplier, or vendor can have a negative impact on an otherwise-solvent firm.[27]

So What Are the Banks Doing About Y2K?

Most banks realize that the extent of the Y2K problem cannot be understated. BankBoston, for example, which got started back in 1995 on its Y2K program, had this warning about the Y2K situation among banks:

> **Y2K Readiness in Banking**

> It has taken us two years to experience and overcome some of the project management complexities associated with the Year 2000 challenge. Knowing that all financial institutions must address the very same issues that we have faced with much less time remaining, I am concerned with the general preparedness of the rest of the financial services industry. In my discussions with other banks, customers, and service suppliers, I feel that unless comparable programs to BankBoston's are put in place within the next few months, the effect will adversely impact even those that are adequately prepared.[28]

It's too bad not every bank has worked as hard as BankBoston. Our research indicates that there is a disturbing pattern developing among banks that, if unchecked, will spell disaster for the sector.

The Big U.S. Banks Are Geared Up . . .

The good news is that most large, publicly traded U.S. banks recognize the danger from Y2K. Analysts appear to be in agreement that while major U.S. banks are at greatest risk from Y2K because of their financial intermediary status, they are the farthest along of any industry in tackling the problem.[29] A study by Paine Webber of thirty large U.S. banks found that the repair programs were proceeding on schedule.[30] Our research also shows that big banks aren't skimping on the costs of Y2K as they snatch up what remaining legacy system specialists remain in the pool of available programmers. These costs often come directly out of existing information technology budgets and aren't expected, in and of themselves, to have a material impact on profits.

Chase Manhattan in New York is a good example of how seriously big banks are taking the Y2K threat. Chase established its Year 2000 Program enterprise-wide in 1995. There are some 300 Chase project plans to deal with over 3,000 business applications made up of 200 million lines of code. In addition, Chase is tracking over 1,000 major third party vendors for compliance and has identified over 3,000 unique external interfaces to test.[31] Chase expects to spend upward of $363 million on its Y2K fixes.[32]

Bank of America began its Y2K assessment back in 1994 and had its project office going by 1996. Bank of America expects that its Y2K costs could run upward of $550 million,[33] with most of the money earmarked to pay an army of 1,000 full-time Y2K computer debuggers. Why so many? Bank of America programmers need to check 90,000 desktop personal computers and remediate 200 million lines of code from nearly 300 different software packages.[34]

Citicorp (now merged with Travelers into Citigroup) expects that its total Y2K bill will be $650 million, spread out over the three years prior to the millennium.[35] With so much money spent, Citibank began to tout its Y2K program as a *competitive advantage*, implying that its systems would be up and running normally: "We've decided to take this onerous task, which has to be done, and turn it to a marketing advantage. . . . We intend to be Year 2000-compliant before any other bank. European banks, especially, are much more focused on European Monetary Union than on Year 2000."[36]

We hate to break it to them, but if massive Y2K problems develop among those same European banks, or with the customers and intermediaries they also deal with every day, no amount of code fixing is going to spare Citibank from the bug's bite.

Cost estimates among big U.S. banks continue to be revised upward as testing proves more expensive and time-consuming than originally anticipated. Experts warn that the repair costs per line are rising quickly. From $1.10 in 1996, Y2K repair cost per line is expected to reach around $6.70 in 2000.[37] Bank of America has revised its cost estimates considerably, up from earliest estimates of $250 million in 1997, to $380 million in 1998, to around $550 going into 1999.[38] The following chart was provided by the *Wall Street Journal* on some of the major U.S. bank cost estimates and revisions:

ESTIMATE ($ millions)

Bank	Current Estimate (11/98)	Previous Estimate
Bank One	350	315
BankAmerica	550	500
Bankers Trust	220–260	180–230
Chase Manhattan	363	300
J. P. Morgan	300	250
National City	65	40
Wachovia	80	55
Wells Fargo	300	273

Note: Previous estimates for Bank One, BankAmerica, and Wells Fargo are based on figures for predecessor companies.[39]

From this it is clear that *money* is not the issue among major banks.

. . . But Not Everyone Is Onboard

Unfortunately, some banks aren't getting the message. According to Weiss Ratings, Inc., which took a survey in the fourth quarter of 1998 of U.S. commercial banks, savings banks, and savings and loans, 12 percent of these institutions are behind schedule in their Y2K programs.[40] These numbers are relatively on par with the numbers prepared by the FDIC in June 1998, which found that 13 percent of bank Y2K programs either were "unsatisfactory" or "needed improvement." It is also in line with a finding by the Office of the Comptroller of the Currency, which inspected around 2,260 of the 2,600 banks it regulates and found that some 14 percent of them had made "unsatisfactory" progress in Y2K programs.[41]

12 to 14 percent of banks are behind schedule

While these numbers may on their face appear positive, we are still talking about *more than 10 percent* of the banking sector at serious risk of mission-critical failures if the trend continues. Computer chaos in this many systems could shake the entire industry to its core. Some analysts warn that if just 5 to 10 percent of the world's bank payment systems failed on January 1, 2000, it would cause a global liquidity crisis.[42] We certainly hope that, come the end of 1999, a lot fewer banks are in the "unsatisfactory" or "needs improvement" columns. But if these banks are behind in their programs now, as resources become scarcer and vendors commit themselves to existing Y2K programs these banks may find themselves further out in the cold.

The situation among U.S. credit unions is also troublesome. The National Credit Union Association has been investigating the state of readiness among the nation's credit unions. The concern is that credit unions, which are typically small, privately held or non-profit institutions, may lack the resources to conduct thorough Y2K remedial programs and are not as heavily regulated as the nation's banks. Nevertheless, a substantial amount of the public's money rests in their care, and Y2K problems could start like a brush fire from non-compliant credit unions. The NCUA has found that credit unions in Texas appear to be the least prepared for Y2K; a disturbing eighty-nine credit unions in that state were rated as "needs improvement" as late as the fourth quarter of 1998. New York also rang in with troubling results, with the most number of credit unions rated to be "unsatisfactory" by the NCUA. Perhaps the most alarming statistic, however, is that the number of credit unions ranked "unsatisfactory" by the report had *risen* 20 percent over the prior quarter's figures.[43]

The Fed Steps Up to the Plate . . . Sort Of

The FDIC, which insures deposits at over 11,000 banks and savings institutions, has itself not had a trouble-free Y2K program. In 1997, it fell behind its self-imposed deadlines, having failed to complete an assessment of its own systems by the end of the third quarter of that year. Instead, the assessment would be finished six months behind schedule in March of 1998, leading House leaders to note that the FDIC was setting a poor example for the institutes it oversees.[44]

The FDIC also admitted that it got a late start in assessing the Y2K compliance efforts of the 6,200 banks it directly supervises. It had set itself a June 30, 1998, deadline for wrapping up initial assessments of its member banks, but toward the end of that deadline, it was scrambling to complete the task. In the final hundred workdays before June 30, 1998, the FDIC still had 4,000 banks to check on, meaning on average over forty banks every day. To make matters worse, the General Accounting Office issued sharp criticism of the review process, leading a chagrined FDIC to go back and recheck the 2,000 banks it had already visited.[45] This pattern of government inefficacy should by now seem eerily familiar to readers.

This history of rushed evaluations draws some doubts over the otherwise relatively optimistic assessment of the FDIC examiners, who claimed to have finished the task on time at the end of June 1998. The assessments broke banks down into three *Enough time* groups: around 88 percent of member banks were found *to evaluate?* to be making "satisfactory" progress, some 12 percent "needed improvement," and less than 1 percent were found to be "unsatisfactory."[46] The FDIC also worked with state banking regulators to conduct on-site assessments of all state nonmember banks. We wish we could tell you precisely which banks are behind the curve, but the results of these on-site reviews remain strictly confidential.[47]

Financial Institutions Fret

Some institutions and companies that deal regularly with the banking sector at large are also making doubly sure that banks do their best to come into full compliance. Visa International, for example, has basically all of its credit card compliance testing complete. Visa deals with around 14,000 banks, and it processes some fifty million electronic transactions daily from its fourteen million point-of-sale merchant terminals. With so many possible origination points for Y2K glitches, Visa can't say with certainty that its own network will remain unaffected, so it is doing its best to minimize problems with its banking partners.[48]

The Federal National Mortgage Association (Fannie Mae) is understandably concerned about the status of banks and other mortgage lenders with which it does business. Fannie Mae is the cornerstone of the $4 trillion U.S. housing industry. As a   *A line in the* buyer and investor in the secondary home mortgage   *sand* market, Fannie Mae deals constantly with primary mortgage lenders—banks, S&Ls, credit unions, state and local housing agencies, and mortgage companies. Fannie Mae drew a line in the sand when it comes to the compliance of its primary bank lenders. It has warned that "lenders must ensure that the internal systems they use to do business with us are Year 2000–compliant *no later than March 31, 1999* in order to maintain their status as approved seller/

servicers."[49] In other words, Fannie Mae quarantined the bug-infected in order to maintain the Y2K health of the others.

Others have taken up the call to keep out the noncompliant from the system. In August 1998, Bank of Korea announced that commercial banks that fail to address the Y2K problem would be denied access to the interbank settlement system. The reason was simple: "Banks that have computing network systems with the [Y2K] glitch problem unsolved could wreak havoc on the interbank settlement system," stated a Bank of Korea official.[50]

The Fed and some state regulators have also quietly drawn up plans to declare Y2K noncompliant banks to be "technologically insolvent" and force them to merge with other institutions

The Fed will shut 'em down

or move their deposits to healthy banks.[51] Regulators seem ready to come down hard. As early as November 1997, the FDIC and the Georgia Department of Banking and Finance issued a cease-and-desist order against three banks owned by Putnam-Greene Financial Corp., in Eatonton, Georgia, citing unreliable electronic information systems that could not process data correctly after December 31, 1999.[52] The banks were given three choices: sell, install new software, or hire a service bureau to handle data processing.

In Massachusetts, state regulators have warned banks and credit unions that they will face a series of penalties, including suspension or removal of directors and officers, if they fail to comply with federal Y2K guidelines.[53]

The market may also operate to force closures and mergers of banks failing the Y2K litmus test. In fact, it has already claimed its first victim. CoreStates Bank could tell you about the impact of Y2K, if it were still around. Its Y2K problems were a major factor in its board's decision to sell the bank to First Union. CoreStates faced "substantial exposure and risk" in trying to make its computer systems Y2K-compliant, while First Union was "substantially farther along," according to CoreStates' former chairman.[54]

No Time to Test?

By the end of 1998, most banks were still in the stage of fixing their systems and hadn't begun the testing phase. The Federal Financial

Institutions Examination Council warns, however, that testing is expected to "consume 50 to 60 percent of the time, funding, and personnel needed to make financial institutions Year 2000 ready."[55] Fed Governor Kelley puts the estimate even higher, saying that testing "will consume more than a year and absorb as much as 70 percent of Year 2000 resources."[56] If these numbers are right, this bodes badly for banks.

Bank of America, for example, promised that testing would begin on December 31, 1998. But if a year's worth of testing sounds like a generous safety margin, consider that Bank of America began its Y2K program some *five years* ago. If you were to use the FFIEC guidelines on testing as an industry standard, Bank of America would come up short. Many Asian and European banks aren't even close to finishing their fixes, so testing will have to be postponed until sometime in late 1999.

Banks face additional complications when they proceed to test their systems. Most of the critical, at-risk programming cannot be tested without a number of other banks, financial institutions, payment systems, and clearinghouses participating. Coordination among these parties is problematic due to the varying states of remediation work and the lack of a strong international coordinating body.

Even more worrisome are reports that companies believing their systems to be fully remediated and Y2K-compliant continue to have serious problems. This is because much of the work already done was less than perfect: improper date formats were "either missed, not converted, or converted wrongly," according to one consulting firm doing verification work for large U.S. and European corporations.[57] U.S. computer services company Unisys has blasted the quality of testing generally, noting that supposedly fixed programs were still dangerously infected. "Some of the issues we found would have taken their systems down," noted the Unisys Year 2000 program manager.[58]

The importance of testing was not lost on Annapolis Bank and Trust. That bank, hoping to get a head start on the Y2K crisis, instituted a new ATM system that was billed as "Year 2000-proof." Unfortunately for the bank, the new system, provided by a U.S. vendor, froze out scores of debit card holders, put some check cards out of commission for a week, and delayed certain electronic transactions for

When the solution is as bad as the problem

several weeks. Over a hundred complaint calls came in as bank officials scrambled to get cash to customers who couldn't access their
accounts.[59] This bank's experience underscores the fact that the
untested solutions to Y2K may present as many problems as the bug
itself.

Not Forever Holding Our Peace:
Why Banks Should Not Be Wed

Another complicating factor is the rash of bank and financial institution mergers taking place as the century draws to a close. These
include the gargantuan Citicorp/Travelers merger, the union of Bank
of America and NationsBank, the marriage of Bank One and First
Chicago, the pairing of Wells Fargo with NorWest, and most recently
Deutsche Bank's buyout of Bankers' Trust. When banks merge, computer systems have to merge, too, so that the systems can talk to one
another perfectly. This is part of the benefit of the merger, because it
allows for cost and job cuts. But programmers are hit with the double
task of fixing Y2K and melding the systems together. This has put a
strain on resources, and in some cases the merging companies have
decided to pursue independent Y2K fixes.[60]

On the other hand, some have begun to predict that bank mergers
will all but dry up in the latter half of 1999. The pace of mergers will
be slowed by a dropoff in demand as the non-Y2K-compliant nature
of the systems of potential acquisitions becomes more evident. "When
you are talking about a [small] bank, you are never sure how close
they are to compliance or how long it will take to get your system
into their branch," explained one bank executive, whose bank was
known for its aggressive purchases of community banks. "If the problems are worse than you think, you can risk fines and other regulatory
action."[61] Indeed, federal regulators are expected to raise doubts over
the wisdom of any merger that could result in a crash of an otherwise
compliant bank's systems as the millennium approaches.

The Problem Over There

Despite all the concerns over the banking situation at home, we hear
again a familiar refrain: They are nothing compared to what's in store

for the rest of the world. There is a growing consensus that foreign banks are behind—sometimes far behind—in Y2K compliance. Even industry optimist Fed Governor Kelley has admitted that foreign banks appear to be lagging their U.S. counterparts.[62]

In Asia, the problem began with lack of early attention. High-tech experts point out that computer types weren't

Y2K *ADDED* RISK FACTOR
Foreign Banks Not Compliant

influential enough with management to get them to focus on how serious the problem was, particularly as more pressing concerns such as the financial crisis gripped the region. Asia's tight labor markets have also made computer personnel resources relatively scarce. And Asian banks rely on computer systems that have been customized to such an extent that foreign consultants can't be of much use.[63]

Of particular concern is the situation among banks in Japan, which is plagued by a nationwide recession and whose banks are still adjusting to sweeping deregulation. Japanese banks started their Y2K programs a lot later than U.S. banks. One of the world's largest banks, the Bank of Tokyo–Mitsubishi, began its repair program in *April 1997*, a full twenty-two months after its U.S. competitor, Chase Manhattan.[64]

Y2K spending among larger Japanese banks is just a *fraction* of what U.S. banks are spending. Allocations among big Japanese banks range from $29 million to $71 million to fix the bug, compared to Y2K budgets at major U.S. banks, which run as high as $650 million.[65] A survey of around fifty smaller Japanese banks in the first half of 1998 revealed that their *total* budget for Y2K was only around $250 million—less than half of Citicorp's budget alone.[66]

A fraction budgeted

The situation is grim enough that Moody's Investor's Service, which issues credit ratings worldwide, has expressed public doubts over Japan's bank readiness. In a report issued in 1998, it stated, "Moody's is concerned that the Japanese bank executives do not appear to be taking the potential problems as seriously as the managements of other global institutions. . . . Unlike other global banks, the Japanese say they do not have any major problems, and how they achieved that happy state of affairs is something of a mystery."[67]

Japan's Financial Supervisory Agency worries that smaller Japanese financial institutions and credit unions rely heavily on outside support for their computer software and haven't established clear schedules for their Y2K remediation programs.[68] This situation is similar to the one among smaller U.S. banks. The problem is compounded in Japan, however, where the resources of even fewer vendors will have comparatively less time to achieve compliance.

Japan is not the only major U.S. financial partner to drop the ball. European banks may also wreak Y2K havoc in the global financial system. European financial institutions spent 1998 scrambling to deal with conversion to a common currency, which was unfortunately timed to begin in early 1999. An otherwise confident Alan Greenspan—who is usually known for his discretion and understatement—left a huge question mark hanging when he noted that he was "concerned about the ability of software programmers in Europe, whose minds are on the shift to the Euro" to be able to complete Y2K fixes.[69] Maybe we're lucky no one was paying attention yet. Statements like this in late 1999 will send bank stocks skidding.

Other Fed governors have pointed out that the Euro conversion has competed with Y2K for information technology resources and the attention of management.[70] Y2K is expected to require three times the effort (and money) that the Euro conversion did, and the fact is, there simply isn't enough time, will, and money remaining.

We are further concerned that the recent *successful* transition for the Euro may lull many in Europe into a false state of complacency with respect to Y2K. While we are heartened by the fact that a computer conversion program of this magnitude can be accomplished without disruptions to the markets and the flow of commerce, we can only credit the vast amounts of money and effort put in by the participating countries in Euroland.

Moreover, the Euro transition, even if largely seamless, does not mean that Y2K will go well in a similar fashion. Euro conversion was relatively "narrow and deep," affecting a limited number of computers and systems. Y2K, on the other hand, is "wide and shallow," requiring simple fixes but sprouting up everywhere, often in unexpected ways. Experts have pointed out that the two issues, while sharing some similarities, are not coextensive enough for there to be much crossover benefit. Still, the fact that there have not been major cases of Euro-related snafus renews our faith that human ingenuity and hard work can overcome the most significant of challenges, including Y2K.

It is, in our minds, a question of whether enough time and resources remain.

As things stand, the consensus is that European banks, particularly in Germany and France, are behind those in the U.S. "German banking supervisors do not and cannot even dare to guarantee that banks will be fully compliant," conceded Edgar Meister of the Directorate of the Deutsche Bundesbank.[71] Unless a herculean effort is undertaken immediately, the chances of a seamless Y2K transition for European banks are low indeed.

Follow the Money

The problems with overseas banks are part of a larger phenomenon of lack of Y2K preparedness in other parts of the world. In chapter 7, we discuss the failure of foreign governments and industries to prepare for Y2K and what those failures could mean for the U.S. economy. But for the banks that deal regularly with international customers and partners, the consequences could be particularly severe.

Y2K *ADDED* RISK FACTOR

Foreign Exposure

Large U.S. money center banks often have substantial foreign exposure in the form of at-risk commercial loans, unstable markets, and potential currency exchange losses, to name a few. The impact on bank earnings from global economic turmoil in 1997 and 1998 was significant—much worse than many had anticipated. But Y2K's impact on those same regions could make the 1997–98 crisis look like a mere precursor.

In its report on the probable global economic impact of Y2K, Goldman Sachs singles out multinational money centers as being at greater risk than large U.S. regional banks, which engage in comparably less international trade.[72] We think this is sound advice, and it is consistent with everything we have seen in interdependent bank business systems and Y2K.

Money Centers Beware

We would steer far clear of international money center banks that have high foreign operations exposure. Most of this information is buried somewhere in the annual reports and SEC filings of these companies, some of which we have been able to ferret out for you. We should warn that the companies we recommend investors avoid are among the

Y2K Stock Shocks

most well-respected and well-known banks in the business, so our advice may discomfit some investors. Remember, it's not that we think their internal Y2K programs are inadequate. Rather, we are concerned over their high Y2K exposure in their roles as global financial intermediaries and over their dependence on other at-risk sectors, particularly overseas commercial borrowers.

U.S. Money Center Banks With Foreign Operations Exposure

Topping our list of concerns is Citicorp, now merged with the Travelers Group into industry giant Citigroup (symbol: CCI). Technically, Citigroup has too many operations to be considered a "bank"—it really is a full-service financial firm, offering property and casualty insurance, investment services, credit cards, and banking. Focusing on its banking operations, we see a lot of risk. Citigroup's well-known Citibank banking unit is the world's largest issuer of credit cards, on top of being a full-service bank with a presence in over 100 countries—including all of the countries we have identified as risky. Profits in 1998 were severely impacted by volatile world markets, and Citicorp's corporate businesses and portfolios bear those scars already. Indeed, Citicorp's global corporate banking segment posted a $127 million *loss* in the third quarter of 1998, compared to a profit of $417 million from the same quarter in 1997.[73] The turmoil will only increase in 1999 and 2000 under Y2K, and we advise investors to stay clear of this stock.

Another bank not to bank on is Chase Manhattan Corporation (symbol: CMB), formed in 1996 from the merger of Chemical Bank and Chase. Chase offers a full range of banking and investment services in over fifty countries in Asia, Europe, the Middle East, Africa, and North and South America.[74] Like Citicorp, Chase earnings are suffering from declines in its global bank division revenues, which fell 20 percent in the third quarter of 1998. We expect the problem to get worse under Y2K in late 1999 and 2000. As of September 30, 1998,

Chase had outstanding foreign commercial loans of $34.3 billion, or around 39 percent of its total commercial loan portfolio. Its "nonperforming assets" are even more telling: as of the end of the third quarter, $559 million—or about 58 percent—of these were foreign loans.[75] The number and extent of foreign nonperforming loans are likely to increase, perhaps dramatically, when Y2K hits.

BankAmerica Corporation (symbol: BAC), another company born of merger (NationsBank and Bank of America), is a major money center bank likely to be hit with serious Y2K woes. BankAmerica has operations in twenty-two states and forty countries. In 1997, before the merger, Bank of America (which has most of the foreign exposure between the two merging companies) had foreign loans of $27.4 billion out of $166 billion, or around 16.5 percent.[76] While this is a lot less than its rival, Chase Manhattan, it is not insignificant. What's more, BankAmerica's foreign exposure is in Asia, Latin America, Eastern Europe, and Russia,[77] where Y2K programs lag significantly.

The Bank of New York Company, Inc. (symbol: BK), has a global presence as well as a dominant share of the New York tristate area. Their foreign operations concern us most; Bank of New York operates in twenty-six countries around the world. As of the end of 1997, a full 32 percent of their total interest-bearing deposits were foreign in origin.[78] Around 41 percent of its $36.5 billion loan portfolio at the end of 1997 was in its foreign offices.[79] As with many other U.S. money center banks, this is a recipe for disaster during the Y2K crisis.

J. P. Morgan (symbol: JPM) bills itself as a global financial leader and international banking company, but in the world of Y2K this description gets turned on its head. In addition to banking and finance advisory, its lines of business include market making, asset management, equity investments, and proprietary investing. Its client base is about 50 percent foreign, with Asia and Latin America comprising around 20 percent of total client revenues.[80]

BankBoston Corporation (symbol: BKB) may have the most advanced internal Y2K program around, but that doesn't change the fact that it derives a substantial amount of its revenue from its overseas operations, primarily in Latin America. It is one of the largest foreign banks in both Argentina and Brazil, where Y2K problems are rampant. Over 28 percent of its loans are sitting outside of the United States, again mostly in Latin America.[81] This more than offsets the positive marks that BankBoston gets for its early start on and good handling of its internal Y2K program.

Bankers Trust Corporation (symbol: BT), which is being acquired by Deutsche Bank, has enormous international exposure, operating in over fifty countries worldwide. Bankers Trust has already been hammered by market turmoil in Asia and emerging countries in Eastern Europe, the Middle East, and Africa. In those markets, Bankers Trust posted losses in the third quarter of 1998 in excess of $300 million.[82] We expect the situation to worsen under Y2K before it improves.

Rounding out our list of at-Y2K-risk U.S. money center banks is Republic New York Corporation (symbol: RNB). Republic New York offers banking services in South America, Europe, Asia, and the Carribbean, in addition to its branches in New York and Florida. Foreign deposits made up over 56 percent of its total deposits as of the end of the third quarter of 1998. Its foreign loan exposure is lighter, however, making up over 28 percent of its loan portfolio in the same period.[83] Republic New York also has high cross-border exposure, particularly in Brazil, which is a Y2K basket case.

Foreign Money Center Banks

Foreign money center banks trading on U.S. stock exchanges are also high risks. These include the behemoth Bank of Tokyo–Mitsubishi, Ltd. (symbol: MBK), which we mentioned earlier as being a low Y2K spender relative to its U.S. competitors. Even if Tokyo–Mitsubishi can resolve its internal problems, its worldwide exposure and domestic Japanese company risks make it a strong sell in our view.

Barclays PLC (symbol: BCS) operates over 1,000 branches in seventy-five countries besides its native United Kingdom. Its foreign interest-earning assets (e.g., loans) came to around one-third of its total, while its interest-bearing liabilities (e.g., deposits) were close to 40 percent of the total in 1997.[84] Barclays has also taken major earnings hits from and writedowns of its operations in Southeast Asia and is likely to experience similar pain through the Y2K crisis.

Other foreign money center banks to avoid include Banco Santander, S.A. (symbol: STD) (5,000 offices in thirty-two countries, particularly South America); Royal Bank of Canada (symbol: RY) (presence in thirty-four other countries); Westpac Banking Corporation, Ltd. (symbol: WBK) (exposure in Asia and the Pacific Islands); Corporación Bancaria de España, S.A. (symbol: AGR) (at risk in Latin America); and the Australia and New Zealand Banking Group Limited (symbol: ANZ) (operates throughout Asia, Europe, and the Middle East).

Other Money Center Banks

A handful of other money center banks don't have as much direct international exposure that Y2K could exploit. These include such well-knowns as Bank One Corporation (symbol: ONE), Wells Fargo and Company (symbol: WFC) (now merged with Norwest), First Union Corporation (symbol: FTU), and Fleet Financial Group, Inc. (symbol: FLT). Other smaller money centers that will fare relatively better under Y2K due to their more insulated nature include KeyCorp (symbol: KEY), SunTrust Banks, Inc. (symbol: STI), and PNC Bank Corp. (symbol: PNC). All of these stocks we would tend to underweight them rather than completely avoid.

Regional Banks and Savings and Loans

While we predict that regional banks and savings and loans will fare better than their large, international money center counterparts, our concerns over banking in general still lead us to consider these equities an "underweight." Among the largest we would watch out for are the following:

Northeast
Mellon Bank Corporation (MEL)
State Street Corporation (STT)

Midwest
U.S. Bancorp (USB)
National City Corporation (NCC)
Fifth Third Bancorp (FITB)
Comerica Incorporated (CMA)

Southeast
Regions Financial Corporation
    (RGBK)
SouthTrust Corporation
    (SOTR)

Mid-Atlantic
Wachovia Corporation (WB)
BB&T Corporation (BBK)

Southwest
Mercantile Bancorporation, Inc.
  (MTL)

Pacific
Canadian Imperial Bank of
  Commerce (BCM)
Union BanCal Corporation
  (UNBC)

Savings and Loans
Washington Mutual, Inc.
  (WAMU)
Golden West Financial
  (GDW)
Charter One Financial, Inc.
  (COFI)
GreenPoint Financial Corp.
  (GPT)

Concluding Thoughts

We wish that we could offer a more upbeat prognosis for bank operations and earnings through the Y2K crisis. Again, it is entirely possible that every last bank will beat the deadline and that no major problems will erupt. It is also possible that foreign markets won't be significantly disrupted and that banks won't see additional foreign nonperforming loans. Remember, however, that stocks take *risk* into account, and we think the risk of major problems in the banking sector is high enough to warrant considerable caution and in some cases decisive protective measures.

SIX

ANSWERING THE CALL? Y2K AND THE TELEPHONE COMPANIES

The Year 2000 issue is possibly the most critical problem we have ever faced at AT&T.

—A. John Pasqua, program management vice president,
AT&T Year 2000 Program

[T]he potential losses and disruptions that could accrue from noncompliant telecommunications systems could be staggering.

—Joel C. Willemssen, director, Civil Agencies Information Systems,
Accounting and Information Management Div., U.S. GAO

The United States is the world's most advanced—and most dependent—producer and consumer of telecommunications and information technologies. The Y2K threat to our communications network is second only to the danger posed to our electric power grid. Indeed, telecommunications are like the central nervous system of modern society: Without the ability to talk to one another and transmit information, society as we know it could not continue.

It should come as no surprise that the telecommunications sector, and especially the telephone companies (the "telcos"), are at high Y2K risk. After all, advances in telecommunication technology have all been made possible by computers and the microchip. Automation permits customers to link seamlessly from one network to another in a fraction of a second, placing calls and sending faxes and data anywhere in the country or, for that matter, the world. Serious Y2K disruptions to the automated processes in telecommunications would slow our data exchange to a useless trickle. It would also devastate telcos.

The very fact that the industry is called a telecommunications *network* should also set off warning bells to Y2K-minded investors. Even more than the electric utilities, telecommunication companies rely upon each other for effective delivery of their services. The telcos form an interlaced network of local, regional, and international carriers that are physically hooked together through lines, switches, and computer systems in a system even more complex than our national power grid.

But telcos also have many things going for them in the Y2K battle. Like the banking sector, major telcos have been credited with taking an aggressive and relatively early stance against Y2K. Major telcos have spared no expense or personnel to eradicate Y2K from their systems. Telcos are also highly organized, with no less than three cross-industry working groups busily coordinating remediation efforts. Unlike electric utilities, telcos are not worried about increases in the cost of any raw materials, and unlike health care providers, telcos don't worry much about massive exposure to lawsuits due to failing equipment. Most importantly, unlike banks and the airlines, telcos likely will not face a crisis of customer confidence before Y2K even strikes. After all, people are not going to unplug their phones just because they are afraid calls won't get through. These considerations make telcos relatively better off from a *financial* standpoint than any of the other sectors we have discussed so far.

The question for investors is whether telco service will continue uninterrupted. The honest answer to this question is "No one knows for sure." While the Y2K problem itself is deceptively simple, the consequences of Y2K failures in telecommunications can be "complex, unpredictable, and in some cases very serious," according to the FCC.[1] If you ask the telcos themselves, they will tell you that they expect business as usual come January 1, 2000. Not surprisingly, Y2K experts and government watch groups are often not as optimistic.

By now, you know the drill. We'll start by running through the primary Y2K risks for the telecommunications industry in terms of time sensitivity, automation, and interdependence. We'll then discuss the state of readiness of the industry as a whole. There are some troubling *added* Y2K risk considerations, such as the small telcos, lack of customer preparedness, and the poor situation overseas that lead us to disfavor the telecommunications sector as a whole. In conclusion, we'll issue our *stock watch* for several major publicly traded telcos.

Call Anytime, Anywhere

It's no secret that *time* matters a great deal to the telcos. After all, most of the money they make is from toll charges that are based on the *duration* of the call and the *time* it was placed. Y2K could distort time-sensitive calculations, resulting in ridiculous billing errors that show calls being decades long. However, this is more of a nuisance than a serious threat; most if not all publicly traded telcos will at a minimum be able to fix how their computers keep track of the date.

Y2K RISK FACTOR
Time Sensitivity

A more relevant and troublesome aspect of telco time sensitivity is the global, round-the-clock nature of the operations of telcos. Almost anyone anywhere in the world can use the phone to call anyone else anywhere at any time of the day. We take this luxury for granted, both in our personal calls and in our business communications. But in implementing Y2K programs, telcos are limited because they can't perform any *live Y2K tests* of their networks. After all, the phone companies (like the utilities) can't tell customers to stay off the phones while they take them offline and turn the clocks forward to 2000 to run some tests. This means no one will know if the system is actually compliant until the networks are brought together and forced to operate on January 1, 2000.[2]

No live tests possible

Reliability and continuity are the buzzwords of the telecommunications industry. Bellcore, for example, has a reliability standard that is extremely stringent, requiring 99.9999 percent "up time" in its normal operations. (Thus, switch reliability standards only permit 3 minutes of downtime per switch per year.)[3] On top of telephone availability, we also tend to take telephone reliability for granted. We expect never to have to wonder whether calls will go through, even though it wasn't that long ago, for example, that placing or receiving calls overseas to certain developing countries was basically a crapshoot.

Telcos and Public Confidence

The Telecommunications Act of 1996 was designed to bring greater competition in the telecommunications marketplace, and to some extent we are seeing more aggressive carrier marketing and customer switching. If Y2K causes persistent problems in connecting on the first try, this could result in angry customers ready to switch carriers, even if it is not the fault of the originating carrier that the call could not be placed properly. As the impact of increased competition is more widely appreciated, reliability will become an even greater consideration to telcos. In general, Y2K reliability issues tend to favor rather than hinder big, publicly traded telcos. But if the phenomenon of dead lines or failed calls is widespread, expect eager media coverage of the snafus, some customer defections, and modest pressure on share prices.

Still, in comparison to some other sectors, such as banks and airlines, telcos face few of the public panic pressures that Y2K could bring about. After all, we all have to make phone calls, but we don't necessarily have to have all our cash in the banks or fly across the country in January 2000. From this perspective, telcos are *not* subject to major public perception risk under Y2K.

It's no secret that computers pervade every aspect of telecommunications today. Computers control telco switching and transmission systems. Computers also control satellite ground equipment, customer voice mail, private branch exchanges, and even telecommunications equipment such as "repeaters" that lie on the bottom of the ocean. AT&T found, for example, that 20 percent of its Worldwide Intelligent Network needed software updates. At risk were high-capacity switches, signal transfer points, switches and routers for Internet service, and data transmission lines.[4] Computers also control adjunct processors and database-management systems,[5] which are used to track customer information and all-important billing information.

Y2K RISK FACTOR
Automation

A Bellcore survey of carrier networks and large corporations found that 75 percent of voice networking equipment, 25 to 35 percent of data networking devices, and almost 100 percent of network management devices contain date-sensitive processing in them.

A high percentage at risk

The kinds of date-sensitive functions included the following:

- service routing and scheduling
- message reporting
- network administration and management
- system clock maintenance and restoration
- event/alarm time-stamping
- history sorting and reporting
- security (e.g., log-ins and passwords)
- user interface displays and user input
- logging of information
- reports
- data processing functions[6]

These numbers and systems demonstrate why the primary Y2K threat to telco automation lies in their networking technology. Local and international carriers use networks to process, track, record, and route calls, both internally and with one another. Before we discuss Y2K problems at the network level, let's break down how networks are constructed and look at some of the basic building blocks.

Network "elements" permit the storage of call information in databases and the switching and transport of voice and data through communication interfaces. Most elements contain computers and associated internally developed software, as well as vendor-supplied software and application programs. (See Figure 6.1.) All of this hardware and software is potentially at risk from Y2K, so each and every network element has to be checked thoroughly for possible Y2K problems.[7]

The number of elements in use by the telcos is mind-boggling. Bell Atlantic, for example, has over 350 kinds of elements that it has deployed *tens of thousands of times* across its own networks.[8]

Elements in turn are strung together using computer software and hardware to form what are called "functions" or "functional clusters." (See Figure 6.2.) Clusters of elements faciliate such tasks as call routing and customer contact. Each cluster in turn must be Y2K-compliant, meaning each element can interact successfully with others in the cluster.

Finally, functional clusters are connected up in a *network* that per-

Figure 6.1   Telecommunications Element

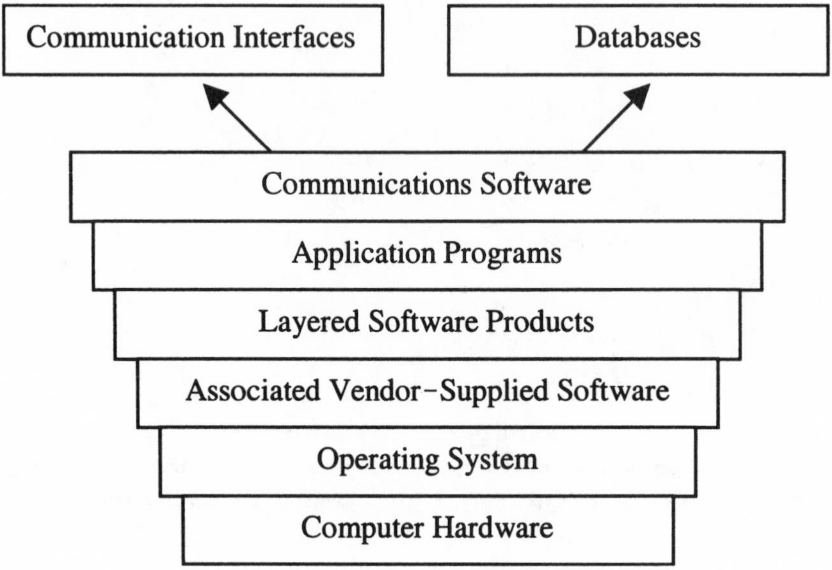

Communication Interfaces	Databases

Communications Software

Application Programs

Layered Software Products

Associated Vendor–Supplied Software

Operating System

Computer Hardware

mits the telco to perform its core operations of processing, tracking, recording, and routing calls. (See Figure 6.3.) In most cases, there is not a lot of date-sensitive information in the call processing or data routing capabilities of networks. Rather, date sensitive information tends to crop up in operations, administration, and maintenance of networks. Still, each separate piece of the network needs to be made Y2K-compliant, either by the telco itself or by the equipment manufacturer who supplies the network equipment. For the clusters to communicate, transfer data, and interface correctly, the connections between them also must be checked for Y2K problems.

What all of these layers mean is that remediating telecommunication systems is painstaking, needle-in-the-haystack type work, with

We have a problem, but where?

thousands upon thousands of haystacks. This of course translates into lots of dollars needed to pay lots of programmers. It also means that Y2K contingency planning for telecommunication networks is problematic. After all, if a call does not go through, it is very difficult to pinpoint whether the problem occurs at the interface

Figure 6.2   A Functional Cluster

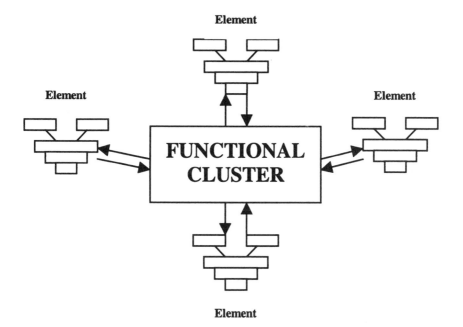

between networks, at the functional cluster level within a network, at the network element configuration, or within a particular part of a network element. And given the high number of networks, the number of possible permutations of how a call is routed is unfathomably high.

This also makes *testing* of all possible automated routes and failure points practically impossible, even apart from the fact that the system cannot be taken off-line to be tested. GTE puts the number of tests it would have to run to test *all combinations* of its automated equipment and operating systems at *10 to the 29th power.*[9] Rather than test each and every network component, most telcos have established labs where "dummy" networks—complete with switches, data links, and simulated peak loads—will attempt to replicate the real networks.

But are telcos up to the task of debugging such complex, multilayered networks? Industry optimists have pointed out that technology upgrades and changes are standard affairs for the telcos, and the Y2K

Figure 6.3   Simple Carrier Network

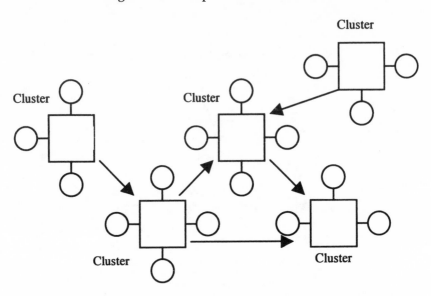

fix is not something totally unfamiliar. For example, telcos are constantly asked to add new area code prefixes. Carrier networks are always being upgraded, developed, and maintained. There is, after all, little that is static in the world of telecommunication technology. But development of new systems and technology usually is *incremental* in nature and occurs in a stable environment. Y2K shakes up information technology in telecommunications because it forces telcos to reintroduce modified systems into a *highly unstable* environment.[10] In addition, unlike most technology upgrades that address specific regions or implement particular solutions, Y2K is a problem that infects all aspects of automated telecommunications, from the hard drives of PCs to the networking software interlinking huge companies' systems.

The telcos will be the first to admit that the task is extremely daunting.[11] Voice and data transfer has to occur nearly instantaneously. Nearly everything has to be checked. Our concern, as we discuss later in this chapter, is that not every telco in the world is up to the task, given the costs and resources involved, not to mention the time remaining. This could mean serious problems for even the most prepared of telcos.

When you make a phone call from your office to another state, every link in the communication chain has to work perfectly for that call to go through. Your call starts from your telephone itself. It usually then passes through a "private branch exchange" (in essence, your company's switchboard) before heading on to the central office switch of the local carrier.

Y2K RISK FACTOR
Interdependence

From there it travels through the local carrier's network components and systems and is routed to an interexchange carrier or carriers. The carrier then sends the call along long distance trunk lines or through more modern microwave, fiber-optic or satellite facilities. The call then drops to another local exchange carrier's central switch, then to the switchboard of the company you are calling, and finally to the phone of the call recipient.

This entire process is completed in just milliseconds. It involves the software and equipment of multiple companies, from carriers to manufacturers. And the next time you place the same call, it is highly *un*likely that it will take the same exact route again.

Y2K problems anywhere along this route could mean disruption or failure of your call, which translates into lost business for the phone company. Compounding the problem is the fact that a failed call will likely result in one or more redial attempts, thus adding to the burden of a given central office switch.

Like the banks, telcos usually depend on outside vendors for their computer software and equipment solutions. Most of the millions of network elements, information systems, and computers used by telcos were purchased from third parties. Telcos need to work with and depend on these parties to ensure compliance of each type of system. Manufacturers of customer-premises equipment must also achieve compliance or calls might never even get onto the phone lines.

We have already seen that how well a carrier's networks will fare under Y2K depends on how well each cluster operation performs, which in turn depends on how well each network element operates, which in turn depends on how well each piece of the element performs.[12] This also means there are at least three different Y2K business challenges for the telcos with respect to outside parties.

First, telcos must be sure their vendors provide compliant elements, which are the building blocks of the network. Second, the telcos must work with their outside network system integrators to bring the elements into compliant networks. The problem is, Y2K remediation of integration systems can only begin *after* the various network elements have been certified to be free of Y2K. Third, the telcos must coordinate their network-to-network interfaces. This can only be done once each of the separate networks has been certified as Y2K compliant. This highlights the difficulties of bringing the entire telecommunications industry into Y2K compliance, since each piece of the puzzle has to be in place before moving on to a higher level.

These levels of interdependence make planning Y2K programs problematic at best. It also makes for tricky contingency planning, since the telcos have to be ready for failure at any point along the network.

The Big Companies

There certainly is no shortage of spending on Y2K fixes among the major U.S. telephone companies. Seven of the largest carriers are expecting to spend around $2 billion, according to their SEC filings.[13]

Y2K Preparedness Among Telcos

If you survey the public statements of the telcos with respect to Y2K preparedness, a very rosy picture is painted indeed. For example, AT&T likes to point out that it launched its Y2K program in the fall of 1996. It is one of the biggest Y2K spenders, having plunked down more than a half billion dollars by the end of 1998, with its total Y2K costs projected at a whopping $900 million.[14] AT&T is busy remediating 3,000 internally developed applications and 800 externally purchased network elements made up of switches, network control points, and signal transfer points, but reassures customers that its completion rates are in the eightieth percentile.[15]

Rival MCI plans on spending around $400 million to fix its systems.[16] It plans to "push back the development of new products in order to get ready for the year 2000" and to complete its Y2K program sometime in early 1999.[17] And long distance carrier Sprint began its Y2K program some three years ago. It has completed its assessment and inventory phases and boasts that it is "well into" its remediation and testing, according to its Y2K disclosure statement.[18]

Among some of the Baby Bells, SBC has assigned 400 people specifically to its Y2K program. It has budgeted around $250 million and hopes to be ready by mid-1999.[19] Bell Atlantic has budgeted $300 million and has targeted June *Billions spent to* 1999 as its completion date, allowing for six months *beat the bug* of testing.[20]

Still, there is no shortage of Y2K critics of the telecommunications industry. For example, Triaxsys Research LLC, a research company that ranks industrial sectors according to their Y2K preparedness, puts telecommunications dead last in Y2K program completion progress, noting that most began to focus on the problem only two or three years ago.[21] And Gartner Group has warned that the telcos are overly optimistic in their assessments of their likely success beating Y2K.[22] AT&T has itself acknowledged the potential for failure across its systems, which may account for its increased spending on Y2K. On balance, however, we are fairly sure that the big phone companies will be able to fix nearly all of the Y2K problems their *internal* systems given their current commitment of resources. As we show later in this chapter, this might not matter, since it is forces beyond the control of the telcos that would cause the serious business interruptions.

Talk Amongst Yourselves

The telcos deserve kudos for their early realization that coordination amongst themselves would reduce each company's overall Y2K work. The good news is, large carriers are well into the intercompany testing phase. The Telco Year 2000 Forum is made up of eight large regional local exchange carriers: BellSouth, Ameritech, GTE, Southern New England Telephone, Cincinnati Bell, US West, SBC, and Bell Atlantic. It has been performing interoperability testing since 1998.

The carriers are supervised in their testing by Bellcore, which is a recognized leader in Y2K solutions and compliance. Bellcore claims Y2K compliance in all of its software systems products, including operations support systems and network systems supporting maintenance, provisioning, and other management function for local telephone services.[23] In its interoperability tests, Bellcore is using a two-level approach that tests first within each company's network elements, and then in selected groupings of network elements.[24] It expects to release a full report sometime in early 1999. However, preliminary test results are somewhat encouraging. Tests performed in October 1998 on the intra-LATA (local access and transport area) service equipment showed problems only occurred in seven out of 1,000 test cases. These problems were considered "minor" and were referred to the equipment vendors for resolution.[25] This reliability rate is far below that normally employed by Bellcore, but it doesn't appear to spell massive problems for the telcos.

The Alliance of Telecommunications Industry Solutions, whose mission it is to advance new technologies, similarly has begun internetwork operability tests, utilizing network configurations that cover some 90 percent of the country. ATIS is also using Bellcore as its contracted interoperability tester. The ATIS report is due out in the second quarter of 1999.[26]

Bellcore's involvement with both coordination efforts also means there is a strong team of experienced experts in network reliability working on the Y2K problem. Many of these same experts participated in the dismantling of Ma Bell years ago and logged countless hours taking apart whole networks and then stringing them back together. Indeed, some have argued that because companies like the telcos have a history of emphasizing reliability and continuity of their networks, they are well situated to deal with the possible impacts of Y2K.[27]

Despite these industry-wide task forces, some remain concerned over the lack of any information on internetwork operability, either from these coordinating bodies or from the telcos themselves. Complained one Federal Reserve governor trying to gauge monetary policy in light of Y2K, the telcos "have been very tight with providing information, especially on the testing of interconnectivity between systems."[28] We expect this situation to change by the time reports are released in mid-1999. We hope the news is good, because if it isn't, there won't be enough time left to bring the whole network into compliance.

The FCC

The Federal Communications Commission got started on its own Y2K program back in 1995, and by 1997 it had begun a coordinated effort to review how the industry itself was responding to the crisis. The

FCC established a Year 2000 working group in March 1998 (relatively late in our view).[29]

To keep tabs on the industry, in April 1998 the FCC sent letters to twenty major carriers, which account for over 98 percent of the telephone access lines, asking about the Y2K status of their most critical systems. From the replies to these letters, the FCC learned that at least the major carriers anticipated finishing their remediation, testing, and integration by mid-1999.[30] The FCC recognizes, however, that problems in small carriers abound. "Some are probably in stellar shape, but some are doing nothing," according to Michael Power, an FCC commissioner.[31] In addition, overseas telcos could cause service problems among the major carriers, but there has been no comprehensive program to address these problems.

As the vice president of technology programs at GTE remarked, "Y2K is truly a 'weakest link' problem—the single system or date conversion we miss may be the undoing of the ninety-nine percent we did find."[32] In this sense, telcos are in the same situation as the banks, which know that "ninety-eight percent won't cut it." Indeed, as we pointed out earlier, telcos have even lower acceptable rates of failure.

Y2K *ADDED* RISK FACTOR
Single-Point Failures

The danger posed by single-point failures is nowhere more pronounced than in the telecommunications industry. While communications systems are generally designed to be fault-tolerant, isolated failures have on occasion impacted entire systems. At AT&T alone there are many examples of prior single-point failures. In January 1990, a line of incorrect code caused a cascading failure of 114 electronic switching systems. In June 1991, phone service in several cities, including 6.7 million lines in Washington, D.C., was disrupted for several hours due to a single mistyped character in the protocol code.[33] In April 1998, AT&T suffered a single frame-relay outage that resulted in a temporary loss of service for millions: Corporate customers lost networking capability, retailers couldn't process credit cards payments, and financial institutions couldn't process trades.

Learning from the past

On the bright side, unlike bank or airline data, telecommunications data that is transferred along the networks rarely has date-dependent codes buried in it. In other words, the data itself is not likely to cause disruptions or corrupt otherwise compliant systems. Still, the fact that huge amounts of telecommunications data has to pass through a few key pieces of hardware raises the chances of systemic failures considerably.

The critical question for most telcos is whether suppliers of the equipment they all utilize will be ready for Y2K and will meet the rigid and ambitious schedules of the telcos. Such equipment includes the computerized switching systems at the heart of the intercarrier network. It also forms the basis of all network elements. To get a picture of how worried the telcos are about their manufacturers' schedules, you need only look carefully at the telcos' mandated Y2K disclosures and other public statements on Y2K.

Y2K *ADDED* RISK FACTOR

Supplier Noncompliance

For example, Sprint has targeted June 1999 as a compliance date for its most critical applications "subject to change as Sprint's Year 2000 Program moves forward." What might cause a delay in the program? The wild card is suppliers:

> We are also gathering information from our vendors and suppliers regarding their Year 2000 compliance. While we cannot control nor be responsible for compliance by our vendors and suppliers, we are encouraging their efforts to meet the Year 2000 deadline.[34]

In our view, "gathering information" and "encouraging their efforts" is not very reassuring. Even disclosure-wary attorneys could draft more informative and clear language.

As another example, SBC, the parent company of Southwestern Bell, Pacific Bell, Cellular One, and Nevada Bell, uses the old *small-print* trick at the bottom of its Y2K program summary on its website to leave wiggle room for supplier foul-ups. The small print warns, "Dates are contingent upon our vendors meeting the dates they have quoted us for delivery of Year 2000–compliant software and/or hardware."[35]

SBC does have "contingency plans" in the event those suppliers fail to meet deadlines: "In most cases, if it is determined that the system or software must be compliant, and the vendor does not plan to or fails to adequately upgrade it, *we will contact other vendors.*"[36] MCI warns that suppliers who do not have their products ready will be removed from MCI's network.[37] AT&T is also prepared to switch to alternate suppliers "to replace third-party products or services that fail to meet commitment schedules."[38] Our concern is that by the time it is clear that a key supplier has dropped the ball, there will not be enough time to work with a new supplier to achieve Y2K compliance.

In our experience, when a company feels good about the status of its business partners and suppliers, it tends to trumpet this fact. When there are worrisome delays or uncertainty as to the status of key partners or suppliers, the company will hedge and use words like "gathering information" and "encouraging their efforts."

Listen for what they don't say

So how are the suppliers actually doing? Most *major* manufacturers of telecommunications equipment have had their Y2K programs in place for a long time and are expected to meet their timetables, but no one is giving guarantees. Luckily for the telcos, the number of major manufacturers of primary equipment in the industry is relatively small. Most equipment is made by a small group of manufacturers comprised of Lucent, Alcatel, Northern Telecom, Fujutsu, and Siemens.[39] Others that do significant business with the telcos include DCS and Mitel.[40] However, there are *hundreds* of other suppliers for other equipment and services used by the telcos. The carriers realize that they must get all of the suppliers onboard or run the risk of small problems becoming big headaches.

The primary doubt over equipment manufacturers results from lack of public disclosures. No supplier wants to be first to go public about the Y2K status of critical equipment. One systems engineer at Northern Telecom, a major telco vendor, said his efforts to share information with customers, including "impact statements" providing details on the Y2K status of certain pieces of equipment, were shot down by company lawyers who wouldn't permit the release of the data.[41]

The federal government has also voiced its frustration over its inability to obtain information on the compliance status of telecommunication vendors. The telecommunications program manager of the General Services Administration attempted to put together a database of vendor compliance status to help agencies prepare for Y2K. However, vendors were apparently afraid that disclosures could expose them to legal liability should companies or agencies rely on the information provided but later experience Y2K failures, so they were reluctant to provide the information.[42] We have seen the same situation play itself out in the medical device field with similarly troubling results.

Another factor in supplier compliance is testing. Because most telcos buy their networking equipment from outside suppliers, many are relying on those suppliers to perform not only the remediation but also the testing of network equipment. Most telcos will also independently test and verify many of the network components, but the critical work will be left in the hands of suppliers. Thus, not only are remediation schedules dependent on the schedules of the suppliers, but testing schedules can only be met if the suppliers come through as well.

Sizing Up the Problem

Even if the manufacturers come through in the end for the big telcos, another worrisome factor is the status of the smaller telcos. The sheer number of telecommunication companies in operation is a factor. When most people think of phone companies, they come up with the Baby Bells, plus some major providers like MCI, Sprint, GTE, and AT&T. In fact, there are another 1,300 or

Y2K *ADDED* RISK FACTOR
Small-Carrier Noncompliance

so small to mid-sized telecommunication companies, which provide critical service to rural or underserved areas of the country.[43] These smaller companies handle only about 2 percent of the nation's telecommunication's traffic, but could account for a majority of the problems, given their relative lack of preparedness.

Problems originating from smaller companies *could* impact the operations of larger carriers. "We just don't know all the ways that the failure of one piece of the network could trigger failures elsewhere in the system," admitted FCC Commissioner Powell.[44]

These smaller and mid-sized telcos often lack the financial

resources, available personnel, and management structure to perform adequate Y2K remediation and testing of their systems. Perhaps more critically, they will be scrambling for the same vendor support as the big telcos, who long ago snapped up valuable vendor commitments of time and personnel.

Little is known about the true state of readiness, or lack thereof, of the small to mid-sized carriers. One of the few comprehensive studies conducted was by the Texas Public Utilities Commission, which provided much of the information on small electric utilities discussed in chapter 4. The survey is somewhat dated, having been conducted in early 1998. The Texas PUC sent 373 surveys to all of the telecommunications companies operating in the state. The response rate was only around 20 percent, but the respondents accounted for nearly all of the access lines in the state.[45]

Generally speaking, the "incumbent local exchange carriers," which provide local phone as well as the core of long distance service in Texas, reported having solid plans and being prepared for Y2K. However, among smaller "competitive local exchange carriers" only one-quarter reported having any plans, written or unwritten, to deal with Y2K. This alarming statistic is tempered somewhat by the fact that CLECs, which only make up 1.2 percent of all local phone service in Texas, have few access line and equipment of their own, as most prefer to use a service link to an incumbent local exchange carrier. Some CLECs, however, reported that they did not intend to address the Y2K problem at all; most, it should be noted, did not even respond to the survey.[46]

Small companies also service a significant portion of the wireless market. SBC acknowledges that its wireless business is at risk from forces beyond its control. When wireless customers travel outside of their home calling areas, calls are carried by "roaming partners." These partners must upgrade and test their systems in order for SBC to continue to offer seamless cellular phone service. But SBC is careful to say little about the progress of these roaming partners, stating only that it has been "diligent in contacting" them to "increase their awareness of the year 2000," and has "asked for their assurance that they are upgrading their networks as well."[47]

Telcos face an added risk that most sectors (with the exception of banks) don't need to consider: Telcos must also work with customers to ensure they take measures to upgrade their systems, including phones, voice mail, local computer networks, and PBXs. As one FCC commissioner pointed out, "It will not do much good if all the telephone companies fix all their networks, but then major corporations and governmental organizations cannot call out of their buildings because their internal systems do not work."[48]

Y2K *ADDED* RISK FACTOR
Customer Noncompliance

Many customers do not realize that they are a vital link in the chain of telecommunications Y2K preparedness; failure to check internal systems could mean customers have shut themselves off from the network. It also means losses for the telcos. Even Bellcore admits that many companies have been "relatively late in recognizing that the Year 2000 problem affects not only their IT [information technology] systems, but their private networks as well."[49]

The level of preparedness among smaller customers should be alarming to telcos. According to Nortel, a manufacturer of phone equipment, while compliance rates are high among big government and large commercial users, they are only between *15 and 20 percent* among all of the company's business customers.

We predict that telcos, like the banks, will start to focus on counterparty failures as a significant risk to their own financial health. AT&T CEO C. Michael Armstrong recognizes the danger of a cascade failure caused by a noncompliant customer's interconnection, but is prepared to draw the line: "We'll refuse the transaction but protect the network," he declared.[50] Unlike customer risks faced by banks, it wouldn't take the failure of an entire business for the telcos to lose a customer, just failure by the customer to address Y2K. Most small businesses have mistakenly deemed Y2K to be strictly a *computer* problem. They simply are not focused on the fact that it could affect things like their phone systems. Often small businesses don't even know where to begin and are surprised when told the process requires checking switches inside walls and closets.[51]

"If you'd like to make an international call, please hang up and try again. If you need help, too bad." The FCC has pointed out that while the United States, Canada, and the United Kingdom appear to be ahead in terms of Y2K telecommunication preparedness, it remains concerned that "some international telecommunications carriers, especially those in developing countries, are just realizing the seriousness of the problem and have not yet taken the necessary steps to prevent system failures."[52] At

Y2K *ADDED* RISK FACTOR
Foreign Telco Noncompliance

the Gartner Group's Symposium/Itxpo 98, CEOs from four of the largest telecommunication companies were in agreement that the biggest problems would occur in voice and data networks of undeveloped countries.[53]

Why should this concern U.S. telcos? Global telecommunications rely upon *transparent, error-free interconnections* among networks, so disruptions in far parts of the world could tie up or hinder valuable network resources. As Tomas Nylund, vice chairman of the International Telecommunications Union Y2K Task Force, put it, "Not dealing with the Year 2000 issue in one country could be as dangerous to that country's partners [as] computer viruses. . . . No one can afford to ignore the problem."[54]

A more direct hit to the bottom lines of U.S. telcos would occur if problems overseas prevented U.S.-based calls from going through, thus wiping out any revenues from those calls. Australia's biggest phone company, Telstra, voices precisely this concern over the flow-on effect for commerce. Said Telstra's managing director of carrier services, "We are probably going to be the best-prepared company in Australia. However, it is our interconnect partners in Asia that concern me. There's no evidence that some of them have started."[55]

Many of the concerns over the status of international efforts to address Y2K in telecommunications have been heard with respect to other sectors. In Europe, for example, industry experts worry that telcos can't tap enough programmer and management resources to deal with both the Euro conversion and the Y2K crisis. In Asia, the economic crisis

All tapped out

is often cited as the reason telcos in that region appear to lag. One Latin American carrier that is commonly singled out for its noncompliant status is state-owned Telebras, the national carrier for Brazil, which is a country with a generally dismal Year 2000 program record.

Problems in the Telebras networks and subnetworks could disrupt or even close off international calls placed to Brazil—a not insubstantial market.

Efforts to coordinate telecommunication Y2K remediation efforts internationally have met with only limited success. The International Telecommunication Union is working to mobilize governments, operators, and carriers worldwide, hoping it can still prevent "the meltdown of international telecommunications services at the turn of the millennium"—which was the dire warning issued by the U.K.-based Telecommunications Managers Association. (Unlike the relatively upbeat U.S. telcos, TMA members are not at all confident of the ability of telcos to fix Y2K problems. In a survey of TMA's members, only 9 percent said they were fully satisfied with the information they had received from operators, and many expressed no confidence in the overall telco Y2K situation.[56])

The international telco response to ITU coordination efforts has been lukewarm at best. For example, the ITU mailed out a Year 2000 questionnaire to its 5,000 members, but the response rate was dismal.[57] Among those that responded to ITU surveys, the situation can only be described as bleak. Some telcos in developing countries reported plans to complete their remediation work in *late 1999*, leaving only a couple of months for testing. But even in some advanced areas, the situation is little better. New World Telecom and People's Telephone Company in Hong Kong plan to finish remediation sometime in the late second or early third quarter of 1999.[58] If testing is supposed to take more than 50 percent of the time in any Y2K program, these companies simply don't have enough time to test even their own systems, let alone test interfaces between carrier networks.

These survey results are supported by an independent survey by British Telecom in early 1998, which found that only 11 percent of BT's interconnect partners in Africa and the Middle East, 23 percent in the Asia-Pacific region, and 43 percent in Europe even had a Y2K program in place.[59] Experts also point out that foreign telcos may have seriously underestimated the costs and tasks at hand. For example, Ross Anderson, a spokesperson from Cambridge University's computer laboratory, has pointed out that both the British and the South Koreans bought similar telephone equipment back in the late 1980s.

British Telecom has spent around $750 million on its Y2K program, but the South Koreans have spent *little to nothing* because they don't see a problem. "They can't both be right," Anderson remarked.[60]

Unfortunately, the fallout from the lack of international carrier preparedness would not be limited to telcos. Companies that do business overseas, international financial transactions, and manufacturing all would be severely impacted by disruptions in foreign telecommunications. "Our networks may not be as critical as a bank's, but we have sixty factories globally with systems that depend on suppliers connected by [electronic data interchange], and those factories cannot be down too long," said a representative from tractor maker Deere and Co. at a special Senate hearing.[61] Bankers echoed the sentiment: "It's fine if the U.S. networks are ready, but so what? We're concerned about operations in Europe and Asia," said the CIO of J. P. Morgan.[62] A general description of Y2K problems around the world follows in chapter 7.

Our general sense is that the financial outlook for telcos under Y2K is better than the other sectors we have covered in this book. However, due to unknown risks from supplier disruptions, customer noncompliance, and overseas exposure, we would rate the sector in general to be an *underweight* on most major U.S. and certain foreign carriers, and an *avoid* for small carriers and most foreign carriers.

Y2K Stock Watch

There are hundreds of publicly traded long distance service providers, domestic and foreign carriers, and wireless communication service providers. Our discussion is limited to larger market cap stocks, but many of the same rationales apply, perhaps even with greater force, to smaller telecommunication companies.

Long Distance Carriers

Industry giants MCI Worldcom (symbol: WCOM) and AT&T (symbol: T) both appear to have the resources and the comprehensive Y2K programs to diminish if not eliminate the internal risk of Y2K disruptions. However, both companies are at risk from supplier noncompliance, failure of their customers to remediate equipment, and

the inattention of overseas partners. Given these competing considerations, we would underweigh both of these stocks, and if it becomes
clear in 1999 that any of the risk factors turn out to be acute (e.g., the
companies are forced to switch suppliers late in the game), we would
unload whatever remaining positions we had until it is clear that
problems are resolved in 2000.

We recommend avoiding smaller long distance companies that *focus*
on international calls for the majority of their business. For example,
Primus Telecommunications Group, Inc. (symbol: PRTL) prides itself
on its international angle:

> Primus seeks to capitalize on the increasing business and con-
> sumer demand for international telecommunications being gen-
> erated by globalization of the world's economies and the
> worldwide trend toward deregulation of the telecommunication
> sector. . . . Primus targets business and residential consumers with
> significant international long distance traffic and other telecom-
> munications carriers and resellers with international traffic.[63]

This strategy will tend to overexpose Primus to risks in countries that
have failed to upgrade their systems in time.

Similarly, Viatel, Inc. (symbol: VYTL), operates a vast international
network reaching 230 countries and territories, with a concentration in
European cities. (It also provides service to North America, Latin
America, and the Pacific Rim.) Viatel's focus is on small to mid-sized
businesses,[64] making it a double-risk in our view.

IXC Communications, Inc. (symbol: IIXC), provides a unique but
in our view high-Y2K-risk business of wholesaling network capacity
and services to other long distance carriers. We are also not very
impressed with the Y2K efforts of IXC (at least so far as they have
been disclosed on its website), which show it far behind other long
distance companies in its remediation work.

Domestic Carriers

We have the same general outlook for all of the large domestic carriers. While industry coordination of remediation and network testing
very much diminishes the chance of serious failures within the carriers'

networks, the risk again can be traced to outside suppliers and non-compliant customer equipment.

Large market cap domestic carriers include SBC Communications, Inc. (symbol: SBC), BellSouth Corporation (symbol: BLS), Bell Atlantic Corporation (symbol: BEL), GTE Corporation (symbol: GTE), Ameritech Corporation (symbol: AIT), and US West (symbol: USW). We would recommend underweighing these companies for now; if suppliers fail to deliver on schedule, consider keeping completely clear of them by late 1999.

Smaller domestic carriers are at high risk of failure, given their relative lack of resources and the nonexistence of coordinated testing. In the absence of strong evidence that a small carrier has made its systems Y2K compliant, we would avoid holding its shares until after it has shown it can operate in the year 2000.

Foreign Telcos

Many shares of foreign telecommunication companies trade on U.S. exchanges. Not enough information exists on the Y2K status of most of these carriers; a good rule of thumb is to underweigh any that are based in countries that are relatively advanced in their Y2K programs (e.g., the United Kingdom, Canada, Australia, New Zealand, the Netherlands, and Sweden) while avoiding any that are based in developing countries (mostly in Latin America and Asia) or countries that have a poor Y2K record relative to their technical development (e.g. Germany, France, Japan). The reason is not necessarily that the telco itself is relatively unprepared, though this is often true. Rather, it is *more likely* that the telco will experience collateral effects on its operations, such as power outages and lack of customer preparedness.

Some of the larger cap foreign telcos we would avoid include Nippon Telegraph and Telephone Corporation (symbol: NTT), Deutsche Telekom AG (symbol: DT), Telefonica S.A. (symbol: TEF), Telecom Italia SpA (symbol: TI), Hong Kong Telecommunications Limited (symbol: HKT), Compania de Telecomunicaciones de Chile S.A. (symbol: CTC), Perusahaan Perseroan P.T. Indonesian Satellite (symbol: IIT), Telefonica de Argentina S.A. (symbol: TAR), Portugal Telecom SA (symbol: PT) and Telebras Holdrs Ads Rep 1 Dep (symbol: TBH).

Wireless Communication Companies

While wireless service is at lower risk in some ways than standard wire service (for example, there is less of a problem in noncompliant customer equipment), it is at higher risk of others (such as the risk of single-point failures, satellite ground systems failures, and noncompliant roaming services). Some of the larger market cap companies include Nokia Corporation (symbol: NOK.A), Motorola (symbol: MOT), France Telecom (symbol: FTE), Ericsson (symbol: ERICY), Vodafone Group PLC (symbol: VOD), AirTouch Communications (symbol: ATI) and China Telecom (Hong Kong) (symbol: CHL). Our recommendation is to underweigh these stocks until after it is clear they will be able to operate without disruption in the year 2000.

Concluding Thoughts

Telecommunications is an industry that investors will have to watch carefully. Major U.S. telcos are on the edge of being able to beat Y2K and suffer only minor disruptions, but unfortunately most of the risk lies outside of their direct control. There is still a substantial risk of supplier or customer noncompliance that investors must track carefully through 1999. Until it is shown that telcos can operate reliably through the millennium change, investors are best off lightening up on this sector in their portfolios.

SEVEN

THE GLOBAL ECONOMIC IMPLICATIONS OF Y2K

For all of the Y2K problems the United States faces, they pale in comparison to what is taking shape in other parts of the globe. With Asia struggling just to get through its current economic malaise, Latin America teetering on the edge of the same cliff, and Europe focusing its attention on conversion to a single currency, it is not surprising that Y2K has been on back-burner status. It will be front page headlines soon.

Just how bad is the situation overseas? The Gartner Group warns that only some two dozen countries are actually working actively on the problem.[1] Fund managers are already warning that companies in emerging markets such as Asia are at risk. In its July 1998 prospectus, one fund noted such companies "may not be applying the same diligence to the Year 2000 problem as are issuers in more mature markets."[2] This is probably a huge understatement. Let's take a quick and scary tour through three other continents to see how things fare with Y2K. You'll soon appreciate how relatively better off we in the United States really are despite the magnitude of our own Y2K problems.

Will the Asian Crisis Deepen?

Y2K in Asia

Asian nations probably are in the worst shape Y2K-wise. Reeling from the economic crises in Thailand, Malaysia, Indonesia, and South Korea, the last thing Asian government and industry leaders want to face up to is another massive attack on their economies. The current economic woes in Asia must seem a far more immediate problem than Y2K. With Japan in its worst recession since the end of World War II, there isn't a lot of money available in the region, even on loan, to help solve the problem. While there are some bright spots (such as Hong Kong and Singapore),[3] our general prognosis for the rest of the region is bleak. In 2000, just as Asian economies are expected to pull themselves out of the financial crisis, Y2K could prolong or worsen it significantly.

The head of the U.S. Central Intelligence Agency office looking into the general issue of Y2K believes Asian countries lag "maybe nine months to a year behind in terms of where the work

Nine months to
a year behind

should be."[4] The best word to describe the situation in Asia as late as mid-1998 was *denial*. At one point, businesses in Taiwan claimed they wouldn't be affected because the island uses a different calendar than the Gregorian.[5] Many Japanese business leaders also expressed a baffling and mistaken belief that since the Japanese calendar is based on the emperor's reign (making it only eight years old), Y2K wasn't going to affect software and chips in Japan.[6] But computer experts point out that most date-sensitive software and chips sold in Asia continue to use the Gregorian calendar as the standard and are therefore at risk of Y2K failure.

In mid-1998, a survey by Merrill Lynch of 460 Asian companies found that most were in the early stages of Y2K preparation, and that 24 *percent* did not expect to make it in time.[7] Even in relatively advanced countries, there is an alarming lack of awareness of and preparation for Y2K. In Taiwan, for example, the Economics Ministry estimates that 40 percent of small businesses have taken *no action whatsoever* to address Y2K.[8] That translates into hundreds of thousands of companies facing *mission critical failures* in the year 2000. The effect of failures of such magnitude on consumer confidence alone is frightening to consider.

The countries that worry us the most are Japan, China, and South Korea, all of which are major U.S. trading partners. Massive system failures in those countries would affect the entire world economy and could pull down the United States despite our best efforts to minimize the effect of Y2K at home.

Japan

As the world's second largest economy and one of the most computerized of nations, you would think the Japanese would be attacking Y2K with a sense of urgency. But there is an almost eerie quiet among Japanese firms, leading experts in the United States and Europe to worry that the problem is *so* bad, nobody dares to talk about it—a situation seen before with billions of dollars of losses in bad Japanese bank loans.[9]

Part of the problem has been a leadership vacuum at the top. An uneasy change in prime ministers during the crucial mid-1998 period left Japanese private enterprise to fend for itself against Y2K. A central office to deal with the Y2K problem was not even established until September 1998.[10] For a long time, Japanese government agencies lacked the kind of *Japan as the chief culprit?* unified support program put in place by other countries like the United States and the United Kingdom. Japanese financial institutes similarly lacked coordination and didn't establish plans to run their first coordinated tests until the end of 1998, well behind their U.S. counterparts.[11] Some experts are beginning to warn that Japan, already low in credibility for failing to address its asset-inflated "bubble economy" in the 1990s, would be the primary source of Y2K-related computer problems around the world in the year 2000.[12]

When the Tokyo Stock Exchange conducted a survey of nearly all of its 1,869 listed firms in August 1998, it found that of the 1,549 respondents, a full 81 percent were still working on reprogramming, and only 9 percent had reported completion of the remediation phase. More ominously, sixteen companies had taken no measures at all, forty-eight were still investigating whether measures were needed, and seventy-nine said that they didn't even *need* to undertake any Y2K fixes. In short, nearly 10 percent of public companies surveyed fell into the *no action* category.[13] It is difficult to see how any publicly traded company, presumably with millions in market capitalization, would not have at least some computers and systems at risk from Y2K.

Like the situation in the United States, the most at-risk sectors in Japan appear to be small to mid-sized business and government services. A survey taken in September 1997 by the Japan Information Service Industry Association found that 67 percent of firms with capital below 100 million yen had no plan to deal with the Y2K issue.[14] And at the critical 500-days-to-go milestone, only some 15 to 20 percent of small and mid-sized enterprises had taken *any action* to fix their Y2K problems, according to one official at Japan's Ministry of International

Trade and Industry. "Add in that many of these companies are among the worst hit by the poor economy, and you can see that many of them would find it quite difficult to do on their own," the official added, noting that MITI was organizing a loan program to help them pull through.[15]

According to a Japanese government survey conducted in April 1998, 62 percent of the Japanese government's computers were not sufficiently prepared for the year 2000. The lagging ministries and agencies, including the one responsible for air traffic control, failed to secure enough funding to complete the tasks in 1998. They will have to complete the fixes sometime after the beginning of the new fiscal year, which begins *April 1, 1999.*[16] This leaves the Japanese government only *nine months* to finish close to two-thirds of its work. Critics warn that in 1999 there will be a critical shortage of qualified programmers around to complete the monumental task, so when the ministries get serious about fixing their systems, they will only exacerbate the shortage.[17]

Nine months to finish two-thirds of the work

The American Chamber of Commerce in Japan has three primary concerns over the financial sector in that country as it deals with Y2K. First, securities and cash settlements are highly concentrated, passing through one of three systems: BOJ Net, JBNet, and the JASDEC service. These systems suffer from lack of central coordination of Y2K programs and could become huge bottlenecks if failures arise. Second, Japan imposes a "no-fail" settlement rule for trades. What this means is that if a firm fails to deliver, it could be suspended from trade by the Japanese Ministry of Finance. This is very *unlike* the situation in the United States, where all kinds of backup procedures and clear rules exist for when trades don't settle. Third, the chamber worries that the complacency of Japanese firms may be related to the ease with which Japan started its calendar over in 1989 at the coronation of the new emperor. But these dates are used for printing, reporting, and display purposes, and are not used for date-based *calculations.* Y2K fixes are much more complex and costly. This complacency may lead Japanese banks and other institutions to treat the crisis less seriously than they should.[18]

Japan's current recession impacts the United States because Japanese buy fewer U.S. imports and invest less money in our markets. This is more or less a knock-on effect, and it is stretched out over a long period of time, giving exporters and market a chance to adjust. But extensive Y2K problems originating in Japan, particularly in electronic data exchange in financial markets, could have a much more direct and immediately harmful effect. If the shutdowns and system crashes in Japan are widespread and substantially affect mission-critical operations, we would have nothing short of a truly global financial disaster. It is doubtful that companies could adjust quickly to the new circumstances, and they would probably elect to stop the engines of commerce dead than try to cut through choppy Y2K waters.

China

China is one of the least prepared of nations for the Y2K crisis. A survey by Merrill Lynch in 1998 found that less than half of Chinese companies expect to resolve their Y2K problems in time.[19] Another survey by International Data Corp. in April 1998 confirms these figures, though the results were better than those of a year earlier, when 69 percent of Chinese companies had not even started any Y2K programs.[20]

Not surprisingly, problems in manufacturing top the list of concerns in China. The good news is that in all of China, there are only around nine or ten million computers. The bad news is that, with over 1.2 billion people, there is, amazingly, still a shortage of programmers. "In China, we do not have today the manpower with the precise skills needed to do this work," lamented one professor who is working for a joint state-private software firm. "We are outsourcing to Americans for the fixes."[21] In fact, the Chinese often paint Y2K as a problem created by the foreigners who sold them their systems, and they seem determined to hold foreign suppliers responsible for fixes, even though there is no strong indication that foreign firms are rushing in to do the necessary work.

How can there be a shortage of people in China?

The situation in government departments also worries analysts, given that so much of China is still state owned and operated. "They are chronically underfunded and understaffed," according to Chris Morris of Gartner Group's Dataquest, which performed a region-wide analysis.[22] They are also getting a *very* late start. In fact, government policies implemented in 1998 didn't require officials to even present

Y2K plans until *March 1999*, leaving only nine to ten months to fix and test their systems.[23]

China's Central Bank is gearing up to provide loans for reprogramming and testing, and government officials have issued vague threats of criminal penalties for organizations that experience Y2K failures. But the Chinese banks themselves appear to be running into problems already. There have been reports of banks being unable to establish three-year fixed rates for depositors as a result of Y2K problems in their computer systems.[24]

The Chinese State Power Corporation had not gotten beyond "general investigations" of their equipment, some of which must be renovated. "Foreign suppliers" will be asked to help where possible. China's electrical infrastructure had already been overwhelmed in its attempts to restore power to flood-stricken areas in the summer of 1998, so Y2K programs were effectively delayed until *September 1998*.[25]

Merrill Lynch also remains concerned with Chinese airlines, which assumed that the national aviation regulators were taking responsibility over the problem, and that systems leased from abroad such as cargo handlers would be fixed by the suppliers.[26] And Chinese shipping companies are positively blasé about the bug. Said one official from the computer center of COSCO, China's largest shipper, "We haven't put [Y2K] high on our agenda." In September 1998, COSCO was still in the process of negotiating the costs for Y2K fixes with its main computer supplier, IBM.[27]

If Y2K shuts down systems in China, the effect on the United States won't be felt as immediately as would a shutdown in Japan. The number of electronic transactions between the United States and China is negligible next to the interconnectivity with Japan. But a long-term threat looms in the form of higher prices on Chinese imports, which account for a huge chunk of the U.S. total. If Chinese manufacturers are hampered by breakdowns in production lines, prolonged blackouts and dead telephone lines, and if Chinese ships can't get loaded efficiently or leave port safely, we could see a spike in the prices of key imports such as textiles and toys coupled with job losses in the distribution and retailing of those imports.

A further and perhaps more serious consequence of a China weakened by Y2K failures would be a continued deterioration of the economic landscape in Asia. For the past few years, China has been one of the only Asian countries to sustain economic growth and not see a devaluation of its currency. If China is dragged down by Y2K, you can expect Asia to have problems for many months.

China's failure to address the Y2K problem in key infrastructure is symptomatic of its general state of denial about the vulnerability of its public sector. During the devastating floods of the summer of 1998, Premier Zhu Rongji's was astonished at the poor quality of Chinese levies, which he said "might as well have been made out of tofu." He might need to come up with even more colorful metaphors to describe the electrical power, telecommunications, and transportation chaos that could occur in China in less than a year's time.

South Korea

Despite an apparent high level of awareness of the risk from Y2K, South Korean firms have gotten late starts in addressing the issue, and they do not appear to be allocating sufficient resources to the problem. A 1998 survey of 3,000 Korean companies conducted by the Computer and Communications Promotion Association of Korea found that while 70 percent of the top managers and information officers believed Y2K could cause "serious" problems if not addressed properly, less than *half* had earmarked any funds for their Y2K programs. Most planned to set aside special budgets *in 1999* to deal with Y2K.[28]

Like other Asian countries, South Korea will face a severe shortage of qualified programmers, a situation compounded by most firms' plans to implement programs in 1999. Some estimates place the number of programmers needed at around 720,000, given the time remaining. The actual number of local experts is only around 17,000, however, so it seems clear that most of the work will not be completed.[29]

Given these clear deficiencies, it is not surprising that the Federation of Korean Industries (FKI) is predicting that Y2K will shave another 1 to 3 percent off South Korea's gross domestic product. "Problems arising from the millennium bug will *A new* be so widespread and rampant that certain economic *depression?* losses could be inevitable, regardless of the amount of government spending to repair the computer glitches," according to FKI economist Lee Ok-joo. The FKI worries that banks could sharply reduce loans in late 1999 out of fear of Y2K, triggering a fresh economic depression.[30]

Southeast Asia

A 1998 analysis of Y2K preparedness by the South-East Asia Regional Computer Confederation indicates that the region should stop thinking about operational contingencies, and instead "needs to look at a business disaster plan." SEARCC noted that in the Philippines, there still has been "no concerted effort to assess the possible impact of Y2K on the country's economy." And in Thailand, Y2K awareness among businesses remains low. SEARCC believes many Asian nations "will not get it right" and is scrambling to create "as soft a landing as possible."[31]

Southeast Asian telcos are at risk, even though they appear to be relatively serious in their efforts to tackle the problem. While all Asian telcos have pledged large sums of money and resources to fix their systems, analysts are concerned that major players in Thailand, Indonesia, and India will be at the mercy of smaller companies to which billing and revenue collection has been outsourced.[32]

In Thailand, the Siam Commercial Bank has 3,283 mission critical systems that will be impacted by Y2K. This means over 2.7 million lines of code to review and fix, and the bank is already admitting that *it will not complete the task on time.*[33] Thailand is plagued by the fact that many of its computer systems were developed internally and modified for use in the Thai language. Original programmers often can't be found, and foreign programmers can't make sense of the tailored programs. Other important Thai sectors are also facing gloomy prospects. Thailand's Petroleum Authority is frustrated by the inattention of its vendors, 70 percent of which didn't even respond to the authority's inquiries. The authority is particularly concerned about its thirty or so vendors that supply and maintain oil and gas piping.

In Singapore, which is roundly acknowledged as being relatively Y2K savvy and computer literate, computer experts have begun suggesting that banks stayed closed on the first four days of the new millennium. Singapore and the rest of Southeast Asia will be among the first to experience computer failures as the world rotates into January 1, 2000. Since Singapore is a major financial center, there have been calls for a bank holiday to minimize the impact of the bug on the region. The problem is, everyone else seems to be catching on to the idea. New Zealand, also geographically positioned to wake up first to the impact of Y2K, has already declared public holidays on the first days of 2000.[34] And Britain's culture secretary has pushed for bank holidays on Friday, December 31, 1999, in addition to the already scheduled bank holiday of January 3, 2000.[35]

Information technology spending in Indonesia was slashed by 80 percent as a result of the economic crisis in that country, at a time when other nations were beefing up their information technology budgets to battle Y2K.[36] By the summer of 1998, for example, Indonesia's state power company had not yet even *started* its Y2K compliance project due to the large costs involved. According to one official, Y2K compliance plans had been drawn up in early 1997, but no strong action has yet been taken.[37]

Investors must take into account, however, that Southeast Asian markets have been beaten down so heavily that there may not be much more room for them to fall. Some countries, such as Thailand, appear on their way to recovery, so the potential for a return to economic malaise must be carefully tracked. We predict that Y2K will push these economies back into recession or depression. Sadly, Indonesia, where economic turmoil has already caused so much poverty and misery, will slip even further into chaos as Y2K strips whatever confidence investors had in the market and whatever faith the people had in their leaders. Southeast Asia may be a great place to invest sometime during the next century, but in the next year you don't want to have any bets on the table in those countries when the Y2K dice roll.

Siesta Time?

Many had worried that the economic crisis which started in Asia in 1997 would spread to Latin America within a few years, and there certainly are signs that it has with the crisis brewing in Brazil. So concerned were market watchers that few noticed the clock ticking down on Latin America's Y2K programs, such as they were. With the millennium around the

Y2K in Latin America

corner, however, analysts have begun to shift their attention to the *inattention* of the region toward the millennium bug.

Latin American countries are characterized by high levels of government involvement in the lives of their citizens. In order to manage bloated pension systems, state-run health care, tax collection and the like, governments in the regions have naturally turned to computers for help. While these computers may not be the most modern of systems, they perform basic, essential functions that are at high risk for Y2K failures.[38]

Also at risk is the region's highly regulated banking sector, which has so far been able to survive the turmoil of the global economic crisis. Serious Y2K problems in the banking system, coupled with glitches in payments of government benefits and pensions, could erode depositor confidence, and we could see runs on banks.

Complicating the matter is that the supply of skilled programmers in Latin America is comparatively small. The United States is taking the lion's share of what available software resources exist in the western hemisphere, what the International Development Bank's deputy controller calls the "Y2K Brain Drain."[39] This drives up costs for countries in Latin America, which are already struggling with fiscal deficits and austerity measures.

In Brazil, it feels like everything is controlled by the government. Government bureaucrats run enterprises from health care to the national oil company, Petrobras. They also manage an enormous federal pension system upon which so much economic activity in Brazil depends. Unfortunately, Brazilians woke up to the Y2K menace quite late, and most institutions didn't take any action whatsoever until sometime in 1998. The fiscal crisis gripping the nation means even fewer resources can be pledged to fix what must be viewed as an abstract information technology problem. In addition, a huge deficit coupled with a harsh austerity package imposed by President Cardoso will make scrounging up money for Y2K even more difficult, just as it is needed most.[40]

We have earlier mentioned the Y2K crisis at Brazil's telephone company Telebras, which was described in 1998 by Merrill Lynch as "woefully uncompliant at this stage."[41] By 1999, the picture had not markedly improved. It will be of little benefit for foreign companies to maintain a presence in Brazil if they can't get through on the phones. Moreover, if computer failures in the financial system exacerbate the economic uncertainty or even cause panic runs, you can kiss certain

U.S. bank earnings (such as those of BankBoston and Republic New York) goodbye.

Aside from powerhouse Brazil, other South American up-and-comers face a tough fight ahead. Leading the charge is Argentina, which according to the *Wall Street Journal* probably has the most advanced Y2K program in the region, in part because of the tough stance of government regulators. The government mandated Argentine banks to come into compliance by the end of 1998 or face fines and suspensions. Government regulators are also seen as having taken a proactive role to bring huge Argentine pension funds into line. However, the situation outside of the major cities in unclear, and no one in Argentina is expecting the millennium change to go off without a problem.[42]

Chile, which usually has a reputation for being among the more efficient of the Latin American economies, is further behind than its neighbors in Y2K preparedness, and observers predict it will run out of time to fix its Y2K problems. While the banking sector appears to have gotten a head start and is keeping pace with banks in the United States, state-owned infrastructure such as water and sanitation as well as state-owned mining giant Codelco face an uncertain future. Most industries were still in the planning phase as late as October 1998, meaning they have *no chance* of completing all of the fixing and testing by the end of December 1999.[43]

Colombia admits that it has a problem, and officials there wish they had gotten started earlier on Y2K. Even if they had, however, many doubt there would have been funds available to address the problem, given the fiscal deficit and slumping coffee and oil prices. State-controlled entities are the primary source of concern. Realizing that they have run out of time to fix the problems, officials are examining contingency plans to minimize the impact of computer failures. Perhaps the only solace that government planners can find is that Columbia, like its neighbors, is relatively underdeveloped from an information technology standpoint, thus lessening the disruptive impact of Y2K.[44]

For Venezuela, the problem appears less critical. Continuity of oil production is key to Venezuela's economy. State-owned Petroleus de Venezuela SA has spend hundreds of millions on its Y2K program, which began back in 1995, and does not expect significant disruptions in basic oil operations. Of course, this presumes that key vendors and partners are relatively bug-free (a troubling assumption), but it doesn't hurt to see that the principal producer is doing all it can to eradicate Y2K. In other areas, the capital city of Caracas appears to have solved its Y2K problems in key sectors of electricity and telecommunications, but the rest of Venezuela is facing the possibility of widespread failures.[45]

Mon Dieu, Not Europe, Too!

As we have mentioned in previous chapters, the timing of European monetary union and the introduction of a single currency could not have been worse from the standpoint of Y2K readiness. As the difficulties in Euro conversion began to use up valuable IT and management resources and the extent of the Y2K problem became more clear, the head of Britain's Y2K campaign suggested early on that the introduction of the Euro in the continental economies should be postponed.[46] The countries participating in the Euro conversion are also dealing with the Y2K crisis, but they "barely have enough time for either job," he noted. "The problem is they both require the same resources—the same people, the same skills, and the same test equipment—and there is a serious shortage of people with the necessary computer skills."[47] His wise suggestion, however, was roundly met with opposition, and EMU plowed forward.

Y2K in Europe

European companies often have to spend *more* on their Euro conversion programs that they have budgeted for Y2K fixes. In the United Kingdom, which itself is not participating in the Euro conversion, systems still have to be brought into Euro compliance, often at enormous cost. Companies such as British Telecom, retailer Dixons, and the Royal Bank of Scotland all disclosed that their EMU costs would exceed their projected Y2K spending.[48] Assuming this phenomenon is widespread, it is small wonder that European industries lag behind the United States in Y2K preparedness.

Despite the obvious shortcomings of their Y2K programs, European businesses inexplicably are *more* optimistic than their U.S. counterparts that their systems can handle the date change. While 98 percent of large American businesses have adopted contingency plans, only 60 percent of European ones made such plans, according to Cap Gemini America.[49] And while U.S. firms had spent around 61 percent of their Y2K budgets by the end of 1998, European firms hadn't even touched more than half of their budgeted amounts.[50]

Insufficient contingency planning

European optimism is particularly baffling given the low level of attention that the Y2K problem has received, particularly among European governments. Despite the existence of huge government systems that dispense critical money for welfare and to run other essential services, by the end of October 1998, European governments (excluding Ireland, the Netherlands, and Sweden) had spent only *5 to 10 percent* of what they need to fix their systems, according to the Gartner Group.[51]

The United Kingdom is probably the farthest ahead in dealing with the Y2K crisis. Experts put the United Kingdom at around six months behind the United States.[52] Public awareness does not appear to be an issue. If anything, Y2K may receive an inordinate amount of British media focus. Awareness, however, does not necessarily translate into action. For example, while the United Kingdom had planned to train and deploy 20,000 "bug busters" to help business reprogram computers, as of the last quarter of 1998, Prime Minister Tony Blair had to concede that only a small fraction of that number had in fact been trained.[53] And poor performance by the United Kingdom's public sector in 1998 led Cap Gemini to remove the United Kingdom from among the seven most prepared nations.[54]

British public confidence was severely shaken when a confidential Y2K memo authored by a high ranking defense official was leaked to the press. That memo argued against cuts in the civilian reserve army in light of the Y2K threat. The memo noted that the reserve army would be needed "to cope with a serious civil emergency" if the Year 2000 crisis required troops to restore lost power, telephone service, and essential services—all possible scenarios, according to the memo.[55] The memo seemed to confirm fears among British critics that the Labour government was not telling the public all it knew about the Y2K problem.

Whether the chances of serious system failures is actually greater in the United Kingdom than in the United States, or whether this is just a result of British pessimism, it seems clear that the British are anticipating and bracing for significant problems. United Utilities, the largest independent utility in the United Kingdom, has warned that there is a risk of systems failures at the turn of the millennium and has developed emergency and disaster plans to be certain it is "ready to cater for impacts of the millennium date change."[56] This somewhat alarming stance is in marked contrast to U.S. utilities, which are at great pains to downplay the possibility of a power failure and never use terms like *emergency* and *disaster*. United Utilities has also issued profit warnings as a direct result of costs associated with fixing its Y2K problems, something no U.S. utility has yet come close to suggesting.[57]

As with the United States, small and mid-sized firms in the United Kingdom are particularly at risk. A government study in October 1998 warned that 40 percent of such firms were in danger of collapse since they had taken little action and had left it till very late to deal with Y2K.[58] Even if the bug itself did not cause total failure, U.K. Action 2000 officials warn that larger companies will use Y2K compliance as a condition in their choice of suppliers, so failure to take action could lead to loss of business by small and mid-sized firms.[59]

Britain is not alone in its Y2K problems, nor are its problems the worst in Europe. As the European Union's largest economy and one that prides itself on industrial efficiency and technical superiority, Germany has been astonishingly lax in addressing the Y2K problem. In fact, some experts put Germany at between *one year to eighteen months* behind the United States in Y2K preparedness.[60] While much of the inattention can be attributed to the drain on German resources brought about by the Euro conversion, for much of the inaction there is simply no good explanation.

With only 500 plus days to go, Gartner Group found that many Germany companies were just getting started.[61] While some 80 percent of major U.S. firms had Y2K programs in *Heads they make* place in early 1998, only *8 percent* of large German *it, tails they don't* firms had any formal program.[62] The situation is so serious that Gartner has predicted a *50 percent chance* of significant systems failure in Germany—the same rating it gives to fellow slacker nation Japan. (In comparison, Gartner gives the United States, Britain, and Australia only a 15 percent chance of major systems failures.)[63]

The only fair way to describe the reaction in France is *baffling*. One of our favorite Y2K stories hails from that country. When a British analyst asked a board director of a leading French bank what it was doing about the millennium bug, the banker declared, "The Year 2000 question is a conspiracy cooked up by the Americans and the British to create a smokescreen and distract attention away from preparations for the single European currency."[64] French political leaders were alarmingly laissez-faire in their approach. "The problems we expect are negligible and will not destabilise the economy," said one French industry ministry spokesman.[65] This attitude should concern the British: The French supply a substantial amount of the U.K.'s electric power.

The Netherlands also appears to be in trouble, despite being relatively aware and concerned about the crisis. A survey by Dutch insurer NCM concluded that it was "already probably too late to avert a millennium bug crisis." It reached this conclusion after polling 2,750 clients and discovering that while most were busily fixing internal systems, only a small percentage of them had taken action with respect to suppliers and customers or had any plans to do so.[66]

So far, Western Europe has managed to escape much of the economic turmoil occurring in the rest of the world. Y2K could change that rapidly if widespread system failures occur in key member countries. As with the situation in Japan, these failures would have immediate repercussions for dependent systems in the United States. As the millennium approaches, expect more attention to be focused on what is *not* being done in Europe to stop the spread of Y2K damage.

Expect the Worst

Russia came into the Y2K picture with several strikes against it. Its battered economy is faced with a financial crisis that pairs a crumbling ruble with soaring inflation. Its economy is still largely in the hands of inefficient state-run enterprises. Its infrastructure—electricity, railroads, telecommunications, and water—are mismanaged and lacking in funding. Perhaps the only thing saving Russia from total Y2K meltdown is the fact that it is significantly less computer-dependent than the West.

Y2K in Russia

The worst situation lies with Russian state-run systems such as telecommunications, defense, energy, and air traffic control. Russian State Telecommunications didn't begin its Y2K coordination program until *May 1998*. It stated positively that the job could not be completed on time. The U.S. Defense Department, anxious to eliminate the chance of a breakdown in communications and a dangerous mistake due to computer failures, proposed sharing early warning information with the Russian Ministry of Defense.[67] And failures in Russia's power generating and transmission plants spell trouble for Germany, which receives around 40 percent of its electricity from Russia.

The need for Russian companies to act appears to have been lost amid the economic and political upheaval in Russia. "The effect on businesses in Russia will be catastrophic if computers are not fixed before January 1 in the year 2000," said Scott Blacklin, president of the American Chamber of Commerce in Russia. A survey by Coopers and Lybrand of fifty Russian companies back in 1998 backs this up. It found that only one-third of those companies were even *aware* of the Y2K problem. And those that were—all large financial institutions— believed that they were more or less immune to Y2K because their systems are largely less than five years old. This ignores the fact, however, that many of these systems contain old software that must be upgraded before the end of the millennium.[68]

Our outlook for Russia, then, is continued misery as the financial crisis is exacerbated by Y2K. The only good news is that further deterioration of the Russian economy is unlikely to have a significant impact on American equities beyond a psychological one, since many of the losses have already been factored into earnings and share values.

Concluding Thoughts

Most nations have looked to the United States for leadership in the Y2K crisis. Where are the magical software applications and Silicon Valley super-chips that will save the world from computer wasteland? Sadly, the United States has been so preoccupied with its own mounting Y2K woes that it has had little time to help out other countries. We have been able to do little except lead by way of example, and on that score, the United States has a less than stellar track record.

In terms of internationally coordinated efforts, the whole world has come up short. The United Nations began to address the issue in earnest too late—holding its first truly international conference in December 1998. And the World Bank and other sources of international funding haven't been of much help, pledging (along with the United States and the United Kingdom) only around $17 million to countries struggling to come into compliance.[69]

We may come to deeply regret that more efforts were not undertaken to coordinate international Y2K efforts and minimize the disruptive impact. Y2K-induced infrastructural collapse, industrial shutdown, chaos in government services, and market meltdown may be unlikely in the United States, but they are a very real possibility in some parts of the world. The feedback effect of problems of such magnitude cannot be underestimated, and investors must be prepared for significant Y2K fallout.

EIGHT

THE ECONOMICS OF Y2K

If disruptions are severe enough, we could run into a recession.
—Federal Reserve Governor Edward W. Kelly, Jr.

By now it should be clear that Y2K will have a serious impact on key sectors of transportation, health care, electric power, banking, and telecommunications, not only in the United States, but around the world. So what does all this mean in terms of the United States economy? Could Y2K spell the end of the bull market? Could we see inflation, high interest rates, and a recession in the United States?

To answer these questions, let's go back to the 1970s again to the closest analogy to Y2K there is in recent history. The OPEC oil embargo caused a sudden spike in oil prices, basically overnight, on October 17, 1973. This had an initial impact on the industries most dependent on oil, such as transportation and electric utilities. But it quickly rippled out to other industries, including manufacturing, construction, and textiles, as the cost of making and shipping products rose. Manufacturers had to either eat the extra costs or pass them on to consumers in the form of higher prices on the shelves. In fact, they did a little of both, so we soon saw a bad combination of lower company earnings and higher consumer prices.

The feedback effect caused soaring inflation and led to a global recession. The economic contraction in 1973–74 saw real gross domestic product drop 3.7 percent from peak to trough. Economists called this combination "stagflation" because it was a period of inflating prices but stagnant economic activity. The shock to oil prices also turned out to be a shock to the economy precisely because so much of production and delivery was directly—and indirectly—connected to the price of oil. It is certainly something none of us wants to experience again.

Enter Y2K. Because the world has never experienced a phenomenon quite like this one, it is difficult to predict the economic consequences. But as we said at the beginning of this book, and as we've shown throughout, the situation could be *very* bad. So much of our prosperity depends on computers and automated systems, it's hard to imagine how we could get by without them now. In a worst case scenario, we would get set back to a time when computers weren't in control of production, transportation, financial markets, and communications—in other words, sometime in the 1970s before the information technology revolution.

Noted economic predictor Dr. Edward Yardeni, who is the chief economist for Deutche Morgan Grenfell and was named the *Wall Street Journal*'s forecaster of the year in 1997, has been warning of a Y2K recession for some time. Dr. Yardeni expects that problems in business systems, utilities, and government services will shave 3 to 4 percentage points off of the U.S. gross domestic product. "I see a very intense recession lasting twelve months," Yardeni said to a gathering of financial analysts in Kansas City. "I don't think it's doomsday, it's just a nasty, wicked recession."[1]

There are, of course, plenty who disagree with Dr. Yardeni. For example, before the same gathering of analysts, Gabrielle Napolitano, vice president in portfolio strategy for Goldman Sachs, predicted that economic activity might slow down a bit, but the economy will remain strong. But even Mr. Napolitano agreed that not enough information exists to make a clear prediction, and there are plenty of unknown risks.[2]

If Y2K turns out to be as damaging as the OPEC embargo was in the 1970s, there would be a deep recession. The Dow would fall around *40 percent*. That's to somewhere in the 5,000–6,000 range, so we're talking trillions in lost market value. (Dr. Yardeni has predicted a Dow low of 6,400.)[3] And a 3 to 4 percent drop in real GDP today means hundreds of billions of dollars lopped off the economy, on top of the hundreds of billions already spent to fix the problem.

Sound far-fetched? Not if you consider that the oil price increase was pretty much the *sole* precipitating factor for the 1973–74 recession.

With Y2K, oil supplies are at risk of severe shortages. But so are spare parts, coal, medicine, steel, rubber, chemicals, and food, to name a few. Add to that the risk of electric power shortages, failing banks, and a snarled telecommunication network, and it's a powerful mix of negatives. Any *one* of them is enough to set off a chain reaction similar to what we saw in 1973. Is it possible that all the Y2K problems will be fixed? No. It is possible, however, that enough will be fixed to deaden or at least soften the impact of the failures we do see. Every bit of code fixed between now and the year 2000 makes the situation a little bit better. At the current rate of progress, the Gartner Group has predicted a 15 percent change of serious mission critical failures in the United States, and fifty-fifty chances in places like Germany and Japan, on which our economy depends. To us, this makes the picture quite clear: Do you want to be basking on the beach if the experts predict even a *reasonable* chance of a tidal wave?

When your neighbors and coworkers shrug and say that they'll wait and see before taking any measures to protect their assets, just remember the Y2K *multiple detonation effect*. The economy is like a high-rise building, and Y2K glitches are like sticks of dynamite that could go off. Ask yourself if you'd much rather be standing outside the building in case all those little Y2K bombs go off.

Inflation, Shmation

Inflation is barely on most economists' radar maps, particularly since the start of the Asian economic crisis. Even the once inflation-wary Fed has conceded that inflation isn't likely to be much of a factor in the last few years of the millennium. In fact, for the first time since the 1930s, the experts are furrowing their brows over the possibility of a *deflationary* cycle (with consumer prices actually dropping!) and are thinking of emergency measures to reinflate world economies without causing them to overheat.

Y2K's Effect on Prices

But will we have overall inflation or deflation under Y2K? It's a commonly asked question. Our advice to investors is: Don't get caught up in it, because it could lead to the wrong conclusions. When the chips are all counted, we predict an unusual mixed bag on the inflation front, with

Key commodity prices could rise while credit markets deflate

some key prices (such as energy, food and raw materials) going up while credit markets continue to deflate. Rather than dwell on overall inflation or deflation, a more important question to ask is, what does this mixed bag mean to company earnings, the stock market, and interest rates?

The thing to keep in mind is that Y2K will make it *costlier* to do business across the board. Throughout this book, we have provided examples of how Y2K will impact critical bottlenecks and just-in-time operations in the supply chain. The breaks and disruptions in supply can go all the way down to the foundations of our economy and affect energy and raw materials—the building blocks of production. It could then impact subassembly and manufacturing because failures in automation will drive up labor costs.

Now let's add something to the mixture. Let's say that industry wisens up to the threat to the supply chain sometime in 1999. If we are correct, many will begin to *stock up* on supplies. Hospitals will keep extra pharmaceuticals. Electric utilities *Just-in-case* will store additional oil and coal. Tire makers will stock *will replace* rubber and steel. And so on. It's understandable behavior, *just-in-time* and likely to be mirrored by consumers the closer we get to the year 2000. In fact, top officials at the Fed are already talking about this likely outcome. At a speech given at the 1998 Annual Economic Symposium, the Fed's Y2K expert, Edward W. Kelley, Jr., gave this startling prediction:

> One area in which uncertainty about Y2K readiness is likely to have noticeable effects on economic activity in 1999 is in the management of inventories. As the millennium approaches, I expect businesses will want to hold larger inventories of goods as insurance against Y2K-related supply disruptions. Such a shift from "just-in-time" inventory management to a "just-in-case" posture is likely to prompt an increase in orders and production during 1999.[4]

Others in the know appear to agree. At the first Y2K summit held by President Clinton's Y2K council, Senator Bob Bennett warned industry leaders of the possibility of a "classic inventory recession" brought about by the "urge to stockpile."[5] Coca-Cola Co., which worries about international supply lines, in a recent SEC filing has stated that its contingency planning now includes "stockpiling raw and packaging materials, increasing inventory levels, securing alternate sources of supply, and other appropriate measures."[6]

From an economic standpoint, this also means is that there may be *demand*-based pressures on prices even before Y2K hits full force, since there will be more purchases competing for the same goods.

Now, the bad news. It is *possible* Y2K could give you the worst of both worlds. Demand for certain commodities could rise as industries and consumers prepare for the impending crisis, and *A double whammy?* then supply could fall off sharply as Y2K snarls transportation and delivery systems around the world. This is really a double-whammy for the cost of doing business, and it probably means higher producer prices.

Company Earnings Hit Hard

With increased costs, manufacturers have two basic choices. The costs can either be absorbed by the manufacturer or passed on down the supply line, ultimately to the customer.

Y2K's Effect on Share Prices

Under the first scenario, U.S. manufacturers eat the increased costs of doing business while doing their best to keep prices down for consumers. They do this because they are in a competitive situation and markets are tight. Lately, their foreign competitors, particularly in Asia, have the benefit of selling things cheaply to the United States in part because their currencies have fallen so far and could fall even further after 2000. U.S. firms could conclude that it is better to hold the line and post bad earnings now than to give up long-term market share. But remember that stock prices are the discounted *current* value of *future* company earnings. The closer we get to 2000, the more clear it will be that company costs will rise as a result of Y2K. Assuming consumer prices remain constant or even continue to fall, this is a classic squeeze play on earnings. Net result: Stock prices fall *in anticipation*.

Under scenario two, consumers wind up paying for the extra costs, which are reflected in higher prices on store shelves. Costs might get passed along to consumers because there simply is little *room* for them to stay low. Remember that efficient, automated production has the benefit of keeping costs *down*. Companies downsize in order to reduce costs and improve earnings. It's extremely expensive for companies to do things manually, or to do everything themselves instead of farming tasks out. But while passing along Y2K cost increases to consumers may spare company earnings temporarily, it does no one any good in the long term. Increased store prices mean consumers buy *fewer* items for the *same amount* of money. It doesn't take long for this decrease in items sold to feed back into lower economic indicators and lower earnings for companies. So the net result is the same: Stock prices fall in anticipation.

Company earnings and share prices will also be put under some pressure from direct Y2K remediation costs and, more importantly, the *opportunity costs* of information technology budgets earmarked for Y2K. Robert Stansky, the manager of the nation's largest mutual fund, Fidelity Magellan Fund, is very concerned about the possible impact of Y2K spending on earnings. "I'm truly scared about the year 2000," Stansky told a group of business journalists in November 1998. In his view, Y2K diverts resources away from capital spending on corporate growth opportunities and therefore reduces the likelihood of continued double-digit earnings growth, which have driven the U.S. stock market ever higher. Incidentally, Stansky is also glad that January 1, 2000, falls on a Saturday, when the markets will be closed.[7]

Y2K opportunity costs have the attention of the pros

Which Way Are They Headed?

This is an important question for the average American. Falling interest rates boost stocks in part because they lower the cost of corporate borrowing while making buying other investments (like money market funds or government securities) relatively less attractive. Falling rates are also good for the housing market because more people are likely to buy in order to take advantage of lower monthly payments. On the other hand, people who keep their money in banks—typically retirees—earn less interest on their deposits. Lower interest rates also make the U.S. dollar less attractive to foreign investors.

Y2K's Effect on Interest Rates

Our prediction—shared by most economists—is that interest rates are likely to stay low through 2000 as central banks try to keep economies from sliding further into recession by making sure there is plenty of money around to use. But after Y2K strikes, governments will be faced with a dilemma.

On the one hand, they will be seeing prices on basic building blocks like oil and food on the rise, and this will translate into higher producer prices. Since nobody hates inflation more than the Fed, under normal circumstances rates might go up to cool things down. On the other hand, central bankers will also be looking at falling economic indicators and corporate earnings disappointments, which normally would indicate that the economy needs a shot in the arm by way of *lower* interest rates.

So what's a central banker to do? In some ways, the Fed is not able to affect much by way of monetary policy when there are supply-side shocks to the economy. As the Fed admits, "Because such events tend to raise prices and reduce output, monetary policy can attempt to counter the losses of output or the higher prices, but cannot completely offset both."[8]

It is not so hard to see, however, that the trend will continue to favor lower rates, even after Y2K hits. The thinking goes like this: Y2K is causing inflationary pressures. But this is a cost-side problem, not a problem of an overheated economy. Lowering interest rates is not likely to cause prices to rise appreciably. In fact, it may have a net impact of keeping prices lower by permitting businesses to better survive the crisis period. Some have predicted that the Fed will move to drastically cut rates in anticipation of the crisis in order to encourage banks to lend to companies striving to fix their computers in time.[9] Indeed, if banks do not step up and offer liquidity to companies perceived as struggling with or falling victim to Y2K, the knock-on economic effect could be devastating. One influential Fed governor, Robert Ferguson, has dubbed this the "Y2K Shadow" and described it as follows:

We predict continued lower rates

> Financial market participants, and entire countries, may find that capital will become scarce, or at least dear, if they are not seen to be making sufficient progress toward resolving this problem. The uncertainty surrounding preparedness for Year 2000 may make

markets less liquid as institutions seek to insulate themselves from risk with counterparties who are thought to be unprepared. The financial cost of this is not clear, and I am not one of those forecasting recession as a result of a Year 2000 slowing, but we know from recent events that a flight to liquidity can have severe repercussions in the real economy.[10]

Translation: We think the Fed will favor lower interest rates to maintain market liquidity through the Year 2000 crisis. Already, we have seen European banks moving in concert to lower rates in order to maintain economic growth in the European Union. And European bank officials have hinted that some banks will have to make further cuts down the line.

But will lower rates keep stock prices supported? Only partially. Investors know that the stock market generally loves low interest rates. So lower interest rates could be a counterweight to dismal earnings reports. But lower interest rates are unlikely to completely stop the hemorrhaging from stocks and a downturn in the economy, since we doubt they will be able to lower the cost of doing business enough to offset the damage from Y2K. Just ask the Japanese, who have lowered interest rates to almost zero but haven't prevented a recession brought on by other fundamental problems in their economy.

If the Fed governors are already planning for squeezes on liquidity, you can bet that they are looking at lower rates through 1999 and beyond. This demonstrates that under Y2K investors can't afford to follow old formulas about interest rates, even under the shadow of inflation. Inflation at the producer level means higher interest rates *unless* it is supply-side in origin, since there is the danger that higher rates could result in recession. Lower interest rates mean higher stock prices *unless* earnings are overwhelmed by higher costs, which is possible with supply-side price shocks. Y2K is the kind of monkey wrench that requires investors to put aside their traditional reactions and take a look at the nature and origin of economic problems.

Let's Bond

In the murky world of Y2K investing, money is likely to move away from volatile equity markets into more stable government securities (i.e., U.S. Treasury notes and bonds). As we explain in this section, investors need to be aware that not all government instruments will

Y2K's Effect on Government Securities

be equal when the crisis hits. While we recommend keeping a healthy portion of your portfolio in U.S. government securities, we are wary of state and local bonds and would step very carefully through that minefield.

U.S. Government Securities

Traders who move their money into the U.S. government securities market early may be glad they did, for three reasons. First, U.S. Treasury notes purchased in 1999 may bear interest rates that by 2000 or 2001 will look relatively attractive, assuming the Fed continues to lower rates in anticipation of liquidity problems and a possible recession. This will push up the face value of the note or bond, meaning investors can sell them for a profit or continue to get relatively good rates of return.

Second, if money heads out of stocks, as we predict, U.S. Treasury securities would be among the primary beneficiaries as investors seek safe havens. The only risks to investors are that the U.S. government might default on its payments and renege on its guarantees (in our view a statistical impossibility unless we have total economic meltdown) or that consumer prices might rise significantly and eat into fixed income payments (possible, but again not as likely as a continued deflationary trend).

The preceding two reasons are typical of those in any situation where interest rates are coming down and there is market uncertainty.

Y2K-induced depositor withdrawals could result in lower rates

However, a third reason why government securities will be a good place to park your money is more unique to the Y2K crisis. *Substantial depositor withdrawals* in 1999 raises the possibility of active Federal Open Market Committee purchases of government securities, which would drive rates lower and face values of U.S. Treasury notes higher. Because withdrawals of such magnitude have not been anticipated before, we are in totally uncharted waters here. To show why FOMC activity could mean lower bond rates and higher bond prices, we need to explore a complex web of reserve supply and demand, interest rates and government securities.

The amount that all the banks have in reserve is called the reserve *supply*. It is made up of borrowed and nonborrowed reserves. Borrowed reserves are what the banks borrow from the Fed in emergency situations to cover their needs. Nonborrowed reserves are what the banks themselves put aside in case of unusual depositor withdrawals.

Normally, the supply of reserves drops in the latter part of the year anyway due to depositor withdrawals for the holiday shopping season. In 1999, this phenomenon will likely be compounded many times by Y2K fears. The Fed will be most interested in maintaining *stability* of reserve supply and demand, something that economists call reserve "equilibrium." That is the magic point at which the pressures on reserve demand are balanced out by changes in reserve supply. It is important for the Fed to achieve equilibrium, or as close to it as possible, so that it can maintain its influence and move interest rates in the direction it desires.

A high demand for reserves would put upward pressure on interest rates, particularly on the *federal funds* rate. This is the rate of interest charged between banks for the use of reserves. In other words, it is the rate that a bank loaning excess reserves charges to a bank in need of more reserves. To keep the federal funds rate level or moving downward, the Fed will want to increase the reserve supply so there will be more money out there for banks to swap.

One strategy would be to lower the *discount* rate. The discount rate is the rate of interest that the Fed charges banks for their borrowed reserves. The discount rate has been described by commentators as "largely symbolic" because banks typically only turn to discount window loans after exhausting all other reasonably available funds. Banks don't like to use the loans because they are often perceived as a sign of weakness.[11] But as Y2K problems mount and depositors get nervous, the discount rate may come to be *quite* important in 2000. In fact, the Fed has already moved aggressively to lower the discount rate, and it appears to be paving the way for emergency bank loans, perhaps in expectation of a strong need in 1999. Increased use of the discount window by banks would raise the *borrowed reserve supply* and to some extent balance out increased demand for reserves. It would also reduce the need for banks to borrow from one another, thus lowering demand for loans under the Fed funds rate, which would tend to reduce upward pressure on that rate.

The Fed will also look to increase the *nonborrowed reserve supply* by injecting more money into bank reserves. To do this, the Fed normally moves in and begins to buy up short term government securities such as T-bills (government securities with terms between three and twelve months) and near-term obligations such as T-notes (terms from two to ten years). This increases the total supply of reserves. Why is that? When the Fed buys government securities, the sellers of those securities deposit the checks they receive from the Fed at their banks, the banks then present the checks to the Fed, and the Fed turns around and credits the reserve accounts of the banks, thus adding to the overall reserve supply. This is a typical tactic of the Fed when there is an aberration in the system that is driving the supply of reserves away from the Fed's target.[12]

These three considerations—lower interest rates, flight to safety, and likely activity by the FOMC—all favor the U.S. government securities for those who can beat the crowd to market.

State and Municipal Bonds

From what you have seen in previous chapters, the situation with the federal government and Y2K is pretty appalling. But we are confident that, however bad the situation gets, the U.S. government will be able to meet its debt obligations. The bad news is, the same cannot necessarily be said for state and local governments, where the Y2K situation is sometimes much worse. For investors, this means troubled waters in the municipal and state bond markets, which traditionally are placid, tax-free seas on which to float your assets.

Just as banks are concerned about the Y2K preparations of their commercial borrowers, so should citizens and investors be concerned about the Y2K programs of the state and local agencies that are borrowing money from the public through the issuance of bonds. Despite the importance of the issue, Y2K denial appears to run high among local governments. According to a survey by Public Technology, Inc., less than half of local governments in the United States even thought they *had* a Y2K problem back in 1998.[13] Local governments that have looked in earnest at the Y2K problem are often shocked at its extent and at the projected costs of the fixes. The price tag is sometimes so hefty that it threatens the viability of other essential programs and operations. But officials who don't own up to the Y2K threat face an even bigger price tag and the specter of crushing legal liability should critical systems begin to fail, causing widespread problems in basic services and functions such as emergency services, transportation systems, tax collection, and crime prevention.

Either way, investors should be concerned that Y2K could affect local government credit ratings, which in turn affect the ability of local governments to borrow and raise money. These ratings are published by investor services such as *Keeping an eye* Moody's and Standard and Poor's to help potential *on credit ratings* bond buyers assess the risk of default by the issuer. Unlike federal government securities, municipal bonds are not backed by guarantees and so are inherently riskier. Unfortunately, a poor credit rating could result either from underestimates of the high cost of Y2K fixes or from failure to fix systems at all. So until recently, local governments have said little to illuminate the public on the extent of their problems.

In the fall of 1998, an alarmed Government Accounting Standard Board passed stricter rules, requiring state and local governments to report the amount of money and resources they have devoted to the Y2K problem.[14] The SEC has gotten involved as well, warning local bond issuers that they must disclose possible Y2K problems that could affect their debt service payments or affect the issuer's creditworthiness.[15] You can expect that lawyers are busy drafting up "boilerplate" language that downplays the significance of the Y2K threat while "disclosing" the potential downside risk, much as was done with corporate disclosures. For example, the State Public Works Board of the State of California inserted this paragraph into its disclosure statement for a bond issuance for prisons in Monterey County:

> Although the [Department of Information Technology] reports the state departments are making substantial progress overall toward the goal of Y2K compliance, the task is very large and will likely encounter unexpected difficulties. The state cannot predict whether all mission critical systems will be ready and tested by late 1999 or what impact failure of any particular IT system(s) or of outside interfaces with state IT systems might have.[16]

Not exactly helpful. We expect that as the end of 1999 approaches, these types of disclosures are likely to mirror those of corporations, which typically boast that all mission-critical applications will be fixed, but that there is no way to predict how the impact of unprepared vendors and customers will play out.

So how bad exactly *is* the Y2K problem at the state and local levels? Now that the states are required to give fuller disclosures of costs, we can tell you that the projected costs to state government are significant. New York's first public estimates of state government Y2K costs ran to $114 million. California's initial estimate to fix its 640 statewide systems was more than twice that, at $240 million,[17] a figure that by December 1998 was revised upward 21 percent to $290 million.[18] Texas rang in at $208 million for its 436 key state systems, and the other big states of Florida and Illinois have respectively put the number at $90 million and $114 million (up from an earlier estimated $69 million) for their Y2K fixes.[19] Remember, these numbers cover only *state* systems and do not include what the cities and counties must separately spend, which is usually in aggregate many times the total for the state.

But the numbers only tell part of the story. The full extent of Y2K is still being uncovered bit by bit, day by day. In New York, for example, a September 1998 survey by the state comptroller's office discovered that 26 percent of the state's cities, 54 percent of towns, 48 percent of villages, and 61 percent of fire districts didn't even have any plans in place at that time to address Y2K.[20] Financial systems were at substantial risk, with 31 percent of survey respondents predicting problems with their systems.[21] Neighboring New Jersey's survey results were also revealing: Only *one in five* government entities had fully prepared to deal with the Y2K problem, and only a little more than half even considered it a serious problem.[22]

At the local level among counties and municipalities, the results are disappointing to say the least. As the *Wall Street Journal* reported, despite an estimated price tag of $1.7 billion among counties to fix their Y2K problems (with most of this hit coming out of counties' general funds), only around one-third had even completed the *inventory* process by December 1998.[23] More alarmingly, *half* of the nation's 3,069 counties didn't even have *plans* to deal with the problem, according to a survey by the National Association of Counties. At highest risk were emergency service systems such as 911.[24] Massive failure of those systems across the country would be "a major catastrophe," according to the Association's president, Betty Lou Ward.[25]

In California, which is roundly acknowledged as being a leader among states in Y2K preparedness, while 74 percent of its counties and municipalities had Y2K plans in place by the end of 1998, only 42 percent had actually set aside any *money* to implement those plans.[26] Further, the state auditor's report in August 1998 found that some state agencies were between one and three months behind schedule and that departments were not making adequate plans for testing, had not focused sufficiently on data interface issues, and lacked business continuation contingencies.[27] Only 50 percent of mission-critical state systems, such as those that monitor departments such as fire and police, were believed to be in good shape by the end of 1998.[28]

A plan is nice, but money is better

Among cities, the Y2K battle often has taken on a tone of desperation. Washington, D.C., for example—whose protracted financial woes has meant no upgrades of antiquated systems for many years—has already conceded that it will not fix all the glitches, and that the transition to 2000 "absolutely" will result in some system failures. According to the district's acting chief technology officer, "We came late to the game, and we came with a pile of stuff."[29] Apparently, they also came with a lot of political dead weight. According to the inspector general, the city's Y2K program was "frozen in place" because of delays in decision-making and late payments to consultants. There was also confusion over who was in charge. As the U.S. General Accounting Office concluded in a June 1998 report, "Bottom line: The district faces a great risk that its systems will not be ready on time."[30] The impact on city services? A retreat to backup systems, meaning in some cases manual operations.

Nevertheless, Washington, D.C., has ambitious plans to replace computers in a host of departments, including budgeting and bill payment, personnel and payroll, real estate and income tax collection, business and land-use permits, driver's license and motor vehicle registration, pension payments, purchasing, student information, and police and fire communications, including dispatch services. The cost? Estimates in 1998 put the fixes at around $200 million, but the late status of the repairs is likely to make costs escalate.[31]

To take another example, Denver worries that the unexpectedly high cost of Y2K, estimated at $15 million for 1998 and another $28 million in the years following, could wipe out its surplus for the 1998 fiscal year, once all other spending is accounted for. If Y2K costs went much higher—as well they could given the nature of fixes and diminishing human resources to fight the bug in 1999—it could cut into Denver's $50 million in reserves, which would affect the city's credit rating.[32] Ominously, when the mayor's chief of staff was asked when the city's then-eighteen-month-old Y2K program would be finished with its corrective measures, she responded, "December 31, 1999."[33] Let's hope she was joking.

Local law enforcement around the country may have its hands full as problems mount. In Sacramento, tests on computer systems had surprising results: when the clocks were set forward to the new millennium, a computer controlling the jail cell doors interpreted that something catastrophic had happened and proceeded promptly to *unlock all the doors.*[34] A different problem in Frederick County, Maryland, would have netted the same result: Officials discovered that the computer would have miscalculated release times for inmates and let some out by mistake.[35] Also at risk are emergency response services that depend on local telecommunications and transportation systems to operate seamlessly.

In recognition of the threat to basic services posed by Y2K, some local governments have put eyebrow-raising contingencies into place. In Los Angeles, for example, the police department has asked the city council to set aside $4.5 million for overtime pay to keep as many as 300 additional police officers on the streets at the turn of the millennium. The extra officers are needed in case, for example, emergency systems fail or there is widespread looting. (Los Angeles has budgeted $100 million for its total Y2K-related programs—a modest figure compared to, say, New York City's $300 million.)[36]

Perhaps because it, too, recognizes the potential for problems in local services across the nation, the Clinton administration has begun to coordinate Y2K efforts of regional emergency response centers. The centers are run by the Defense and State departments, intelligence agencies, and the Federal Emergency Management Agency. They will be brought together to address problems that citizens, communities, and states might face as a result of Y2K.[37]

While such measures may alleviate concerns over emergency

response preparedness, it does nothing to diminish what we perceive as serious financial exposure at the local level. In sum, investors should proceed with the utmost of caution prior to investing in bonds issued by state and local government entities. Our advice is to stick with federally backed government securities until after the crisis is well past.

Flight to Safety

Economic uncertainty makes investments such as gold and the U.S. dollar attractive because they are classic safe harbors for investors. Y2K is uniquely likely to breed panic and over-reaction among investors both at home and abroad. As money streams out of equity markets and foreign currencies, gold and the dollar are the most obvious beneficiaries.

Y2K's Effect on Gold and the U.S. Dollar

Gold

In times of economic instability, gold historically has done well. This is because most of the world's money is what is called fiat money, which has value only so long as the people have faith in their governments. Fiat money can devalue quickly during crises as public confidence erodes, as the Thai baht, Indonesian rupiah, and Russian ruble tumbles demonstrate. Commodity money, on the other hand, has value because of what it is made out of—usually gold, silver, or platinum.

The good news is, gold is still well off its historic highs. In 1997, the Swiss dumped a good portion of their gold on the market, driving the price down well below the $300-per-ounce mark. It traded as low as $283 per ounce on the news. These days, gold is still trading low compared to where it was a few years ago, kept down in part by the selling of massive stores by the Russians and by improved mining techniques that increase the total production supply. Accordingly, the downside risk to owning gold is already somewhat moderated.

It may seem anachronistic to talk about trading in hard gold assets while investors are surfing the Internet to trade stocks electronically. But Y2K is a unique occurrence that may turn the clocks back on a lot of modern practices. In our view it makes sense for investors, even individual ones with modest portfolios, to diversify and reallocate some assets to hold precious metals like gold through the Y2K crisis. We explain how to go about converting some of your cash into gold in chapter 9.

The Dollar

Despite the trend toward lower U.S. interest rates, we also predict the U.S. dollar will gain in strength through the Y2K crisis. Like gold and other precious metals, the dollar is often the beneficiary of a "flight to safety" mentality among foreign investors. These investors will see the United States as relatively well-prepared for Y2K and will be fearful of further weaknesses or even outright devaluations of their own countries' currencies.

If the dollar gains significantly in strength, however, this will put a dent in the earnings of U.S. exporters, whose product prices in foreign countries will rise in tandem. It is also bad news for U.S. multinationals looking to repatriate profits overseas, since the currency exchange environment wouldn't favor conversion to the dollar. Indeed, a stabilized U.S. dollar helped boost corporate profits in the latter part of 1998, which in conjunction with lower interest rates pushed the U.S. stock markets back up to near their record highs. A surging dollar in late 1999 and 2000, however, will again cast a cloud over short-term earnings and therefore the share prices of large U.S. companies.

Aggressive investors seeking to capitalize on global uncertainty can bet on the rise of the U.S. dollar—and the weakness of foreign currencies—in the futures marketplace. Strategies for this and other play are discussed in chapter 10.

Concluding Thoughts

In summary, we predict that Y2K will have a major impact on the economy. A possible scenario follows: At-risk industries begin to experience the early effects of Y2K. Prices and inventories of certain commodities and spare parts start to rise as industry makes "just-in-case" provisions. As the possible effect becomes more widely understood, there is a first wave of stock sell-offs by institutional investors and savvy individuals. The bond market is a main beneficiary as the big money tries to lock in relatively higher rates. Gold also rises as investors, particularly foreign investors, head for hedges and safety. Interest rates continue to fall as central banks try to restore market liquidity, but this doesn't avert a second major downturn in share prices in the last quarter of 1999, nor does it turn back a surging U.S. dollar. The Fed worries about shoring up reserves as banks feel the squeeze of depositor withdrawals. FOMC activity and other Fed action pushes bond prices even higher and interest rates ever lower. A third wave of stock sell-offs occurs after the turn of the millennium when things go haywire with banks, telecommunications, energy, and transportation. Foreign markets are particularly hard hit, and investors worry about the knock-on effect. A flood of lawsuits ensues. Sharp price increases in energy, food, and other essential items put pressure on company earnings, and stocks and prices fall further. The global recession deepens.

Could it be that none of this happens? Sure. Industry could ignore the need to take precautionary inventory measures. Investors could shrug off the warnings, stay invested in stocks and fail to push the dollar and gold prices higher. The Fed could decide that interest rates are low enough because the global liquidity threat is past. Banks around the world could win their battle for depositor confidence and have no need for extra reserves. Industrial and financial operations at home and abroad could miraculously come through unscathed. Earnings could continue to defy gravity, and stocks could continue their long march upward.

The point is that in our view the *chances* that all of the positive developments will come into alignment is low relative to the risk that significant mission-critical failures could cause global economic turmoil. We are already seeing the warning signs. The sheer unpredictability of the Y2K crisis will drive much of the flight to safety. For the risk-adverse, this means precautionary measures are amply warranted.

NINE

Y2K INVESTMENT OPPORTUNITIES

After reading the last few chapters, you might conclude that Y2K survivalist types who are buying generators and heading for the hills may not be so off the mark. In situations like this, it is tempting to turn away from all investment advice altogether and horde cash, bunkering down as if truly preparing for a financial hurricane. Before you do this, remember that many people will make a lot of money *precisely because* there is a crisis in the markets. Astute investors can take advantage of bad times as well as good.

In this chapter, we'll discuss some of the basic opportunities that exist, even for the average investor who doesn't want to, or can't afford to, get into the riskier options and futures plays we discuss in chapter 11. The opportunities fall into four basic categories: short selling, Y2K contingency companies, Y2K fix-it stocks, opportunities in gold, and what we call (for lack of a better term) our "after the Y2K dust settles" stock picks.

If you are convinced that many of the industries we've identified are at risk, rather than simply underweighting or avoiding the stocks we've listed, you can take the extra step of *short selling* them. More experienced investors know that short selling is an easy way to take advantage of downward pressures on a stock. We anticipate that short positions on stocks will gain in momentum as we approach the end of 1999. This in and of itself will put downward pressures on certain shares. It also means that the potential for panicked short-position covering is increased, making overall risk to short sellers somewhat higher.

Y2K STRATEGY
Short Selling

Short selling involves what amounts to borrowing shares from your broker. After borrowing the shares, you sell them in the market and receive money from the buyer. At some point, however, you need to buy those shares back and return them to your broker. It is your hope that you will be able to buy them back cheaper than where you sold them.

For example, suppose you short sold 100 shares of XYZ Airlines in mid-1999 at $65. Your broker would loan you those shares and sell them for you in the marketplace. Your account would receive $6,500, less some commission. This would in effect be a $6,500 loan from your broker, which would start to accrue interest as soon as the trade settled.

Say in late 1999, the Transportation Department were to ban flights to certain parts of Asia and Latin America for the first few weeks of 2000 due to concerns over incomplete Y2K programs with the air traffic control systems in those regions. XYZ, which derives a higher percentage of revenue from its flights to those countries, sees its stock fall from $65 to $50 a share in the frenzy of selling that ensues. Meanwhile, oil prices shoot up as several oil exporters report unspecified Y2K problems at drilling sites and pipelines. Jet fuel rises in tandem, sparking a new wave of selling. By the end of January 2000, XYZ is trading at $44 per share.

You call your broker and arrange to *cover your short position.* This means you are buying the 100 XYZ shares back and returning them to your broker. You pay $4,400 for the stock, plus some commission. You have a profit of $2,100 on the trade, less whatever you paid in commissions and interest. The math looks like this:

Proceeds from short sale:	100 × $65 =	$6,500
Cost to buy shares back:	100 × $44 =	$4,400
Total profit:	100 × $21 =	$2,100
(Less interest and commission)		

There are two principal risks to short sellers. One of course is that the stock will go up in price. If this happens, you will wind up paying more to buy them back than for what you sold them. What's more, if the stock has been heavily shorted but defies naysayers and continues to rise, short positions will get *squeezed* further as nervous traders move quickly to cover their positions, pushing the price up even higher.

The other risk is that the stock *does little to nothing,* dragging out the term of the short-sell position. Traders caught in these share-price doldrums will find themselves paying hefty interest to their stock-brokers with no offsetting gains.

Short selling can be highly rewarding in a down market, but there is, as you can see, significant (and, in theory, unlimited) downside risk to your short position. To limit this risk, consider putting in "stop loss" orders in which your broker will automatically buy the stock you have shorted back if it breaks past a certain price in an upward move.

Our Picks for Best Shorts

The best stocks to short during the Y2K crisis are those that have enjoyed continued strong earnings through 1998 and 1999 and whose share prices have not already been discounted heavily. These stocks are the most likely to take the non-Y2K-minded investors by surprise. Of course, by the time you are reading this book, the financial picture for many companies may have changed dramatically, so it is important to take a look at their current prices and to view their stock price histories to see that they are indeed still near their historic highs.

But even stocks that have experienced stock price weakness could continue to be further battered by the Y2K crisis. Based on Y2K risk exposure, we have compiled a list of stocks on which we would strongly consider holding short positions going into the new year. We call this list the Y2K Terrible Twenty based on the risk to their industry and their relatively high exposure within that industry:

American Airlines (AMR)
BankAmerica Corp (BAC)
Bank of Tokyo-Mitsubishi (MBK)
Beverly Enterprises (BEV)
British Airways (BAB)
Chase Manhattan (CMB)
Citigroup (CGI)
CMS Energy Corporation (CMS)
Columbia/HCA (COL)
Delta Airlines (DAL)
Duke Energy (DUK)

FPL Group (FPL)
Federal Express (FDX)
KLM Royal Dutch Airlines
  (KLM)
Northwest Airlines (NWAC)
Pacific Gas and Electric (PGE)
Primus Telecommunications
  (PRTL)
Telebras (TBH)
Tenet Healthcare (THC)
United Airlines (UAL)

Again, these are only some of the many stocks we believe will fare relatively poorly under Y2K, holding all other considerations constant. Whether to actually take out a short position depends on many factors that must be considered at the time of the short sale, so consult with your broker before trading.

Preparing for the Worst

Before turning your back on long positions in equities entirely, there are a few sectors (besides the lawyers and the programmers) that stand to actually *benefit* from the Y2K crisis. In particular, companies that provide consumers with contingency services or products are likely beneficiaries. For example, companies offering *human services* such as temp agencies and security personnel agencies will stand to profit from Y2K problems in other more computerized industries.

Y2K "Contingency Companies"

We should caution that we expect these companies to do a stellar business in late 1999 and through 2000, but for that business to level or drop off after the crisis is past. A short-term rise in their stock prices is possible as investors look for possible beneficiaries of the Y2K crisis.

You Can Take This Job and . . . Fill It!

Temporary service companies may see demand for their personnel rise sharply as companies scramble to implement contingency plans, correct billing errors, field customer service inquiries, and return to manual operations in many systems. The number of able hands available on loan from temp agencies is expected to shrink as companies snatch up whatever warm bodies are still unassigned by early 2000. This is expected to buoy the near-term profits of temp agencies.

There are dozens of publicly traded temporary service companies. The largest in the world is called Adecco SA (symbol: ADECY). Based in Europe, it has more than 200,000 clients in 3,000 offices around the world. The second largest temp service is Manpower, Inc. (symbol: MAN), which is probably more of a household name to U.S. residents. It places over two million workers worldwide and services critical professional and technical industries—those most likely to be hit by computer failures brought on by Y2K. Most investors have also heard of Kelly Services, Inc. (symbol: KELY), which provides 750,000 workers to over 200,000 customers. Kelly also has a strong presence in information technology personnel as well as other professionals.

We like Romac International, Inc. (symbol: ROMC), which has some specialties in manufacturing and health care personnel services as well as information technology and finance. Personnel Group of America, Inc. (symbol: PGA), has a full 55 percent of its temp service sales in the information technology sector. Robert Half International, Inc. (symbol: RHI), focuses on administrative, accounting, finance, and IT—a good mix for the demand likely to be created by Y2K.

And here's an interesting possibility: Labor Ready, Inc. (symbol: LRW), provides short-term *unskilled* labor for freight handling, construction, and light industry. If the machines stop moving, people will be called in to do things the old fashioned way. Labor Ready is well positioned as a beneficiary of the clocks being turned back.

The following is a list of other large, publicly traded temp service companies. Remember that we think the sector as a whole is likely to outperform the market because of Y2K. Each stock we discuss or list should still be looked at by you individually and should also be assessed on traditional criteria of price earnings ratios, earnings potential, average stock price, and the like. *Always consult with a broker before trading.*

Company	*Symbol*
ACSYS, Inc.	ACSY
Administaff, Inc.	ASF
AHL Services, Inc.	AHLS
Alternative Resources Corp.	ALRC
CDI Corp.	CDI
Metamor Worldwide, Inc.	MMWW
Modis Professional Services	MPS
Norrell Corp.	NRL
Novacare Employee Services, Inc.	NCES
Olsten Corp.	OLS
On Assignment, Inc.	ASGN
RCM Technologies	RCMT

Remedy Temp, Inc.	REMX
SCB Computer Technology, Inc.	SCBI
Select Appointments (Holdings) PLC	SELAY
SOS Staffing Services, Inc.	SOSS
Staff Leasing, Inc.	STFF
Staffmark, Inc.	STAF
StarTek, Inc.	SRT
Vincam Group, Inc.	VCAM
Volt Information Sciences, Inc.	VOL
Westaff Inc.	WSTF

Providing Security for the Y2K Insecure

With systems going haywire—or even at risk of going haywire—companies will be keen to increase security staffing at their facilities. When security codes and card readers malfunction, doors and elevators fail to operate properly, telephones go dead sporadically, or the power goes out in a building, companies will be only too happy to pay a little more to have extra hands around to make sure security isn't compromised and that safety is made a top priority. At the turn of the century, expect security guards to become a scarce commodity. One banker in Massachusetts who is planning on leaving the door to his vault ajar reports being told that security guards in the weeks leading up to the end of 1999 are already in short supply.[1]

There are plenty of security companies that are publicly traded. But investors need to make sure that they are looking at security *personnel* companies rather than makers of the same electronic security systems that could go on the fritz at the beginning of the millennium. The top security personnel company is Borg-Warner Security Corporation (symbol: BOR), which employs around 65,000 security guards under the well-known brand names of Burns, Wells Fargo, and Globe. Borg Warner focuses on industrial, financial, and government markets, all perfect Y2K niches.

Our other picks include Pinkerton's, Inc. (symbol: PKT), which has worldwide offices for its security services business. You can find Pinkerton's guards in a lot of hospitals (you'll find more of them after the millennium, we'll bet), as well as in government buildings, commercial and industrial complexes, and in traffic control. Wackenhut

Corporation (symbol: WAK) provides general security services as well as specialty services in airport security (remember, this is a growth market under Y2K) and nuclear power plants (ditto). Command Security Corporation (symbol: CMMD) has around 3,500 guards placed in industries likely to be affected by Y2K, including aviation (Command Security apparently does a big business in airline preboard passenger screening).

The reason we aren't recommending a lot of other security firms is that these firms sell the same systems that could fail, either because of internal chip problems or because of a break in the link of services such as 911. It is worth considering, however, that there may be a boom market for companies that make people feel more prepared for Y2K. These include manufacturers of guns, dried or canned foods, safes, solar cells, and diesel generators.

When investors consider opportunities during the Y2K crisis, what often springs to mind are the software tools companies performing

Y2K Fix-it Companies

Y2K remedial services, which have seen a truly stellar couple of years. Indeed, whole indexes have been constructed around this bonanza, and some of these companies have already seen phenomenal—if sometimes short-lived—increases in shareholder value.

Other authors have covered this ground and made predictions, sometimes with mixed results. Firms specializing in Y2K fixes and technical consulting will do an amazing business this year and next, but we should warn that many of their projected earnings have already been reflected in their stock prices.

But for some of these firms, Wall Street has determined that they are one-trick ponies whose earnings will not be sustainable much beyond the crisis itself.[2] In some cases, the price earnings ratios are simply too high to be supported realistically. Take high flyer Viasoft (symbol: VIAS), once touted as a beneficiary of the millennium bug due to its year 2000 software fixer software, which at one time was one of the only options in a hot market. At least one Y2K author had boldly labeled Viasoft a "defensive investment" during the Y2K crisis,[3] and *Business Week* even went so far as to identify it as one of their Top Tech Bets in its June 1997 issue.[4] But competition from other companies and decreased demand for its product brought earnings disappointments, and the stock which had traded at over $65 a share in August 1997 was trading below $5 by October of 1998.[5]

Still, the chance that Y2K remediation firms will outperform other stocks in the near term is high. Rather than pick and choose among the dozens of firms out there and risk buying a lemon, investors seeking to bet on an upward move of the overall stock prices of these firms can put their money into the Y2K Fund from HomeStates Mutual Funds. The Y2K Fund invests in thirty-two companies that perform Y2K remediation work. This fund is up sharply since its inception, so there is some downside risk. For information, contact the fund at 888-Y2K-FUND (888-925-3868) or its website at www.y2kfund.com/snapshots.htm.

More aggressive investors can trade options on the de Jager Year 2000 Index (symbol: YTK). This is an index whose "puts" and "calls" are traded on the American Stock Exchange. We should warn you that, like the Y2K Fund, this index and the nontraded Bloomberg Year 2000 Index (covering a larger segment of companies) have seen astronomical increases in the last few years, so there is significant downside risk.

The de Jager Year 2000 Index is made up of the following twenty companies:[6]

Company	Symbol
American Management Systems, Inc.	AMSY
Analysts International Corp.	ANLY
CIBER, Inc.	CBR
Computer Associates International, Inc.	CA
Computer Horizons Corp.	CHRZ
Computer Sciences Corp.	CSC
Compuware Corp.	CPWR
Data Dimensions, Inc.	DDIM
Electronic Data Systems Corp.	EDS
EMC Corp.	EMC
Information Management Resources, Inc.	IMRS
INTERSOLV, Inc.	ISLI
Keane, Inc.	KEA
Mercury Interactive Corp.	MERQ

PeopleSoft, Inc.	PSFT
PLATINUM Technology, Inc.	PLAT
Sterling Software, Inc.	SSW
VIASOFT, Inc.	VIAS
Unisys Corp.	UIS
Zitel Corp.	ZITL

Strategies for buying options on this and other indices are outlined in chapter 11.

Golden Opportunities

In the previous chapter, we briefly discussed how uncertainty in global markets could lead to a flight to safety among investors and spell a boom for gold. Gold is also a good hedge against inflation, which could be a factor if disruptions to key commodities like oil occur.

Y2K and Gold

In this chapter, we show how the average investor can capitalize on the possibilities of a spike in the price of gold. Basically, investors have a choice of owning actual gold or owning gold-related equities or funds. For high-risk takers, we outline some basic strategies in chapter 11 using leverage in the futures and options markets to maximize your profits.

The banks hold gold in bullion, but most small investors can simply buy gold coins, which are in denominations easier for small investors to handle. We recommend buying broadly traded coins from established mints to avoid questions of purity. Gold coins from these mints include, for example, the American Eagle, the South African Krugerrand, the Canadian Maple Leaf, and the Austrian Crown and Vienna Philharmonic.

For Y2K purposes, we recommend against buying *rare* gold coins. For our purposes, "intrinsic" value or "spot price" of coinage is much more relevant than the "numismatic" or "rarity" value of coins. The price of coins is determined daily and is linked to the price of gold in world markets. This can be found in every business newspaper or on-line with relative ease.

Investors shouldn't have to pay much by way of commission on gold coins. That means going to smaller shops, sometimes in your own neighborhood. Don't get sucked in by flashy television promotions by rare coin dealers. If you buy standard minted coins, you will pay a premium to the mint—sometimes as high as 3.5 percent. To reduce this cost, consider Austrian Crowns, which have low premiums relative to their price.

Some gold dealers offer depository services, but many dealers still require you to take personal delivery of gold coins. If storage is an issue for you, you can buy through firms who hold the coins for you or deposit them with firms like Brinks. We prefer reputable firms like Monex, which can be reached by phone or on the Net as follows:

Monex
4910 Birch Street
Newport Beach, CA 92660
Tel. 800-949-GOLD
Website: www.monex.com

Gold Stocks and Gold Funds

If you're more comfortable buying paper instead of actual gold, you can still play the gold market by purchasing select gold stocks or gold funds. Gold stocks do well when the price of gold rises, and gold funds tend to follow suit.

We should point out that these stocks have been beaten up badly as central banks (particularly Russia's) continued to sell gold through 1997 and 1998. Y2K could spur renewed interest in these companies, but we should also remind you that they may face many of the same Y2K problems in their mining and delivery systems as many other large companies. Nevertheless, if gold prices rise as we expect them to do, these stocks and funds are likely to outperform the market.

Below is a representative sample of gold stocks. Remember: Check with your broker before trading.

Gold Equities	Symbol
Barrick Gold	ABX
Battle Mountain Gold	BMG
Coeur D'Alene Mines	CDE

Echo Bay Mines	ECO
Franco-Nevada Mining Corp.	FN
Hecla Mining Company	HL
Homestake Mining Company	HM
Newmont Mining Corp.	NEM
Placer Dome, Inc.	PDG
Tech Corp.	TO

There are also many gold funds to choose among. The following is a representative sampling, but funds close out, merge, and open constantly, so check with your broker or contact the fund directly. Also, before buying, make sure you check all additional fees, including fees for redemption, what is called a "12b-1 fee" and any deferred sales charges, which can be quite stiff.

Gold Funds	Symbol	Load	Phone
Amer. Century Global Gold	BGEIX	None	800-345-2021
Bull and Bear Gold Investors	BBGIX	None	800-847-4200
Capiello-Rushmore Gold	CRGDX	None	800-343-3355
Fidelity Select Gold	FSAGX	3.00%	800-544-8888
Franklin Gold I	FKRCX	5.75%	800-342-5236
Franklin Gold II	FRGOX	1.00%	800-342-5236
Gabelli Gold	GOLDX	None	800-422-3554
Invesco Strategic Gold	FGLDX	None	800-525-8085
Lexington Goldfund	LEXMX	None	800-526-0056
Monterey OCM Gold	MNTGX	4.50%	800-251-1970
Oppenheimer Gold and Special Minerals A	OPGSX	5.75%	800-525-7048
Oppenheimer Gold and Special Minerals B	OGMBX	None	800-525-7048
Pioneer Gold A	PIGDX	5.75%	800-225-6292
Pioneer Gold B	PBGDX	None	800-225-6292
Pioneer Gold C	PCGDX	None	800-225-6292
Scudder Gold	SCGDX	None	800-225-2470
SoGen Gold A	SGGDX	3.75%	800-334-2143
USAA Gold	USAGX	None	800-382-8722
Van Eck Int'l. Investors Gold A	INIVX	5.75%	800-826-1115
Van Eck Int'l. Investors Gold B	GRFRX	5.75%	800-826-1115

Just as what goes up inevitably comes down, what has been badly pushed downward eventually will come back up. Such is the probable situation with U.S. equities. Many of the stocks that may be badly beaten up during the Y2K crisis will stage a comeback, and we are basically quite bullish on many long-term outlooks.

After the Y2K Dust Settles

But which stocks will stage the best comebacks? We are going to make a prediction here: In our view, certain *technology stocks* are likely to be the first and finest beneficiaries of the Y2K recovery.

Here is why: The market for non-Y2K-related software and for new hardware is likely to be depressed through 1999 and early 2000 as companies devote their attention to Y2K fixes and existing systems instead of upgrading or buying new software programs and machines. This means that these companies are among the earliest *hit* by Y2K fears, but also will be the earliest to *recover*, in our opinion, because once the Y2K bug is past, information technology managers will go on a buying spree to make up for the slowdown caused by Y2K.

The drop-off in orders for 1999 is already affecting some companies' near-term earnings forecasts. For example, Computer Associates (symbol: CA), whose earnings were in line with expectations in the second quarter of 1998, saw its share price nevertheless fall over 30 percent in a single day after it warned of future earnings shortfalls, brought about in part scaled-back customer purchases of software, given their existing expenditures on Y2K.[7]

Similarly, Hewlett Packard's (symbol: HWP) earnings in 1999 are expected to be impacted by Y2K as companies work on existing systems, according to an analysis by Merrill Lynch. The analysis noted that earnings are "back-end loaded" and "users could freeze second-half budgets due to Y2K,"[8] a warning that helped send Hewlett Packard shares tumbling in November 1998.

The sales and earnings slowdown in technology through 1999, however, is expected to right itself in mid-2000. In a survey of senior CIOs and IT managers of Fortune 500 companies conducted by Morgan Stanley Dean Witter, around one-third reported having *deferred new projects* because of Y2K projects. While this is not great for earnings in 1999, sometime after the crisis is past, *spending will pick up once again.* In fact, 57 percent of respondents to the survey indicated that they have a post-Y2K backlog of projects to address.[9]

Indeed, many IT managers may be so distraught by the effects of Y2K (and the likely impact of incomplete or bug-filled Y2K fixes) that they will gladly junk their legacy systems in favor of newer, bug-free systems. They likely will have the support of upper management as well, which will come to realize the consequences of relying on outdated equipment for core operations. We therefore forecast a surge in interest in new hardware sales beginning in mid-2000.

There are a few factors that investors should consider, however, that could put a damper on earnings of technology companies. First, there is an unknown level of risk due to legal liability. Experts are predicting a bonanza for lawyers after critical systems begin to fail. We expect most of the lawsuits will name the makers of the software and hardware as in part responsible for the failures. However, early legal victories appear to give vendors a slight advantage in arguing that the liability should not extend to them.

Second, if the situation overseas deteriorates further, this will impact sales of high-tech products. But again, we expect the Y2K situation to have a severe near-term impact on overseas economies, but for them to stage a recovery after the dust settles.

Finally, we predict IT managers will require high-tech firms to certify their software and hardware as being free from the Y2K bug, a new kind of "clean" standard in IT. Companies will probably also require their vendors and partners to impose the same standards to ensure data exchange can take place reliably. Resurfacing occurrences of Y2K after the crisis is supposedly past will absolutely slaughter some firms.

Our advice to shareholders is to wait until just after the crisis has passed before picking up technology shares. When will this be? Our best estimate is that the worst of the Y2K crisis will be over by the end of the first quarter of 2000, that the markets will spend another quarter or so digesting the damage, and that the money will flow back into high-tech equities by mid-2000. We therefore expect that there will be some excellent bargains available in technology stocks around the middle of the year 2000.

Internet Stocks

When computers start to get blamed for every problem under the sun in the year 2000, we predict that there will be a mass exodus from the high-flying Internet super-stocks of 1998 and 1999, which as this book goes to press are often trading at price-earning multiples that are hard to justify. The thinking behind a sell-off might go something like this: Y2K infects computers, and it will disproportionately affect telecommunications; the Internet is a marriage of computers and telecommunications; therefore the Internet is at major risk, along with the profits of Internet companies.

Here is the problem with that logic: True, the Internet depends on telecommunication and a distributed worldwide network of computer terminals. But that great thing about the Internet is precisely its distributed nature. If the Internet were a living organism, it would be more like a giant amoeba than an advanced animal with a heart, brain, and nervous system. If computers foul up in one part of the organism, they may go down for a while, but it doesn't affect the larger health of the system. And even where there are some bottlenecks through which a substantial amount of data transmissions flow, failures at these junctures are not expected to be long lived, and the Internet should be back up and running in short order.

Moreover, most of these companies operate on programming developed after the Y2K threat became clear, so the likelihood of internal disruptions is relatively low. And because *information* is what these companies deal in, there aren't the same worrisome issues of long-term supply chain disruptions. Just as many turned to the Internet for solutions when Galaxy IV failed as a way *around* their bottlenecked systems, we predict that many companies will see the advantages of distributed, information-based networking on the Internet and insist that their IT departments bring them up to speed on the information superhighway.

This suggests continued high growth and earnings for Internet portal companies, netware, internet connectivity equipment, integrated telecommunications companies, and consumer Internet commerce. Remember that most Internet stocks have reached stellar prices not because of expectations over short-term profits but over their long-term outlooks. In fact, many of these companies have yet to see any profits at all. Instead, investors are betting that years from now, these companies will be the super-engines of the U.S. economy and will be worth hundreds of times what they are today. If, as we expect, there is an overall panic over technology stocks, with the technology-heavy NASDAQ leading the sell-off of equities, once the Y2K dust begins to clear (probably sometime in mid-2000) we predict there will be some nice buying opportunities in Internet-related stocks.

Concluding Thoughts

The Chinese have a saying: "When all under heaven is in chaos, the opportunities abound." In fact, the Chinese word for *crisis* (*wei ji*) is composed of the two words for *danger* and *opportunity*. So should investors view the Y2K crisis next year when the computers wreak havoc under heaven.

TEN

PROTECTING ASSETS

A lot of us have benefited from a soaring stock market, rising property values, low inflation, and low interest rates. We've been able to refinance homes, get easy credit, take an additional vacation, and add to our Christmas shopping lists. Our prospects for retirement in style look good . . . for now. Ninety percent of investors should be looking to protect their assets during the Y2K crisis rather than speculate. Most investors want to know how to insulate their gains from the devastation of Y2K and the possibility of a global Y2K recession. The following quick checklist will tell you whether you fall into this category:

Do you:

- Worry about being able to making mortgage or credit card payments?
- Buy stocks and bonds mostly through mutual funds?
- Invest in order to put your kids through college?
- Have under $100,000 in total investments (excluding property)?
- Count on your portfolio for your retirement?
- Prefer to keep what you have rather than risk it trying to make quick money?

If you answered yes to *any* of the above questions, our recommendation is that you to consider yourself someone seeking to *protect assets* from Y2K. This means that you will be taking some simple but straightforward steps to reallocate your assets, and then waiting until the crisis is over before coming back in, probably at prices much lower than where you sold.

It is probably no surprise that the most defensive strategy would be to liquidate all of your equity holdings and keep everything in cash—and hidden under your mattress. We certainly don't advise that anyone take such extreme measures. A more practical solution is to make some general and commonsense reallocations within your portfolio. These include lightening your equity holdings considerably, buying U.S. government-guaranteed securities, keeping a healthy reserve of cash and cash equivalents, and even taking some positions in tangible assets like gold.

Even investors who don't perform major restructuring on their portfolios can benefit, however. By avoiding or underweighting the sectors we have discussed in the previous chapters, or by hedging against downward moves in the markets, investors looking to protect their assets will have already gone a long way already toward minimizing their risk from Y2K.

What follows is a quick reference chart of at-risk equities to help you shape a Y2K-ready portfolio. Remember that the recommendations below relate only to the question of how we think Y2K will affect earnings and share prices *holding all other factors equal*. There may be other factors that weigh as heavily or even more heavily into the equation than Y2K, but those would take a far more comprehensive analysis of the fundamentals and technicals of the stock, and they are beyond the scope of this book.

We won't tell you about price earnings ratios, fifty-two-week moving averages, or other factors that could affect earnings and stock prices. Our expertise is in Y2K only. So before making any trades, consult with your broker about the underlying strengths and weaknesses of the stock.

If you own one of the stocks we have discussed in this book or that is listed below, you should first ask yourself why you like the stock. If you have a good reason (for example you admire the company's products or its management, like the way the company has grown, or think it is a safe, long-term investment), then ask yourself if what we have said about the probable effects of Y2K changes any of those views.

If you are on the fence as to whether to hold the stock or sell it, to the risk-adverse investor we advise selling at least some of it before the end of 1999 or hedging against a downward move. You can always buy it back when the crisis is over, hopefully at a lower price than you sold it. We don't think that the equity markets are going to be a happy place to be in the last quarter of 1999 and the first quarter of 2000, so having a bit of cash ready to come back in when the markets settle down isn't a bad idea in any event.

Finally, while there are other companies in these sectors that we have not listed, they are smaller cap stocks whose equity prices tend to be more volatile for a host of reasons outside of Y2K. If a stock you own belongs in one of the sectors listed below but isn't part of our list, you can still ask yourself many of the same questions about its prospects under Y2K. Remember that we think that air transport, health care, electric utility, banking, and telecommunications are going to fare worse—or at least be more volatile—than other major sectors, so conservative investors should think twice about keeping their money locked up in these kinds of equities.

Air Transport in general has us concerned, particularly because of problems at airports and in air traffic control. In addition, the more international exposure an airline or air courier has, the worse we think it will fare in 2000.

UNDERWEIGHT

Major U.S. Airlines

Low to Medium International Exposure
Alaska Airlines (ALK)
America West Airlines (AWA)
Southwest Airlines Co. (LUV)
TWA World Airlines (TWA)
US Airways Group (U)

Regional U.S. Airlines
AirTran (AAIR)
Atlantic Southeast (ASAI)
Comair (COMR)
Mesa Air (MESA)
Mesaba Airlines (MAIR)
Skywest Airlines (SKYW)

Air Couriers,
Moderate International Exposure
Airborne Express (ABF)

AVOID

Major U.S. Airlines

High International Exposure
American Airlines (AMR)
Continental Airlines (CIAB)
Delta Airlines, Inc. (DAL)
Northwest Airlines (NWAC)
United Airlines (UAL)

Foreign Airlines
Air Canada (ACNAF)
British Airways (BAB)
Japan Airlines (JAPNY)
KLM Royal Dutch (KLM)

Air Couriers,
High International Exposure
BAX Global (PZX)
FDX Group (FDX)

Specialty/ATA Services
Airnet Systems (ANS)
Atlas Air (CGO)

Health Care companies are at risk, but the most vulnerable are hospitals and long-term care providers due to their dependence on at-risk medical devices and their exposure to problems in the Medicare and Medicaid reimbursement system.

UNDERWEIGHT

Physician Practices
Phys. Mgmt. Companies
MedPartners (MDM)
PhyCor (PHYC)
ProMedCo (PMCO)

Other/Specialty Services
AmSurg Corp (AMSG)
HEALTHSOUTH (HRC)
Magellan Health Services (MGL)

Health Maintenance Organizations
Managed Care Companies
Amer. Medical Security (AMZ)
First Commonwealth (FCWI)
Foundation Health Systems (FHS)
Health Power, Inc. (HPWR)
Humana, Inc. (HUM)
Maxicare Health Plans (MAXI)
MedicalControl (MDCL)
Mid-Atlantic Medical Services (MME)
Oxford Health Plans (OXHP)
PacifiCare Health Systems (PHSY)
RightCHOICE Managed Care (RIT)
Safeguard Health Enterprises (SFGD)
Sierra Health Services (SIE)
Trigon Healthcare (TGH)
United Healthcare (UNH)

AVOID

Hospitals
Columbia/HCA (COL)
Health Management Association
   (HMA)
Province Healthcare (PRHC)
Tenet Healthcare (THC)

Long-Term Care
Beverly Enterprises (BEV)
Genesis Health Ventures (GHV)
HCR Manor Care (HCR)
Integrated Health Serv. (IHS)
Mariner Post-Acute (MPN)
National HealthCare (NHC)
Sun Healthcare (SHG)
Vencor (VC)

With Electric Utilities, the issue is fuel supply. We advise staying clear of nuclear power dependent utilities, while reducing exposure to utilities that are highly dependent on coal and oil shipments for their generating plants.

UNDERWEIGHT

Moderate Fuel Supply Risk
Allegheny Energy (AYE)
American Electric Power (AEP)
Central and Southwest (CSR)
Conectiv (CIV)
DPL, Inc. (DPL)
DTE Energy Company (DTE)
Energy East Corp. (NEG)
Florida Progress Corp. (FPG)
LG&E Energy Corp. (LGE)
Mid-American Energy (MEC)
NIPSCO Industries (NI)
PacifiCorp (PPW)
Puget Sound Energy (PSD)
Southern Company (SO)
Texas Utilities (TU)
Western Resources, Inc. (WR)

AVOID

High Fuel Supply Risk
Carolina P&L (CPL)
Consolidated Edison (ED)
Dominion Resources (D)
Duke Energy (DUK)
Entergy Corp. (ETR)
FPL Group (FPL)
Niagara Mohawk (NMK)
Northern States (NSP)
Pacific Gas and Electric (PGE)
PECO Energy (PE)
Pinnacle West (PNW)
PP&L Resources (PPL)
Rochester G&E (RGS)
SCANA Corp. (SCG)
Unicom Corp. (UCM)

Independent Producers With Overseas Exposure
AES Corporation (AES)
CMS Corporation (CMS)

The admirable Y2K preparations of the Banking sector are counter-balanced by its high level of automation and interdependence. In particular, money center banks with higher than average exposure to global financial problems should be avoided.

UNDERWEIGHT

Nat'l. Money Center Banks
Bank One Corp. (ONE)
First Union Corp. (FTU)
Fleet Financial Group, Inc. (FLT)
KeyCorp (KEY)
PNC Bank Corp. (PNC)
SunTrust Banks, Inc. (STI)
Wells Fargo and Company (WFC)

Regional Banks
BB&T Corp. (BBK)
Canadian Imperial Bank (BCM)
Comerica, Inc. (CMA)
Fifth Third Bancorp (FITB)
Mellon Bank Corp. (MEL)
Mercantile Bancorporation (MTL)
National City Corp. (NCC)
Regions Financial Corp. (RGBK)
SouthTrust Corporation (SOTR)
U.S. Bancorp (USB)
Union BanCal Corp. (UNBC)
Wachovia Corp. (WB)

Savings and Loans
Charter One Financial, Inc. (COFI)
Golden West Financial (GDW)
GreenPoint Financial Corp. (GPT)
Washington Mutual, Inc. (WAMU)

AVOID

Int'l. U.S. Money Center Banks
BankAmerica Corp. (BAC)
BankBoston (BKB)
Bankers Trust (BT)
Bank of New York (BK)
Chase Manhattan (CMB)
Citigroup (CCI)
J. P. Morgan (JPM)
Republic New York (RNB)

Foreign Money Center Banks
Australia and New Zealand Bank
   (ANZ)
Bank of Tokyo-Mitsubishi (MBK)
Banco Santander, S.A. (STD)
Barclays PLC (BCS)
Corporación Bancaria de España
   (AGR)
Royal Bank of Canada (RY)
Westpac Bank Corp. (WBK)

Large Telecommunication companies may be ahead of the curve on Y2K compliance efforts and spending, but their interdependencies, particularly with smaller telcos, suppliers, and foreign operators, make them a risky investment.

UNDERWEIGHT	AVOID
Major Long Distance Carriers	*Smaller Carriers With*
AT&T (T)	*International Exposure*
MCI Worldcom (WCOM)	IXC Communications (IIXC)
	Primus Telecom (PRTL)
Domestic Carriers	Viatel, Inc. (VYTL)
Ameritech (AIT)	
Bell Atlantic Corp (BEL)	*Foreign Telcos*
BellSouth (BLS)	Compañía Telefónica de Chile (CTC)
GTE Corp. (GTE)	Deutsche Telekom AG (DT)
SBC Communications (SBC)	Hong Kong Telecom (HKT)
US West (USW)	Nippon T&T Corp. (NTT)
	Perusahaan Indonesia (IIT)
Wireless Communications	Portugal Telecom, S.A. (PT)
AirTouch (ATI)	Telebras (TBH)
China Telecom (Hong Kong) (CHL)	Telecom Italia, SpA (TI)
Ericsson (ERICY)	Telefónica Argentina (TAR)
France Telecom (FTE)	Telefónica, S.A. (TEF)
Motorola (MOT)	
Nokia Corp. (NOK)	
Vodafone Group PLC (VOD)	

Keeping Stock

After everything you have read so far, it may be tempting to sell every stock you own and keep clear of the markets. This is certainly a valid decision, but it isn't necessary. If you sell off a good chunk of your stock and stay partially invested, and then the market falls as we predict, you will be happy that at least you got out of as much as you did.

Of course, markets could continue to head upward. There is certainly a chance of that. We happen to think it is small and that keeping most of your money invested in this market is not worth the risk, given the uncertainty. But *any* market predictions are just that—predictions. There will be plenty of people out there, many with vested interests in a continued bull market, who will hasten to tell investors that the Y2K bug is a bust and that markets have nothing to fear. They could be right. We happen to think, based on our research, that they are dead wrong.

If you want to keep money in the market, consider lightening up on risky areas. Also, take advantage of some of the opportunities we identified in chapter 9 in personal service firms like temp agencies and security personnel and in technology stocks that are set to rebound after the crisis.

A Small Slice of Your Portfolio Pie

The stock market may be in for a sharp downward move in the latter part of 1999 or early 2000 given the looming Y2K crisis. Risk-adverse investors in particular should steer far clear of stocks. In total, we recommend keeping between 0 and 20 percent of your money in stocks, depending on your level of risk tolerance. But keep your eyes open: Once the crisis is past, there will be excellent buying opportunities.

A Good Hedge on Your Financial Shoulders

Under conditions of inflationary pressures, market uncertainty and global crisis, investors typically head for the hedges. Hedges are intended to offset the full impact of an event such as an inflationary spike. To hedge against the effects of inflationary pressures, big institutional investors often prefer sophisticated financial instruments. For

example, inflation usually means higher interest rates, which can be hedged by the pros with futures contracts. Inflation also usually means lower stock prices, which can be hedged with index options.

Under Y2K, however, some of these instruments aren't guaranteed to work so well. Remember, we are predicting that inflation at the producer levels will not necessarily set off higher interest rates. Investors seeking to hedge against inflation by betting interest rates will rise might wind up getting hit twice: Once when Y2K-induced inflation kills stock prices, and again when interest rates nevertheless continue to fall, wiping out hedge positions.

Stop-Loss Orders

Complex futures and options may be beyond the level and reach of the average investor trying to keep his or her money safe from the ravages of Y2K. One simple solution is for investors to protect what remaining stock positions they hold with *stop-loss orders*. These are standing instructions to your broker to automatically sell your stocks if prices slide beyond a given point. Many on-line trading services permit traders to set up stop-loss orders on their accounts with a few clicks of a mouse. Stop-loss orders can cost money to maintain, but they are like buying Y2K insurance. Talk to your broker about how to establish them, and by all means get them into place before the third quarter of 1999, when the extent of the Y2K problem will become clearer to everyone.

Writing Call Options

Another option for people who are not able or willing to sell a lot of their stock at once (for example, because of tax consequences) but who remain worried about the downside risk is to *write call options* on their stocks. This is a somewhat complicated procedure, so you need to consult with your broker carefully about it. In a nutshell, if you own a stock, you can often protect that stock from downside risk in the *options* market. An "option" is a contract that gives the owner the right, but not the obligation, to buy or sell a stock at a specific price for a defined period of time. Options on major stocks are traded every business day and the information on them is printed in business journals.

Writing call options is a perfect hedge for risk-adverse small investors. A "call" is a kind of option that gives someone else the right to "call away" stock at a given price called the strike price. A "covered call" means that, as the writer of the option, you actually own the stock you are optioning out. The buyer of your covered call is betting that the price of your stock will rise above the strike price.

For example, let's say you own 100 shares of General Motors. You don't want to sell or can't afford to sell the stock outright, even under the threat of the Y2K crisis. Assume GM is selling for around $70 a share in mid-1999. You write a covered call option with a strike price of $75. A buyer somewhere who thinks GM will rise above $75 will pay you cash today (called the "premium") for your call option. Let's assume he pays you a $300 premium.

If the stock is at $75 by the expiration date, there is no reason for the buyer to exercise the option, and you will pocket the $300 premium. If the stock falls to $65 a share, there is even less reason for the buyer to exercise the option, and your losses on the stock are insulated somewhat by the premium you earned by writing the call:

Present value	$ 6,500	($65 × 100)
Value when call written	$ 7,000	($70 × 100)
Loss	$ (500)	
Plus premium received	$ 300	
Net loss	$ (200)	

The drawback is that if the price of the stock *rises*, you miss out on the upswing. For example, if the price rises to $80 and the stock is called away by the buyer of your call at $75, you would have missed out on the chance of making another $200:

Present value	$ 8,000	($80 × 100)
Called away at	$ 7,500	($75 × 100)
Foregone profit	$ 500	
Less premium received	$ 300	
Total foregone profit	$ 200	

Another problem is that no one really knows when stocks are going to drop, and they could rise sharply before they fall. Or, they could fall below the amount you receive for your call. A further consideration is in the term of your option. Generally, the longer the term, the more buyers are willing to pay. If you want to cover your stock positions with calls, we advise that you aim to have your terms extend well into the year 2000 to maximize the amount you receive for your call.

Buying Married Puts

Another way to hedge against a downturn in stocks is to purchase *put options* on the stocks you own, so-called married puts. A "put" is the opposite of a "call." Buying a put on a stock gives you the right to "put" that stock to another investor at a certain price within a certain time period. In other words, for a premium, you can force someone (don't worry, you never actually meet this person) to buy the stock from you at the strike price, even if the stock is well below that price.

Let's take our example of your 100 GM shares. Suppose today GM is worth $70 a share, and you bought a put option on those stocks at a strike price of $75 with an expiration date in December 1999. You paid a $450 premium for the put.

If GM falls in price to $60 a share, you sure are happy you bought that put option. You can force someone else to pay $75 a share for your 100 shares, and you'll receive $7,500. Factoring in your premium, you will have made $50:

Value when put bought	$ 7,000	($70 × 100)
New put value	$ 7,500	($75 × 100)
Gain	$ 500	
Less premium paid	$ (450)	
Total profit	$ 50	

If you didn't buy the put, your stock would have been worth only $6,000, resulting in a loss of $1,000.

Of course, as GM stock falls, your put option rises in value, and you can sell it prior to the expiration date in the options market for many times what you paid for it. This would cushion the blow from the drop in GM's share price. If you are wrong and GM stock goes up, you lose out on some of the upside profit because of the premium you had to pay for the option.

Don't Go Naked

The average small investor looking to protect assets from Y2K shouldn't dive headlong into the options market, especially with so-called naked puts and calls. These are options bought and sold by an investor who does not own the underlying stock.

A naked put is a speculative investment, but at least the risk is limited to the amount paid for the premium. For example, in our above discussion on married puts, let's say you didn't actually *own* any of the GM stock. For the same $450, you bought the right to sell 100 shares of GM stock for $75. If the price of GM stock were to rise above $75, nobody would want your option and it would be nearly worthless as the expiration date draws nearer.

A much riskier (and foolish) investment would be to *write naked calls*. Let's say you wrote a call for 100 shares of GM stock, giving a buyer the right to call the stock away at $80 a share. Instead of falling, the GM stock price defies Y2K logic and continues to rise, say to $100 a share. The stock gets called away, but now you have to come up with the goods. In other words, you have to go out and *buy* that GM stock for $10,000 just to hand it over to someone else who gives you only $8,000. You are out thousands of dollars, lessened only by a small premium you got for writing the call.

Our advice to small investors is to stay clear of uncovered calls and unmarried puts. In fact, only use puts and calls to insure the stocks that, for whatever reason, you can't bring yourself to sell in advance of the Y2K market turmoil.

Cashing In

Cash is never a bad thing to have a lot of when the market falls. After all, you could have been holding loser stocks, and having cash around

> **Y2K STRATEGY**
> ## Cash Positions

means you can come in when you think stocks have bottomed out. Some investors worry that under Y2K the banks are going to screw up so badly that people won't have access to their cash, and that money market funds won't necessarily be Y2K-compliant and could lose whole accounts. Of course, these are possibilities, and the best way to protect yourself is to keep good paper records of your deposits and funds. But assuming there will be some errors, they shouldn't take more than a few days to resolve. Problems *accessing* cash should be ironed out long before you'll want to come back into the stock market as a buyer. (And if the problems have *not* been resolved, this is a good sign you should stay far clear of volatile markets until they are!)

We think that sometime in 1999, stock market investors will start selling off and building up their cash positions. The trick is to beat the rest to the sale and avoid getting trampled in a stampede.

Money Markets

Most people keep their money in checking and savings accounts in the bank. This is fine when the amount of cash you are planning to have around is relatively low. But Y2K-minded investors who plan to seriously build up their cash positions should look at various vehicles that could provide a higher rate of return.

Nonbank *money markets* are probably your best bet. There are over 1,000 money funds with over a trillion dollars in assets. Most money markets even permit you to write checks, provided the amount is over a few hundred dollars (perfect for mortgage and credit card payments). While bank money markets typically only pay investors *half* the current T-bill rate, more competitive money market funds can provide up to twice that rate with the same or smaller risk.

Y2K investors should bear in mind that not all money markets will be equal to the task during the Y2K crisis. Money markets invest in a host of different sectors in order to pay out their competitive rates. These include T-bills, commercial loans to big corporations, various kinds of certificates of deposit (such as jumbo, Eurodollar, and Yankee-dollar), repurchase agreements (overnight interbank loans) and bankers' acceptances (used by banks to finance foreign trade). Unlike bank deposits, not all money markets are not federally insured, and there is a risk of loss, even though it is normally slight.

If you want to play it extra safe, avoid money markets that have high exposure to general purpose investments such as commercial paper, foreign banks and trade, and jumbo CDs (uninsured large deposits at banks). The chance of a default among these borrowers is historically low to negligible, but we can't say for certain what the risk during the Y2K crisis will be. If you do wind up investing in a general purpose fund, ask whether it is insured with limited default insurance.

Also on the "avoid" list are money market funds that bill themselves as tax free (that is, no federal income tax, and sometimes no state income tax). These low-yielding funds typically invest only in short-term municipal obligations, which, as we discussed in chapter 8, are not a solid bet during the Y2K crisis.

We would stick to money markets that invest primarily or exclusively in government securities. The safest bet would be U.S. Treasury funds, which invest only in T-bills backed by the U.S. government. In most states, these funds have the added advantage of being free from state taxes (check with your broker to see if your state qualifies). Companies such as Dreyfus, Fidelity, T. Rowe Price, and Vanguard all offer these types of funds and can be contacted as follows:

Dreyfus 100 percent
  U.S. Treasury
Money Market Fund
(800) 782-6620

Fidelity Spartan
  U.S. Treasury
Money Market Fund
(800) 544-8888

T. Rowe Price U.S. Treasury
Money Fund
(800) 638-5660

Vanguard Money Market
Reserves/Money Market Portfolio
(800) 662-7447

For a complete list of 100 percent U.S. Treasury funds ranked by yield, look up the IBC Data website at www.ibcdata. com/mfs/tresretl.htm.

Another consideration is money market expenses. Like mutual funds, money markets charge their investors an annual fee, which averages around 0.7 percent. With money markets paying an average of around 5 percent yields, this fee could be significant. For a look at some low-cost money market funds, check out the IBC website listed above.

Cold, Hard Cash

Aside from money markets, where should investors keep the rest of their cash? You should think about keeping enough cash on hand (we recommend putting it in a personal safe) to get through normal expenses. You probably won't even need the cash for more than a week, but to be on the safe side you might go as high as one month's worth. The chances that Y2K problems will plague ATMs and bank accounts much longer than that are pretty small. If your bank is one of the unlucky few that are forced by the Feds or state regulators to shut down operations, the bank will probably be sold to or merged with a more compliant bank, and your money shouldn't disappear from the computers.

If you insist on withdrawing large sums of cash, keep in mind that there really are other dangers beside Y2K, like losing it or being robbed. One possibility is to put whatever large cash withdrawals you make into your bank's safety deposit box, rather than walk down the street to your home with it. Another is to obtain traveller's checks in lieu of cash.

We also remind you to always keep a good paper trail. The Federal Deposit Insurance Corporation suggests customers keep records of bank deposits, investments, loan payments, and other account activities for at least the first few months of 2000.[1]

Before you keep huge sums of cash in any bank, make sure that the bank is insured by the FDIC. (The vast majority are.) Look for the FDIC signs, sometimes labeled under BIF (Bank Insurance Fund) or SAIF (Savings Association Insurance Fund). If you are lucky enough to have more than $100,000 in cash in a single institution, by all means spread out your deposits among different types of ownership (like CDs, savings, and a separate individual retirement account) or among different banks so that you are completely covered. Bank failures are not out of the realm of possibility during the Y2K crisis, so prudence suggests you not put any amount at risk if you can help it.

So, how much cash should investors hold? We think a good target is 30 to 50 percent of your total assets in cash and cash equivalents.

Fixed-interest government investments may not be glamorous, but the bond market could be a good shelter during the Y2K storm—with a few important exceptions. As a general rule, treasuries will benefit from falling interest rates. When interest rates fall, bond prices will rise as existing bold holders' fixed payments appear relatively attractive. And as long as you stick to U.S. government-backed securities, there is virtually no risk of nonpayment. (On the other hand, as we explain below, the state and local bond market could be in for a rough ride.)

Y2K STRATEGY
Investing in the Bond Market

Treasuries have other advantages. They are free from state income tax, which makes a big difference if you live in a high-tax state. They are also highly liquid, meaning that when you want to buy or sell them, there will certainly be a market. And they can't be *called away* like certain corporate bonds, meaning they can't be retired early just because interest rates are falling.

T-bills

Treasury bills are so highly liquid that some investors consider them to be a kind of cash. If you're thinking of buying a bank CD instead of a T-bill, think again. T-bills earn higher interest rates than most bank CDs, are free from state and local taxes, and are completely backed by the U.S. government. And you could see the face value of your T-bills rise slightly as the Fed takes action in the credit markets or the FOMC starts buying them up. Try doing that with a bank CD.

To understand how the T-bill is priced, look at the *discount rate* on the T-bill. T-bills start at a denomination of $10,000, so if the discount rate is 4 percent, the price to you is $9,600. You send a check to the government for $10,000, and they'll mail you a check for $400. When the T-bill matures, you'll get another $10,000. This means the actual yield is slightly higher than the discount. (In this case, the actual yield is $10,000 divided by $9,600, or 4.17 percent.)

T-bills are also very easy to pick up. Three- and six-month T-bills are auctioned basically every Monday by the U.S. Treasury, with bills issued every Thursday. Every four weeks, they auction fifty-two-week T-bills. They are also sold in secondary markets after they are first auctioned. Look in your local newspaper's money rate section to find the latest auction results and secondary market prices.

How do you buy T-bills? You can buy secondary market T-bills through your bank or your broker, but small investors can also buy newly issued T-bills through a nifty program called Treasury Direct. This permits individuals to participate in auctions along with the big buyers. The interest is sent straight to your bank, and the program even allows for automatic reinvestment of maturing bills into new T-bills of the same maturity. To get a new account request, call or visit your nearest Federal Reserve and ask for Form PD F 5182. Or download the form at the U.S. Treasury's website at www.publicdebt.treas. gov/sec/secform1.htm.

Buying T-bills directly has one drawback, however. You usually won't know how good (or bad) a rate you receive on your auction bid until all bids are settled. In the secondary market, you will always get the rate posted.

U.S. Treasury Notes and Bonds

For risk-adverse investors, we recommend getting into shorter-term U.S. Treasury notes—fixed income assets that are of mid-range maturity, say two to three years. Long-term bond prices, such as those on thirty-year treasury bonds, tend to be more volatile than short-term bond prices. If you are convinced, however, that interest rates will continue to come down through the crisis, you can pick up long-term bonds and hope to sell them for a much higher price than you paid.

The greatest risk in holding bonds is that inflation will catch investors unprepared. If Y2K-induced failures raise the cost of doing business, as we expect, there is a risk of seeing inflation at the consumer level. This wouldn't bode well for any fixed-income asset like a note or a bond. Remember, however, that companies will strive to keep prices competitive in the short term rather than sacrifice long-term market share. We are also predicting that global economic slowdowns will counterbalance inflationary pressures and that central banks will want to maintain market liquidity, leading many, including our own, to keep rates low. In our view, these competing considerations weigh in favor of continued low interest rates and little to no inflation at the consumer level.

In fact, if there is a worsening of the global economy, we could see significant deflation despite increases to manufacturing costs. Deflation is *terrific* for fixed income Treasuries. The last deflationary period we saw was during the Great Depression, when Treasuries became extremely attractive.

If the possibility of Y2K-induced inflation still has you very concerned, there is the option of buying *inflation-adjusted* bonds, which are a recently introduced way to always stay one step ahead of inflation. The idea is simple. The U.S. Treasury will *adjust* the price of the bond depending on inflation, and then make the interest payments based on the adjusted price. The drawback is that the yield is lower, and both the interest and any price adjustments to the bonds are taxable in the year it is credited, even though you won't see the interest until the bond matures.

Government Agency Bonds

For only a little bit of extra risk, you can pick up U.S. government and federal agency bonds that, while not backed by a 100 percent guarantee, are almost certainly going to be covered by Congress in the event of a default by the issuing agency. The good news is, the bonds tend to pay a higher rate. We recommend bonds issued by one of the following government agencies:

- Federal Credit Financial Assistance Corporation
- Federal Farm Credit Bank System
- Federal Home Loan Bank Financing Corporation
- Resolution Trust Corporation
- Student Loan Marketing Association

Note that we have some reservations about *mortgage-backed securities* during the Y2K crisis. Unlike other bonds, a drop in interest rates doesn't necessarily translate into a rise in the price of the bond, since the bond's value is affected by the rate at which people with mortgages refinance or move. Indeed, often the prices of these bonds *fall* with falling rates. For Y2K investors moving into bonds, we therefore recommend staying away from bonds issued by Ginnie Mae (the Government National Mortgage Association), Fannie Mae (the Federal National Mortgage Association) and Freddie Mac (the Federal Home Loan Mortgage Association).

A Big Slice of Your Portfolio Pie

So how much should you hold in T-notes or T-bonds? We think a good 40 to 60 percent of your money can safely be held in U.S. government securities. Be prepared to cash out of these positions once it is clear that the crisis is past. You can buy bonds through your broker or by using the Treasury Direct system, discussed earlier.

No Money In Munis

In chapter 8, we explained why investments in unguaranteed government bonds such as state bonds and munis (municipal bonds) should in general be avoided. We recommend against moving any of your assets into state bonds and munis unless it is absolutely clear that the issuer has completed its Y2K programs within budget and left plenty of money in its coffers to cover all contingencies.

Y2K STRATEGY

When Bonds Are a Bust

Because these contingencies may include lawsuit liability for which the local government cannot get insurance coverage, there is a huge question in our minds over whether any local government will have its reserves completely protected from Y2K fallout. If you are holding munis now, consider selling them if you can't get a strong indication that the credit rating of the issuer is not at risk from Y2K.

If the issuer of your state or muni bond sees a drop in its credit rating due to Y2K problems, this will not only tell you that the issuer is at risk of default, it will also undermine the face value of your bond. We expect to see many credit downgrades during the Y2K crisis, because municipalities are among the least prepared of sectors.

Remember that local governments are required to disclose their Y2K expenditures and detail their Y2K programs, and this information should appear in the risk factors section of any prospectus for a bond issuance. Certainly, before you purchase any new munis, you should review this information carefully, as we think it will be the single most important question for most local government bond issuances as we go into 2000.

If you still want to hold munis, at least make sure there are other protections that the issuer is offering, such as insurance against default.

Some munis are backed by third-party insurers, such as the Municipal Bond Insurance Association and the American Municipal Bond Assurance Corporation. Ratings on bonds insured under these third-party arrangements are based on the strength of the insurer, not the issuer. While these insurance companies are quite strong and well capitalized, it is possible that widespread municipal bond defaults could strain their standing in the eyes of the credit agencies. Finally, if you must own some municipal bonds, you should favor general obligation bonds over special revenue bonds, which are at greater risk of nonpayment.

The states are in a somewhat better situation than the local governments. The threat of liability from Y2K lawsuits usually doesn't run as deeply with states. States are generally immune to this type of liability unless they pass laws making it possible to sue the state for money—an unlikely legislative action piece, we'd venture to guess. States also have broader resources than municipalities and can more easily borrow or go into debt in order to make good on bond payments. Still, states face credit downgrades if their system failures impact upon their ability to collect revenue or make timely bond payments, so there is some appreciable risk in state-issued bonds as well.

Corporate Bonds

Corporations also issue bonds that usually pay higher interest than government bonds due to the fact that they are not guaranteed. Large corporations will be anxious to make sure bondholders are paid, since defaults would have serious long-term repercussions for their ability to borrow money. But even the highest-rated bonds have risk of being downgraded, or even of going into default. In the period from 1900 to 1943, around 6 percent of top-rated bonds defaulted, many during the Great Depression.[2] Lately, defaults of top-rated bonds are almost unheard of, but again we wouldn't rule anything out during Y2K. We wouldn't be surprised if, throughout the crisis, many companies are dealt credit downgrades that could drive down the value of their bonds.

Many corporate bonds are also *callable*, meaning that as interest rates fall, the corporation can close out the bond and force a buyback at its principal value. This takes the upside out of a lot of bond plays, which otherwise benefit from falling interest rates.

We would *certainly* stay clear of any noninvestment grade bonds (rated BB or below). These bonds may attempt to lure you with high interest rates, but the risk is not worth the reward. Where a company has a chance of an upgrade of its credit rating, these bonds sometimes became good speculative investments. But the chance for simultaneous major business disruptions and worldwide bankruptcies and defaults is appreciably higher, so the junk bond market is not somewhere investors will want to be.

Bond Funds

As you might know or could probably guess, there are also thousands of "bond funds" that operate much like typical stock mutual funds. However, because we are recommending investors stick to U.S. Treasuries, it doesn't make much sense to pay fees and get into bond funds that carry only U.S. Treasuries when it is so easy for investors to buy them on their own. We recommend bond funds only for those investors who cannot meet the minimum investment of $10,000 for T-bills.

Go for the Gold

In chapter 8, we discussed why we think holding tangible assets like gold is a good strategy, given the economic uncertainty that Y2K will present. But how much gold should investors hold? That of course depends on the risk tolerance of each investor. In a general sense, gold is riskier than holding dollars, since the downside risk of holding cash is the difference between inflation and interest rates, while gold prices can swing 20 to 30 percent in a year (but usually have a much smaller range). On the other hand, gold has an upside potential that cash does not.

Y2K STRATEGY

Gold Holdings

For risk-adverse investors, we recommend that you keep between 10 and 20 percent of your total cash assets in gold. Sometime after the Y2K crisis passes, you can convert your gold back into cash, perhaps with a nice profit.

What would a Y2K portfolio for investors seeking to *protect assets* look like? We have put a few of them together, designed to correspond to various risk-comfort levels. None of them is designed to make you big sums of money during the Y2K crisis; rather, they are meant to protect your hard won gains of the previous years' bull market. The predominant allocation

Y2K STRATEGY
Sample Portfolios

for all of these portfolios is in U.S. Treasuries, with cash or cash equivalents (including gold) making up most of the rest. We recommend that only a small percentage of your portfolio be in equities. We understand that most people are currently highly invested in stocks, so this is where the greatest number of Y2K asset reallocations will have to occur.

Asset Allocation Recap

Bonds (U.S. Treasuries or U.S. government agency bonds)	Cash (Cash, money market funds, gold)	Stocks (Low Y2K risk, all others hedged)	Hedges (Covered calls, married puts)
40% to 60%	30% to 50%	0% to 20%	0% to 5%

Sample Portfolio One: "I think a serious Y2K recession is coming."

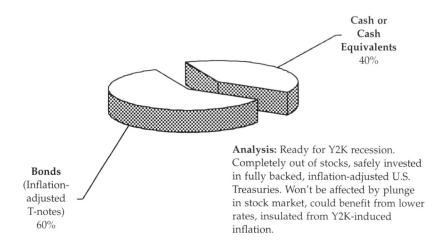

Cash or Cash Equivalents 40%

Bonds (Inflation-adjusted T-notes) 60%

Analysis: Ready for Y2K recession. Completely out of stocks, safely invested in fully backed, inflation-adjusted U.S. Treasuries. Won't be affected by plunge in stock market, could benefit from lower rates, insulated from Y2K-induced inflation.

Sample Portfolio Two: "I think there will be twelve months of disruptions."

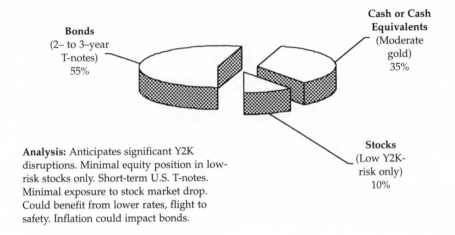

Bonds
(2– to 3–year
T-notes)
55%

**Cash or Cash
Equivalents**
(Moderate
gold)
35%

Analysis: Anticipates significant Y2K disruptions. Minimal equity position in low-risk stocks only. Short-term U.S. T-notes. Minimal exposure to stock market drop. Could benefit from lower rates, flight to safety. Inflation could impact bonds.

Stocks
(Low Y2K-
risk only)
10%

Sample Portfolio Three: "I think there will be six months of disruptions."

Analysis: Middle-of-the-roader. Expects mission-critical failures in certain sectors. Downside risk in stocks hedged with married puts, covered calls. Could benefit from drop in interest rates, some inflation risk.

**Cash or Cash
Equivalents**
(Some gold)
30%

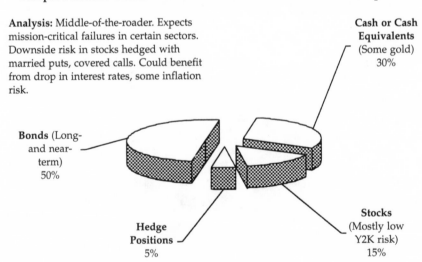

Bonds (Long-
and near-
term)
50%

**Hedge
Positions**
5%

Stocks
(Mostly low
Y2K risk)
15%

Sample Portfolio Four: "I think there will be three months of disruptions"

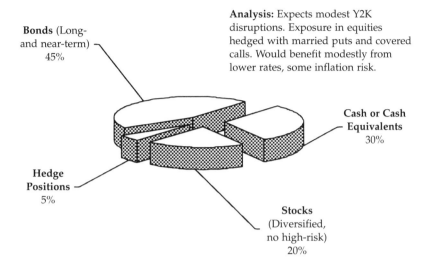

Bonds (Long-
and near-term)
45%

Analysis: Expects modest Y2K
disruptions. Exposure in equities
hedged with married puts and covered
calls. Would benefit modestly from
lower rates, some inflation risk.

**Cash or Cash
Equivalents**
30%

**Hedge
Positions**
5%

Stocks
(Diversified,
no high-risk)
20%

ELEVEN

PROFITING FROM Y2K

From the last chapter it should be clear that investors can take con-crete measures to protect their assets from Y2K devastation. Investors willing and able to take some risks with a percentage of their money, however, can also use the Y2K crisis to *increase* their net worth through *speculative Y2K investing*. Aggressive trading is not for the weak of heart, however. To help you determine if you are ready to use Y2K to make loads of money, ask yourself the following questions:
Do you:

- Have time to track investments and make quick decisions to buy and sell?
- Have enough in other assets to risk losing some or all of the money you use for speculation?
- Have enough cash to cover margins calls, contract shortfalls, and losing positions?
- Feel sure that losing money will not endanger your credit his-tory or force you to lose other assets such as your house, car, or personal property?
- Think that large swings in the markets won't keep you up at night?

If you answered yes to all of the above (and don't qualify as strictly a "protect assets" type from the previous chapter), then you qualify as an investor who could potentially *profit greatly* during the Y2K crisis.

Y2K risk takers will be in for a wild ride through the crisis. The reason for this is simple: Y2K is very unpredictable. From what we have seen, Y2K could have a devastating impact on the global econ-omy and on markets. But Y2K could also be a nonevent, depending on whom you believe. Y2K will constantly be in the news as we approach the end of 1999. Investors will need to keep a close watch on how remediation efforts progress in the key sectors we have discussed. Ultimately, each investor will have to use his or her own judgment about how bad the effects from Y2K will be.

Another tricky aspect of Y2K is that, assuming Y2K will create economic problems, it's hardly clear when markets will start to discount for those problems. Will it take actual system failures for markets to sell off? If so, when will those failures occur? Will depositor withdrawals spark weakness in banks and start a bear market? If so, when will people start to take their money out?

While we can't provide you with hard and fast dates by which you should get your own portfolio in Y2K shape, we do believe that the closer we get to the year 2000, the more investors (especially big institutions) will begin to focus on the problem and discount company earnings—and therefore share prices. We expect that the markets will start to get truly nervous about Y2K sometime after mid-1999. There are a few key dates worth watching:

- August 22, 1999: The Global Positioning System, which is a satellite network operated by the U.S. Navy and used by planes and ships worldwide to navigate, as well as by major international banks to calculate overnight interest, will roll over and reset. Apparently, the system has been counting off weeks since January 5, 1980, but can only "count" up to 1,024 before starting over. Problems with the GPS may be a precursor to the kinds of difficulties Y2K could present. For more information, see the navy's GPS website at www.tycho.usno.navy.mil/ gps_week.html.

- September 9, 1999: This date is entered on many computers as 9/9/99. In many systems, "9999" means "end of file" and will cause computers to stop accepting new data or to roll over.

- September 17, 1999: This is the first of two important "triple-switching" days, when traders experience the expiration of stock option, stock index options, and stock index futures. If Y2K has been on the minds of many, expect particular volatility on this date.

- September 23, 1999: This is the critical "100 days to go" date. Expect media attention to be riveted on Y2K and how much of a disruption the world can expect.

- December 17, 1999: This is the second crucial triple-witching day in U.S. markets. Y2K could be the predominant factor for increased volatility on this date.

On the other side of the crisis, it is hard to predict how long the negative effects of Y2K will *last*. Some experts point out that we will be dealing with computer-related date problems for many years into the new millennium. But that doesn't mean that it will take that long for the economy to recover. We could be back on track in a matter of weeks, or it could take a few months to a year.

We're going out on a limb with this prediction: Our best guess is that the worst of the crisis will strike in January and begin to clear by mid-February. The economic fallout will probably last through mid-2000. Because we think the bear market will begin the third quarter of 1999, the downward pressure will continue for a total of about one year.

This is only an educated guess, however, because so much depends on how much can be repaired prior to the start of the year 2000. But we will be the first to tell you that nobody can give you complete assurances. Anyone who tells you otherwise is lying. The reason is that everything is contigent on how much of a downstream or upstream effect Y2K system failures will have. For example, if Y2K impacts oil production (as we expect it to do), this could be a minor disruption resulting in a blip in the price of a barrel of oil, therefore barely impacting the earnings of utilities and transportation companies for which oil is such a huge factor. On the other hand, if oil production disruption is extensive, oil prices could soar and stay high for an extended period of time. This would absolutely *kill* earnings for companies such as the airlines, as well as drive every manufacturer's costs up.

One thing at least is clear: A lot of money stands to be made by those who can correctly predict the effects of Y2K. Those willing to take some risks could make a great deal of money very quickly. In this section, we briefly outline some of the high-risk, high-potential-return strategies that aggressive investors can employ to build wealth.

One word of warning: None of the discussions below will give you *specific* advice on how much to risk or invest. We can't do this because every investor is different. We do, however, put together some handy sample investment strategies at the end of this chapter that you might find useful in forming your own Y2K investor battle plan.

The futures market may seem too bewildering for most investors, especially when they envision pit callers in the Chicago Board of Trade shouting and hand-signaling their trades. For most investors, trying to figure out the futures market is like looking at a craps table in Las Vegas for the first time. The dice are rolling and lots of money is chang-

Y2K STRATEGY
Trading in Futures

ing hands, but most onlookers have no idea what is really happening.

The concept behind futures is actually quite straightforward, even if the speculative nature of them may prove too heady for most investors. Futures are nothing more than *contracts*. They are promises to make or take delivery of a item at a specific price by a specific time in the future. Thus, futures markets actually act to *reduce risks* for many traders.

For example, a manufacturer that knows that it will require a lot of oil for its production lines six months from now can go to the futures market and lock in the price today for a particular grade and amount of oil. This way, the manufacturer is eliminating the risk that the price of oil will rise drastically, driving up its costs and killing its profits. Sure, the price of oil could fall, and that is the risk the manufacturer takes, but at least it knows that at the price it has agreed to pay for the oil, it will be able to meet its cost and profit targets.

When most people think about *futures*, they think *commodities*. But in addition to commodities like oil, gold, silver, and pork bellies, there are financial futures such as currencies, stock indexes, and interest rates. These are harder for many investors to grasp, since they don't really concern a tangible good that you take or make delivery of. If it makes it easier for you, think of financial futures as a kind of "raw material" that financial markets, institutions, and businesses use to operate, generate trade, and invest. Large financial institutions use financial futures to hedge against risk to their holdings, just as manufacturers and farmers use other commodity futures to plan their business operations.

In addition to the traders that use futures to lock in prices or hedge against price swings, *speculators* abound in the futures market. This is because a very small amount of money put down on deposit can control a very large contract. Speculators never intend on actually making or taking delivery of a commodity. After all, what would you do with

5,000 bushels of corn? Instead, speculators are betting that the prices of commodities will go a certain way, and they hope to make money on the price change, getting out of the market before actual delivery takes place. In fact, 98 percent of contracts made in the futures markets get canceled out before expiration without any delivery whatsoever.

Example of a Futures Trade

Let's assume you wanted to use futures to speculate on the price of oil. One thousand barrels of oil, if purchased outright, would require you to put up in the neighborhood of $12,000 to $13,000 at today's prices. But you can *control* that same amount of oil by buying an oil futures *contract*, with between 2 and 10 percent down.

Let's say the price of oil is $12 a barrel, and you only need to come up with a 5 percent deposit on a contract for 1,000 barrels, or $12,000 × .05 = $600. You call up a commodities broker, place the order, and pay your down payment, or "margin deposit," or "initial margin" (not to be confused with the margin requirements of your account with your stockbroker).

After the order is placed and filled, you wait. Each day, your account is valued based on the price of oil, what the industry calls marking to market. If the price of oil rises by 60 cents a barrel, you are psyched. Your account is credited an amount of 1,000 × $0.60, or $600. It's only a 5 percent gain for the contract, but it's a 100 percent gain for your account. The math looks like this:

Price of oil at time of purchase	$12 / barrel
Contract value ($12 × 1000)	$12,000
Initial margin ($12,000 × .05)	$600
Price of oil after rise	$12.60 / barrel
New contract value ($12.60 × 1000)	$12,600

Congratulations! You have made a quick and tidy $600 profit in the oil futures market. You happily tell your broker to reverse out your position by *selling* a futures contract with the same expiration date, which cancels out the original trade. (While this may seem odd to you, the clearinghouses that take care of this don't really care who is buying and selling which contract, as long as they are for the same commodity at the same expiration date.)

There Are Dangers and Downsides . . .

So, futures sound great, right? But what happens if oil prices move the other way? The effects can be devastating. Let's say the price fell to $11.50 per barrel. Your account would be debited 1,000 × $.50 = $500, leaving you only $100. This is just over a 4 percent move in the price of the contract, but it nearly wipes out your $600 investment.

From this, you can appreciate that futures trading is not for everyone, and even for experienced investors, it should only comprise a modest percentage of your total portfolio. Besides the danger of a sudden downside move that drains your account value, if your account falls below a certain minimum amount, your broker could require you to put up *more money* or be liquidated. This could be repeated (to your horror) every time the price of oil falls.

In fact, we should warn that statistically speaking, the odds are strongly against you; *the vast percentage of futures traders lose money every year.* In addition, you'll soon discover that futures brokers charge much higher commission rates than the average stockbroker—sometimes up to ten times as much. So before you get into the futures market, you need to have more than just a strong feeling that your particular position will pay off.

. . . And There Are Great Opportunities

That said, Y2K will present traders with tremendous opportunities in certain commodity and financial futures. Again, assuming we will see rapid run-ups in commodity prices and the dollar or a precipitous fall in the stock market, foreign currencies, and interest rates, the most difficult question will be *when* these changes are likely to occur. Because markets are anticipatory, the opportunities may arise long before there are any serious indications of Y2K-related failures, probably sometime after mid-1999. Much depends on the level of public and media attention that Y2K is given. As this book goes to print, however, we have already seen increasing attention to Y2K in major broadcast and print media, as well as talk of Hollywood thriller-style movies about Y2K to be released in the summer of 1999. What impact this type of public discourse and hype is having on investor sentiment is anyone's guess, but it is almost certainly going to add to market volatility.

Commodity Futures

Among the commodity futures, we see strong potential for upward moves in the price of gold as nervous investors around the world seek protection from inflation and uncertainty. Gold has been severely price-depressed, in part because of improved mining techniques and selling of gold by Russia, thus the chance of strong downward movements is relatively low while the upside remains high. Our prediction is that the price of gold will rise in direct proportion to the severity of the Y2K crisis, so if the disruptions are as serious as many predict, hang on to your hats and watch gold shoot through the roof.

Among the precious metals, our other bet would be silver, which is also near historic lows. Silver, however, is not traditionally as much of a safe haven in times of trouble, so we tend to view it somewhat less favorably than gold. (Still, we are intrigued by moves by legendary trader Warren Buffet, who in February 1998 bought 20 percent of the world's annual silver production.)

Other industrial metals such as copper, lead, nickel, tin, and aluminum may also rise in price if Y2K disrupts supply. However, if Y2K plunges the world into a deep recession, a drop in demand could be more than enough to offset upward pressures on commodity prices.

The price of oil and other energy commodities such as gasoline, heating oil, propane, and natural gas may see a spike as supplies are limited by Y2K production problems. We temper this prediction somewhat by the same concern we have with industrial metals: it is possible that weak global demand due to continued economic slowdowns will keep oil prices low despite a supply crunch. However, oil is also trading at near historic lows, so the downside risk to traders may be worth the risk.

We are less convinced that the production and delivery of grain, livestock, and other foods such as orange juice and coffee will be affected by Y2K, though this certainly is possible in a worst case scenario. The possibility of bad or good weather, however, probably has a stronger impact on such prices than will Y2K, so these commodities are not viewed as strong Y2K plays. And if it turns out that Y2K *is* so bad as to disrupt the food supply chain for more than a few days, there are other futures positions that would better benefit investors.

Currencies

We anticipate a significantly stronger U.S. dollar as global investors head for quality, much as we saw during the initial stages of the Asian financial crisis. However, it is likely that the Fed will intentionally seek to damper enthusiasm for the dollar. We might even see concerted effort among central banks to stabilize the dollar should it rise too quickly, much as we saw in the summer of 1998. Lower interest rates will also make the dollar relatively less attractive. But despite these efforts to keep the dollar stable or even to weaken it, we predict a surging dollar in the latter part of 1999 as the extent of the lack of preparedness in key countries becomes more evident. Investors seeking to capitalize on this will buy up U.S. dollar futures in anticipation.

On the other side, we forecast weak foreign currencies in nations that are less well prepared, such as Germany and Japan. We could see further weakness in battered Asian currencies, such as the Thai baht and the Korean won. Traders betting against these currencies would come into the market by selling futures contracts on those currencies, predicting their values will fall. Look also for currencies in Latin America, particularly Brazil, to come under pressure.

Stock Index Futures

Speculators betting on a stock market tumble or even a collapse might consider selling stock index futures. The most commonly traded future is the S&P 500. Traders can also bet against stocks by selling futures on the S&P 400 Midcap Index, the American Major Market Index, and the Value Line Composite Index.

Stock index futures are perhaps the most difficult futures to predict in terms of the timing of their major movements. We expect that investors will become fully focused on the Y2K issue in the final quarter of 1999, so it may be prudent to have future positions in place well ahead of that time. As we mentioned earlier, watch out for high volatility on Friday, September 17, 1999, and especially Friday, December 17, 1999, which are the "triple witching days" when stock options, stock index options, and stock index futures all expire and traders rush to offset buy and sell orders.

Well-heeled investors who insist on continuing to hold on to significant equity positions can hedge against potential downside movements in the markets by selling short S&P 500 futures contracts. The dollar value of an S&P 500 futures contract is 500 times the index's current value. So if the S&P is trading at around 1,250, the dollar value of the contract is $500 × 1,250 = $625,000. Again, the amount you would have to put down is just a fraction of this, but it is still in the tens of thousands of dollars. If the market falls, the loss in share value can be at least partially offset by a fall in the value of the contract sold, so that the short-trader can buy it back at a much cheaper price.

Interest Rate Futures and TED-Spreads

Finally, traders can bet on continued falling interest rates by taking positions in the interest rate futures markets. These are even more complex and bewildering than other futures markets, so only experienced investors should swim in these waters. As a straight play, investors can buy U.S. Treasury futures (bills, notes, and bonds) in anticipation of future interest rate cuts as a liquidity crisis deepens. In general, the longer the term of the bond, the more volatile it tends to be, and therefore the more volatile its futures contracts also tend to be.

One strategy, called a TED-spread, we find particularly intriguing, even though it is highly technical and not suitable for the average investor to try. In futures jargon, a "spread" is a pair of futures positions in the same commodity that are completely offsetting, so that one always wins and one always loses. Why would anyone do this? The trick in any spread is to capture the *difference* between the two contracts and have it be in your favor. Risk is reduced, but so is upside potential.

TED-spreads are not really "spreads" per se because they involve betting on U.S. T-Bills futures while betting against Eurodollar futures. (Eurodollars are U.S. dollars deposited and drawing interest in European banks.) A TED-spread seeks to capture the *increasing difference* between the two interest rates.

T-bills are backed by the U.S. government and therefore pay lower interest and cost more. Eurodollars aren't backed at all, and therefore they pay higher interest and are relatively cheaper.

When rates are falling, T-bills futures tend to rise in value more quickly that Eurodollar futures. Because a TED-spread investor has bought T-bill futures while shorting Eurodollar futures, the account value is being credited more from the T-bill gains than it is being debited from the Eurodollar losses:

Hypothetical TED-Spread When Rates Are Falling

Net: Up 10%

On the other hand, when rates are rising, T-bill futures tend to fall more slowly than Eurodollar futures. The account value is increasing faster from the Eurodollar short-sell gains than it is being drained by the T-bill futures losses.

Bottom line: when interest rates move sharply, TED-spreads tend to gain. When interest rates stay stagnant, there is no gain from the spread, and you lose your margin.

One of the nice features of the TED-spread is that the initial margin requirement is low because the amount required by the purchase of T-bill futures is offset by the amount received from the short-sale of Eurodollar futures.

Under Y2K, the TED-spread could be a magical combination. We have already discussed why U.S. Treasuries are likely to be a good place for investors to be. By extension, T-bill futures look bright as

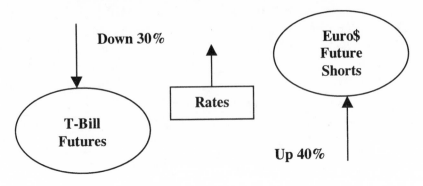

Hypothetical TED-Spread When Rates Are Rising

Net: Up 10%

well. On the other hand, because of the chance of extensive disruptions to the European banking system under Y2K and even the chance of substantial bank failures around the world, any nonguaranteed notes are going to be cheaper and have to bear higher interest rates.

If the Y2K crisis were *really* bad, Eurodollar futures could even conceivably *fall* in value despite a decline in interest rates, particularly if the credit ratings of some of the major issuers are at stake. This would be unprecedented, of course, since it would mean *both* positions of the spread would be winners.

In the previous chapter, we discussed some of the basics of options in terms of puts, calls, expirations, and strike prices. The options market is a tad tamer than the futures market, largely because options are a step further removed from the underlying commodity. Remember that options are only rights, not obligations, to buy or sell. Futures, on the other hand, are the actual contracts: You bought it, it's yours, until you sell it again. And while the upside potential in options is unlimited, the downside risk is generally limited to the amount you put at risk. The same cannot be said for a futures contract, which could continue to suck money into a losing position beyond the initial margin.

Y2K STRATEGY
Trading in Options

Stock options and stock index options are traded in four principal exchanges: Chicago (CBOE) and American (AMEX) (the two major indexes), and two smaller exchanges, Philadelphia and Pacific.

When you put it that way . . .

In terms of options on equities during the Y2K crisis, most traders will be interested in stock *puts*. To review, a put option allows you to "put" stock to another trader (force him or her to buy) at a specific price anytime before the expiration of the option. If you agree that equities in general, and equities in certain high-risk sectors in particular, are headed south both before and during the Y2K crisis, and if you are a risk-taker, you will have your put options ready.

The key to put options is leverage. Rather than sell a stock short, you can use the same amount of money to control a great deal more stock (albeit at much higher risk). Put options cost just a fraction of the underlying price of the equities they control. To illustrate, let's suppose you are convinced that hospital provider ABC, whose stock has been a highflyer through mid-1999, is in deep trouble due to impending Y2K foul-ups in Medicare and Medicaid reimbursements and its own lackluster Y2K program.

ABC is trading at $100 a share, and you think it could go to $70 a share quickly. One option is to sell the stock short, as we discussed earlier. You would borrow 400 shares of ABC from your broker, who would sell them for you and hand you a check for $40,000. If after half a year ABC were in fact trading at $70 per share, you would buy the stock back for $28,000, and you will have made $12,000, less interest and commission charges. The math looks like this:

Proceeds from short sale	400 × $100 =	$40,000
Cost to buy shares back	400 × $70 =	$28,000
Total profit	400 × $30 =	$12,000
(Less interest, commission)		

Now, let's assume instead that you use some money to buy put options on ABC. Assume the ABC January 100 puts cost $225 apiece, so you pick up twenty of them for $4,500. You now control *2,000 shares* of ABC stock (20 times 100). It turns out that you were right about ABC. In December 1999, the HCFA announces that it will not be able to process Medicare payments using existing systems and will have to resort to manual processes until new systems are in place. Meanwhile, major Medicaid programs in key states issue the same dire warnings. ABC stock tumbles sharply.

By the end of 1999 ABC is trading at $70 a share, and you exercise your option to "put" the stock to a buyer at $100 per share, even though you only buy them for $70 apiece. The difference is $60,000. Minus the premium, you have made $55,500, much more than you would have by short selling. The math looks like this:

Premium, 20 puts (controls 2,000 shares)		$4,500
Price buyer must pay	2,000 × $100 =	$200,000
Your cost for the stock	2,000 × $70 =	$140,000
Gross profit		$60,000
Less premium		− $4,500
Total profit		$55,000

Of course, traders typically would have long since sold the put rather than exercise it, and earned about the same amount of money from the rise in the put's value.

Most major stocks traded today have options listed on them, and most of them have many different options. If you think Y2K will seriously impact a particular stock, you can buy a put with a strike price that is at-the-money (a strike price equal to the current trading price) or even out-of-the-money (a strike price lower than its current trading price). These would be considerably cheaper to purchase and could become in-the-money as the price of the stock drops below the strike price.

Our recommendation is that Y2K risk-takers should set aside some of their speculation money to purchase puts on individual at-risk stocks in the air transport, health care, electric utility, and banking sectors. To find out what options are traded on a particular stock, you can look it up in a financial paper (like the *Wall Street Journal, Investors Business Daily,* or *Barrons*) or find it on the Web at http://cboe. pcquote.com/cgi-bin/cboeopt.exe?.

Calling It Like It Is

While we like puts, we are not big on buying calls. Generally, stocks are not going to go up during the Y2K crisis, so having a handful of calls would run contrary to our overall outlook. However, if you like to have a few calls on the table, we would go with Y2K stocks and gold stocks discussed in chapter 9. Or, if you think that Y2K will right itself before the end of 2000, you might pick up some December 2000 calls in some of the more beaten-up stocks.

Because the *seller* of a naked call has unlimited downside risk, we do not recommend that any investor participate in the sale of calls unless they are covered (see discussion in chapter 10).

Stock Market Options

A broader investment strategy for Y2K risk-takers would be to buy *put options* on *major stock indexes.* Stock indexes are a price-weighted collection of individual stocks that are representative of sectors or whole markets. Options markets have taken these bundled stocks and given them a value, making them optionable just like most stocks. Investors following this strategy are betting on declines in the sector represented by the index or, in the case of broad indexes, in the market as whole. One complicating factor, however, is that the lifespan of most stock index options is not long, so timing becomes quite critical.

One index at risk during the Y2K crisis is the Dow Jones Transportation Index (CBOE ticker symbol: DTX), which contains many airlines and air freight companies predicted to have problems under Y2K. The stocks we have recommended against (either avoid or underweigh) comprise around 51 percent of the index on a weighted scale. The index is composed of the following stocks:

Airborne Freight Corp. (ABF)**
Alexander and Baldwin, Inc.
 (ALEX)
AMR Corp. (AMR)*
Burlington Northern Santa Fe
 Corp. (BNI)
CNF Transportation, Inc. (CNF)
CSX Corp. (CSX)
Delta Air Lines, Inc. (DAL)*
Federal Express Corp. (FDX)*
GATX Corp. (GMT)
J. B. Hunt Transportation Services
 (JBHT)

Norfolk Southern Corp. (NSC)
Northwest Airlines Corp.
 (NWAC)*
Roadway Express, Inc. (ROAD)
Ryder System, Inc. (R)
Southwest Airlines Co. (LUV)**
UAL Corp. (UAL)*
Union Pacific Corp. (UNP)
US Airways Group, Inc. (U)**
USFreightways Corp. (USFC)
Yellow Corp. (YELL)

 * *recommend avoid*
 ** *recommend underweigh*

Of course, the Transportation Average also contains many other at-risk stocks that we have mentioned in relation to other industries. These at-risk companies include many of the railroads, which we would underweight.

To play this average, timing is an important consideration. We recommend holding some DTX September 1999 and December 1999 puts. This strategy would take advantage of mounting public concern in the latter half of 1999 over the safety and efficiency of air travel as Y2K is more and more in the spotlight. Your best position, though, would be in March 2000 DTX puts, which you would probably sell in mid- to late January.

The Dow Jones Utilities Average, whose CBOE options ticker is DUX, contains fifteen stocks in this average, made up of electric, gas, and multipurpose utilities. Not surprisingly, the index includes many of the electric utility stocks we have cautioned investors against. Indeed, the stocks we view as riskier (to be avoided or underweighted) make up over 58 percent of the index on a weighted basis. The index contains the following stocks:

American Electric Power
    (AEP)**
Columbia Energy Group (CG)
Consolidated Edison, Inc. (ED)*
Consolidated Natural Gas Co.
    (CNG)
Duke Energy Corp. (DUK)*
Edison International (EIX)
Enron Corp. (ENE)
Houston Industries, Inc. (HOU)

PECO Corp. (PE)*
PG&E Corp. (PCG)*
Public Services Enterprise Group
    (PEG)
Southern Co. (SO)**
Texas Utilities Co. (TXU)**
Unicom Corp. (UCM)*
Williams Cos. (WBM)

* *recommend avoid*
** *recommend underweight*

Note that many of the other utilities in this average also are at risk, but we did not discuss them specifically because they are either diversified across many industries or offer nonelectric utility services.

To bet against this average, we have two recommendations. The first is to buy CBOE DUX put options that expire sometime in December 1999. We are hesitant to recommend September 1999 puts only because the utility sector will probably not receive as much public scrutiny as, say, the airlines. But by December 1999, the cat could be well out of the bag. This timing should permit you to take advantage of any mounting public concern over the *operational* aspect of utilities under Y2K. The second recommendation is to buy DUX put options that expire in March 2000. This would permit you to take advantage of downward movements in stock brought about by poor *financial* performance of the electric utilities, which we think is probable given threats of disruptions in fuel supply and the intermittent shutdowns of nuclear power plants.

Other broad indexes that you may want to buy puts on include the Dow Jones Industrial Average (DJX), the S&P 500 (SPX), the S&P 400 Mid-cap (MID), the S&P 100 (OEX), the American Major Market Index (XMI), and the Russell 2000 (RUT).

In terms of call options, the only ones we would consider include the de Jager Year 2000 Index (YTK) (discussed earlier in chapter 9) and the Philadelphia Gold and Silver Index (XAU). You possibly could go with calls on the oil indexes (OIX and XIO), which could see a rise if the price of oil rises due to supply disruptions. In general, however, we think it is riskier to bet that any stock indexes will move upward, as we will probably be in a down market generally for stocks. So if you are convinced that gold prices will rise, we recommend sticking to betting on the metal itself and not necessarily the companies that mine it.

LEAPS and Bounds

One of the disadvantages of stock and stock index options is their relatively short life spans. For Y2K investors who are looking forward more than a few months, or who are worried about when to time their options trading, there are special investment vehicles we like called LEAPS, which stands for Long-term Equity Anticipation Securities. LEAPS, which trade on the CBOE, are basically what they sound like: long-term stock or index options. They are, like other options, available in both calls and puts.

The nice feature of LEAPS is that they have expiration dates up to three years in the future. That means that the options take longer to expire, so their *rate of price erosion* is a lot slower than the average option. Because the life-cycles of LEAPS are longer, investors don't have to time the stock market movements as precisely—a useful thing not to have to worry about in the Y2K crisis, when timing will be particularly difficult to pinpoint. If the stock market moves downward significantly *any time* between now and, say, January 2001, holders of LEAPS puts on the S&P will see those options appreciate quickly.

Because LEAPS are relatively new, having been introduced by the CBOE only in 1990, there aren't nearly as many available options as there are in the normal stock option and stock index option markets. Another limiting factor is that all LEAPS expire in January, up to 39 months out from the date of purchase. This means that 2001 LEAPS are what most Y2K-minded investors will be looking at. (By the time you read this, January 2000 equity LEAPS will likely have "rolled into" the standard option for that equity after the May, June, or July expiration, depending on whether the option associated with the LEAPS is on the January, February, or March expiration cycle. Translation: January 2000s probably aren't available or worthwhile.)

LEAPS are listed for stocks, stock indexes, and interest rate products. Most equity leap symbols are based on the underlying equity symbol, modified by an L, V, W, or Z. For example, LEAPS on ABC company might be symbolized by LBC for this year, while LEAPS for ABC expiring next year might use VBC. To get a full listing of LEAPS, call 1-800-OPTIONS (at the CBOE).

We naturally are recommending buying LEAPS puts on major market indexes with expirations in January 2001. You can also buy LEAPS puts on highly capitalized companies that you feel are at Y2K risk.

Options on Currencies

In addition to futures on currencies, investors can use options to speculate on currencies. This is somewhat less risky than buying whole futures contracts, since you are limited to the premium you pay. But you can still expect wild swings in this arena when Y2K begins to impact around the world.

As with the futures, we are looking to buy calls on U.S. dollar options while buying puts on foreign currency options such as the yen. Timing is a concern, however. We expect foreign currencies to stabilize and rise through early 1999 as the Asian crisis begins to ebb. Too far into 1999, however, and the probable impact of Y2K will begin to dawn overseas, which could create a demand for dollars and renewed pressures on foreign currencies.

Options on Interest Rates

We are looking at a bullish market for U.S. government bonds, so purchasing the right to buy them at a lower price (buying U.S. Treasury calls with low strike prices) is our general strategy. Again, buying options on interest rate instruments is less risky than the interest rate *futures* market, since your downside risk is limited to the amount of the premium you pay for the call.

If interest rates fall significantly, holders of calls on U.S. Treasuries are going to make *a lot* of money as the price of securities jump higher and yields tumble. As we have discussed before, we anticipate that both foreign and domestic investors looking for a safe place to park their money will be headed for U.S. government-backed securities, so the bond market will be a fine place to have staked out call-option positions. (Incidentally, if you are worried about when interest rates are going to move lower, even though you are sure that sometime in 2000 they will, you might consider buying a January 2001 LEAPS call in interest-rate-related options. Talk to your broker or contact the CBOE for more information.)

Options on Futures . . . If You Can Figure Them Out

Welcome to the world of the abstract. If futures contracts are one step removed from the actual commodity, and stock index futures are two steps removed because the index itself is an amalgamation of a pseudo-commodity, then an option on a stock index future is truly in the realm of the bizarre. Nevertheless, investors who want to limit their downside risk by paying premiums for the right (but again, not the obligation) to buy or sell a futures contract can make a foray into the world of options on futures.

For traders who want to buy precious metals but don't want to have unlimited downside risk, options on precious metals futures actually make good sense, and we would recommend this vehicle over actual futures contract trading. We are looking at gold and silver call options with expirations in late 1999 and 2000; however, we should advise that as this book goes to print, traders have already bid up the cost of these options significantly. Consult your options broker before executing any options trade.

So what would a portfolio of an investor seeking to *build wealth* during the Y2K crisis look like? We can't tell you how much of your money to put into speculative investments, but we should remind you that it should never be more than you are prepared to *lose completely*. Most small traders in futures get burned, especially in their first few invest-

Y2K STRATEGY

Sample Portfolios

ments. What you don't lose by wrongly placed or, more importantly, wrongly timed positions, you could see disappear when your broker takes his commission. In the options market, the risk is limited to your premiums, but there are still high commission rates, and again, the problem of timing is a universal leveler. Before you invest in futures and options, make sure you are completely familiar and comfortable with all of the techniques, limitations, margin requirements, costs, and risks involved. Consult regularly and carefully with your broker.

On the other hand, if you can afford to risk a few thousand dollars, and if you time your winning positions correctly, speculation could make you *very* wealthy. Of course, this money comes from other investors in the market, so for you to hit big, someone else will have to lose big, or some group of people will all have to lose their premiums. That's the way of the world in the zero-sum options and futures markets.

Our sample speculative portfolios are based on generalized investor sentiments. Of course, these portfolios are only examples and are meant only as rough guidelines. You and your broker should decide what strategy and course to plot through the crisis based on your own risk tolerance and circumstances. In the following charts, the speculative investments are represented as a "ring" around your portfolio core. Even speculators should keep the vast portion of their investments in low-risk, long-term investments.

Sample Speculative Position One: "I'm pretty sure markets will fall, but I'm not at all sure when."

Heavy on LEAPS, which are longer-term options, thus reducing the chance that the position will expire worthless

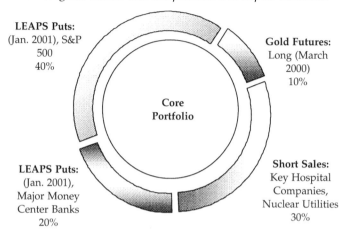

LEAPS Puts:
(Jan. 2001), S&P
500
40%

Gold Futures:
Long (March
2000)
10%

Core
Portfolio

LEAPS Puts:
(Jan. 2001),
Major Money
Center Banks
20%

Short Sales:
Key Hospital
Companies,
Nuclear Utilities
30%

Sample Speculative Position Two: "While things will be bad in the United States, they will be much worse overseas."

TED-Spreads; U.S. dollar calls; foreign currency puts; short sales of foreign at-risk equities

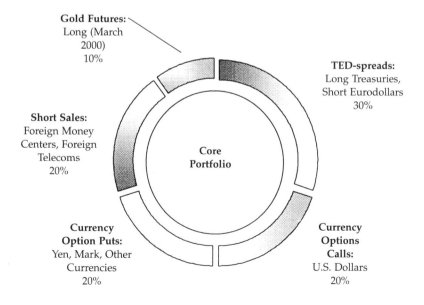

Gold Futures:
Long (March
2000)
10%

TED-spreads:
Long Treasuries,
Short Eurodollars
30%

Short Sales:
Foreign Money
Centers, Foreign
Telecoms
20%

Core
Portfolio

**Currency
Option Puts:**
Yen, Mark, Other
Currencies
20%

**Currency
Options
Calls:**
U.S. Dollars
20%

Sample Speculative Position Three: "People will head for safety and I want to get there first."

Focus on U.S. dollars, U.S. Treasuries, and Precious Metal Futures and Options on Futures

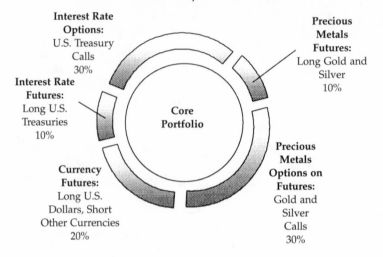

Interest Rate Options:
U.S. Treasury Calls
30%

Interest Rate Futures:
Long U.S. Treasuries
10%

Currency Futures:
Long U.S. Dollars, Short Other Currencies
20%

Precious Metals Futures:
Long Gold and Silver
10%

Precious Metals Options on Futures:
Gold and Silver Calls
30%

Core Portfolio

Sample Speculative Position Four: "We are looking at meltdown in certain sectors."

Buys Put Options on Transportation and Electric Utility Indices; Sells S&P Futures; Buys de Jager Y2K Call Options

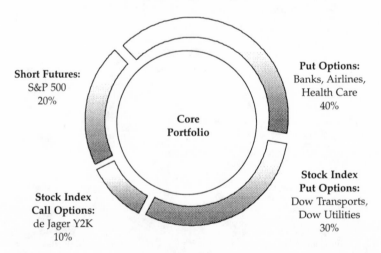

Short Futures:
S&P 500
20%

Stock Index Call Options:
de Jager Y2K
10%

Put Options:
Banks, Airlines, Health Care
40%

Stock Index Put Options:
Dow Transports, Dow Utilities
30%

Core Portfolio

TWELVE

CONCLUDING THOUGHTS: PREPARING FOR THE FUTURE

As millions of computers around the world silently count down toward our collective date with digital destiny, businesses will be left with fewer—and increasingly bleak—choices. Y2K consultants, who have for the past few years advised people to focus on fixing *mission-critical* applications and processes, will soon have to help their clients choose which of these mission-critical systems to save first. In 1999, expect to hear as much about *triage* and *damage control* in certain sectors as you hear about success and compliance in others.

Governments also will face tough choices. Should public officials seek to mobilize the populace in the fight against Y2K by warning of the dangers of inaction, even if this means risking mass hysteria? It is not really so hard a question in our minds. Governments should tell the truth, and should tell it sooner rather than later. If anything is worse than being told the harsh truth, it is being left to speculate over it. There is simply too little time remaining in 1999 for business and government to waste any of it debating how big a problem we have. It is enough for all of us to know that the impact of Y2K must be mitigated, or we are all going to be very, very sorry.

Throughout this book, it has been our goal to help you as an investor get a handle on Y2K. Investors should bear in mind that while many aspects of Y2K are highly unpredictable (such as how badly it will affect us and for how long), there are many general conclusions that can be drawn about its likely effects and disparate impacts on various sectors of the economy.

The principles we have used to assess Y2K risk are not that complex. The key to our approach has been to look at *complex business systems*. Knowing the right questions to ask is more than half the battle in Y2K investing. We have used these questions to pinpoint what we think are the industries most vulnerable to Y2K. There are, of course, many other sectors that could be equally or even more at risk from Y2K. As the end of 1999 draws nearer, it will become increasingly clear to many where the true problems lie.

As an investor, however, you want to stay at least one step ahead by foreseeing Y2K problems before they become clear to everyone else. By using the common sense Y2K assessment guidelines we developed in this book, you can be your own best Y2K investigator and keep from being pulled down in a swirl of millennial business disasters. So when considering your investment in a company in light of the coming Y2K crisis, ask yourself the following questions, which you have seen posed throughout this book:

- Does the company depend on just-in-time operations? Do the company's operations continue around the clock? What are the consequences of delays to those operations? What would happen if there were significant delays in deliveries of critical supplies and parts?

- Is the company susceptible to loss of public confidence? How big a factor is safety to the company? How about reliability? If the media starts to hype Y2K in 1999, will people sell out of the stock just to be out of it?

- Is there a critical bottleneck or threat of single-point failures in the company's operations? Do substantial company operations come together and pass through dangerous choke points? Are revenues disproportionately coming from a single source that itself might be at risk?

- How dependent is the company on computers? Most companies use computers to handle at least their *internal* accounting, payroll, financial planning, inventorying, etc. But does the company's computer dependence go beyond this internal dependence? If the company is a manufacturer, are automated processes like robotics needed to make the product or any of its components? If the company offers a service, are computers critical to providing that service successfully to the consumer? What would happen if the computers had to shut down or became undependable? Could the company do things manually?

- How dependent is the company on others? Does it interact frequently with others in its industry? If so, what happens if those interactions are fouled up? Does the company use many outside vendors and suppliers? Can the company shield itself from business failures of others in the production or service chain? What about business failures of its customers? How much does the company depend on the government or on foreign operations to continue to operate profitably?

Finally, our advice to investors is to get familiar with the Y2K programs of the entities in which they invest. There is a reason the SEC and other regulatory agencies have demanded heightened Y2K disclosures. Visit websites and read through the most recent annual reports. Read what they have to say about critical relationships with suppliers, customers, and government. If you don't like what you see, or you don't get answers to your questions, take measures to protect your investment. Do this sooner rather than later. The worst that can be said of you is that you took decisive action to protect your money in the face of an unknown and highly dangerous threat.

Keep in mind that Y2K is an unfolding story. We will continue to monitor Y2K throughout 1999 and provide updates to our readers on our website, which can be found at www.y2kinvestment.com. We hope that we will have good news to report on the progress of many sectors, but we are also realists, and we expect that in many areas our fears of significant disruptions will continue to be confirmed.

There will be many who will tell you that your concern over Y2K is unjustified, that you are overreacting to the whole millennium thing, or even that by buying this book you are making the problem worse. Unfortunately, it is a mentality like that which set back early Y2K efforts and got us in the mess we are in today.

The philosopher George Santayana warns that those who cannot remember from the past are condemned to repeat it. But to this, we humbly add that those who fail to *prepare for the future* surely are condemned to suffer through it. Preparing yourself and your investments for Y2K is not the act of a fringe survivalist. Such measures are the practical precautions of an informed realist.

Finally, what about the outlook beyond Y2K? We have devoted this book to how to prepare yourself as an investor for the Y2K Computer Crash—what to do before and during the Y2K crisis. When the dust from the millennium storm settles, the investment landscape may be vastly changed, and more opportunities will abound. Stay tuned.

APPENDIX A:
FREQUENTLY ASKED QUESTIONS

Q: **What exactly is the Year 2000 computer bug?**

A: The Year 2000 computer bug, often called Y2K, results from the use of two rather than four digits to represent the date. It has long been customary, even in computer programming, to presume that the first two digits of a date are "19," just as you might see on some checks and forms. Thus, 1980 was simply "80" and 1999 is "99." The problem arises when the clocks turn over to the year 2000, which will read as "00" and be interpreted as "1900" by many computers.

Q: **Why did programmers use two digits instead of four?**

A: There are three reasons commonly given for this. The first is simple economics: They did it to save space. Computers used to be many times larger than today's common desktops, yet they had far less data storage capacity. Data storage was therefore extremely expensive, and programmers needed to do everything they could to limit the size of the data they were inputting, including chopping off the first two digits on dates. The second reason is the result of a mistaken assumption: Programmers and information technology managers assumed that the older "legacy" systems they were implementing would be long gone before the turn of the millennium. Instead, companies and governments have tended to keep them around, adding on to them piecemeal. The third reason is the least forgivable: It was habit. Even after computer space became much more affordable, programmers continued to use only two digits to represent the date, perhaps because that was their routine, or perhaps out of sheer laziness or sloppiness.

Q: What systems are at risk?

A: Any software or microprocessor that performs calculations using a two-digit date format is at risk of Y2K-related failure. At particular risk are systems that process data that is dependent on the current date.

Q: How extensive is the problem and what will it cost to fix?

A: Y2K is much more pervasive than most people believe. Computer systems around the world will need to be upgraded, particularly in critical infrastructure such as telecommunications, transportation, energy, and financial services. Also at risk are manufacturing, delivery, and information systems. The most commonly cited estimates put the worldwide cost of the fix somewhere between $300 and $600 billion.

Q: Why didn't someone do something about this a long time ago?

A: Some programmers predicted over twenty years ago that unless we changed the way we entered date data in our computer systems, we would face this problem in 2000. However, they were largely ignored by both industry and government leaders, who at the time didn't see the importance computers would come to have in our society. More recently, individuals such as Peter de Jager in the mid-1990s have been sounding the warning, but it wasn't until the latter part of this decade that top managers and high level officials took notice and action.

Q: What is the government doing about Y2K?

A: The U.S. government leads the world in Y2K preparedness and spending, but it still may not be enough, we're afraid. The Clinton administration has established a task force on Year 2000 conversion, headed by John Koskinen, who has his work cut out for him. There have been numerous House and Senate hearings on the problem. Certain government regulatory bodies have begun to clamp down on noncompliant companies and sectors. But most of these efforts were implemented a bit late, and it seems clear that at least some parts of the government are not going to make it in time.

Q: What government departments are at most serious risk?

A: According to the Clinton administration's own assessment, the departments of Defense, Energy, State, Transportation, and Health and Human Services along with the Agency for International Development continue to lag in their preparations. For the average citizen, problems with IRS computers may result in botched or the late processing of returns.

Q: What does "Y2K-compliant" mean?

A: This question sets off furious and passionate debates among experts, critics, and IT managers trying to cope with Y2K. In basic terms, a system that is Y2K-compliant means that that it will be able to make the transition and operate without disruption or error after the turn of the millennium. The thorny question arises when you ask whether a *company* is Y2K-compliant. To some, this means that a company's internal systems are themselves Y2K-compliant, but others have pointed out that companies must determine whether suppliers and customers with noncompliant systems will cause otherwise compliant systems within the company to fail. In our view, this definition of Y2K compliance is not very helpful, however, since no company anywhere can claim with 100 percent assurance that every one of its business partners is Y2K-compliant.

Q: What is the issue of the year 2000 being a leap year?

A: Most people know that years divisible by four are leap years, with twenty-nine days in February. Fewer people are aware, however, that there is an exception for years ending in 00, which are typically *not* leap-years under the arcane rules of leap-year accounting. Even fewer people know that there is an *exception to the exception* for the "00 rule" every 400 years. Thus, 1600 was a leap year and 2000 will be a leap year, but 1700, 1800, and 1900 were not. Make sure your computer recognizes 2000 as a leap year.

Q: Is my money safe in the bank?

A: So long as your total deposits in any single account do not exceed $100,000 and your bank is insured by the Federal Deposit Insurance Corporation, then your money is safe. A more important question is whether you will have access to your funds. If you are concerned that your bank will have trouble processing withdrawals, consider keeping around one week to one month's worth of cash in a safe place, such as the bank's safety deposit box. Always keep good paper records of your money.

Q: What else should I do personally to prepare for Y2K?

A: While we do not anticipate widespread power outages, they are possible in some regions, particularly rural ones. People in the northern part of the country in particular should be prepared for possible losses of heat in the dead of winter, though again we think this will be short-lived if it occurs. The Red Cross (not an organization prone to unfounded hysteria) recommends stockpiling of essential food and drinking water, having extra cash on hand, keeping your car gas tank more than half full and being prepared to move to a shelter if the power fails. The full text of the Red Cross's recommendations appears in Appendix C. We also remind everyone to keep good paper records of accounts and bills in case data becomes lost or corrupted.

Q: Will it be safe to fly in January 2000?

A: That depends on where you are flying. The Federal Aviation Administration and the Department of Transportation are at pains to reduce the level of public fear of unsafe skies, and they insist that January 1, 2000, will be business as usual. At the same time, they concede that certain parts of the world are safety concerns and intend to issue warnings or ban flights to or from such regions. In our view, safety will not be compromised greatly in the United States, but you can expect significant delays or even cancellations.

Q: Is my own computer at risk?

A: Most newer computers have been designed with Y2K in mind, but even these may have some small errors that are not at first detectable. Try this simple test. Set your computer's internal clock forward to December 31, 1999, at 11:55 P.M. Turn it off and wait five minutes. Turn it back on and see what date is displayed. On some computers, the date will reset to 1980, which is the default "birthday" for certain chips.

APPENDIX B:
COMMONSENSE PRECAUTIONS
FOR YOUR FINANCES DURING Y2K

At least it can fairly be said that both Y2K optimists and pessimists agree on one thing: *At a minimum* people should become informed about the Y2K efforts of their financial service providers and keep solid records of their finances. But what does this mean in more concrete terms? We have borrowed various pieces of advice from websites, Y2K experts, and government agencies and come up with the following advice.

Here are the questions you should ask of each of your FSPs:

- When did your FSP begin its Y2K program? If it started any later than the beginning of 1998, take your business elsewhere.

- Is it in the testing phase by now? Testing will consume more time and resources than most businesses estimate. If your FSP isn't in the testing phase by early 1999, it won't have enough time to test thoroughly.

- Find out what type of backup records are kept by your FSP. How would these records be used to correct computer problems? If there isn't a backup plan, change FSPs.

- If you keep a deposit with your FSP, make sure it is fully insured by the FDIC.

The following are some basic precautions you can take with respect to your accounts at each of your FSPs:

- A few months before the end of 1999, obtain statements from your creditors detailing your history of payments. Make sure that it includes a breakdown of principal and interest, and also other charges such as late fees. If your loan is amortized, get a statement of how your loan will decrease over time with regular payments.

- Your paper trail should cover at least three months before and three months after January 1, 2000, particularly with respect to significant transactions like mortgages, stocks, and insurance payments.

- Consider taking out some cash—enough to get through at least a week, but maybe as much as a month, of expenses. Do this at least a few weeks before the end of the year. The reason is two-fold, really. The ATM could screw up as a result of Y2K after the turnover. More likely, however, is the possibility that ATMs could run out of money!

- Y2K could affect deposits, so keep deposit receipts that your ATM or teller gives you on all deposits within the six-month window described above. Check these against your periodic statements and immediately report (in writing) any discrepancies.

- Same thing goes for checks. Keep canceled checks as proof of payment. If your bank doesn't currently mail you copies, ask them to start. If you bank on-line, print out downloaded records and include the date on the hard copy.

- Credit card receipts and cash advance receipts should be kept around longer than usual, too. Compare these to your monthly statements and immediately report any discrepancies. In the months leading up to the end of 1999, try to keep at least one card that has an expiration in late 1999 in case a merchant has difficulty processing your cards that expire in or after 2000.

- Payments sent by mail should have some sort of record, so consider using a certificate of mailing during the critical period. These are available at your local post office.

- Keep a list of your important account numbers with each of your FSPs, as well as with service providers such as your electric company, garbage collector, water company, and local and long distance provider. If there are problems in service, you will need these numbers handy. Be prepared to be on hold a long time on the phone, however, if service is interrupted.

- Other accounts have a high probability of being disrupted, since many of the computers these records are kept on will fail to be upgraded in time. Keep good records of, for example, frequent-flier mileage accounts, memberships at health clubs, extended warranties, auto clubs, membership shopping clubs, Internet service providers, etc.

- Get a copy of your credit report for one of the three major credit bureaus. It might cost you up to eight bucks, but it's worth it. Report any errors immediately. You can call them at the following numbers:

Equifax:	800-685-1111
Experian:	800-682-7654
Trans Union:	800-916-8800

APPENDIX C:
Y2K EMERGENCY PREPAREDNESS

Experts give all kinds of varying advice on how people can prepare for a Y2K emergency. Rather than choose the advice either from the Y2K Pollyannas or the Cassandras (and risk being accused of being too alarmist or too lax in our judgment), we thought we would just go to the authoritative source on emergency preparedness: the Red Cross.

The Red Cross posted the following recommendations on its website for what precautions the average person can undertake to prepare for Y2K:

- Check with manufacturers of any essential computer-controlled electronic equipment in your home to see if that equipment may be affected. This includes fire and security alarm systems, programmable thermostats, appliances, consumer electronics, garage door openers, electronic locks, and any other electronic equipment in which an embedded chip may control its operation.

- Stock disaster supplies to last several days to a week for yourself and those who live with you. This includes having nonperishable foods, stored water, and an ample supply of prescription and nonprescription medications that you regularly use. See your family disaster supplies kit for suggestions.

- As you would in preparation for a storm of any kind, have some extra cash on hand in case electronic transactions involving ATM cards, credit cards, and the like cannot be processed. Plan to keep cash in a safe place, and withdraw money from your bank in small amounts.

- Similar to preparing for a winter storm, it is suggested that you keep your automobile gas tank above half full.

- In case the power fails, plan to use alternative cooking devices in accordance with manufacturer's instructions. Don't use open flames or charcoal grills indoors.

- Have extra blankets, coats, hats, and gloves to keep warm. Please do not plan to use gas-fueled appliances, like an oven, as an alternative heating source. The same goes for wood-burning or liquid-fueled heating devices that are not designed to be used in a residential structure. Camp stoves and heaters should only be used out of doors in a well-ventilated area. If you do purchase an alternative heating device, make sure it is approved for use indoors and is listed with the Underwriters Laboratories.

- Have plenty of flashlights and extra batteries on hand. Don't use candles for emergency lighting.

- Examine your smoke alarms now. If you have smoke alarms that are hard-wired into your home's electrical system (most newer ones are), check to see if they have battery backups. Every fall, replace all batteries in all smoke alarms as a general fire safety precaution.

- Be prepared to relocate to a shelter for warmth and protection during a prolonged power outage or if for any other reason local officials request or require that you leave your home. Listen to a battery-operated radio or television for information about where shelters will be available.

- If you plan to use a portable generator, connect what you want to power directly to the generator; do not connect the generator to your home's electrical system. Also, be sure to keep a generator in a well-ventilated area, either outside or in a garage, keeping the door open. Don't put a generator in your basement or anywhere inside your home.

- Check with the emergency services providers in your community to see if there is more information available about how your community is preparing for any potential problems. Be an advocate and support efforts by your local police, fire, and emergency management officials to ensure that their systems will be able to operate at all times.

APPENDIX D:
Y2K RESOURCES

Federal government information:

- Y2K toll-free information hot line: 1-888-USA-4-Y2K (1-888-872-4925). There is a recorded message with information twenty-four-hours a day. Information specialists are there to assist from 9:00 A.M. to 8:00 P.M. Eastern time, Monday through Friday.
- Consumer questions: 1-202-FTC-HELP (1-202-382-4357). The Federal Trade Commission will provide you a brochure containing answers to typical consumer questions.
- President's Council on Year 2000 Conversion website: http://www.y2k.gov.
- General Accounting Office (GAO) reports and publications on the year 2000 computing crisis: http://www.gao.gov/y2kr.htm.
- Federal Aviation Administration (FAA) Y2K information: http://www.faay2k.com.
- Federal Deposit Insurance Corporation (FDIC) Y2K information: http://www.fdic.gov/about/y2k/.
- Federal Reserve Board of Governors Y2K information: http://www.bog.frb.fed.us/y2k/.
- Securities and Exchange Commission (SEC) Year 2000 information: http://www.sec.gov/news/home2000.htm.
- North American Electric Reliability Council (NERC) Y2K information: http://www.nerc.com/y2k/.
- U.S. Nuclear Regulatory Commission (NRC) Y2K information: http://www.nrc.gov/NRC/NEWS/year2000. html.

- Food and Drug Administration (FDA) Y2K medical device compliance information: http://www.fda.gov/cdrh/yr2000/y2K intro.html.
- Health Care Financing Administration (HFCA) Year 2000 information on Medicare and Medicaid programs: http://www.hcfa.gov/y2k/.
- Federal Communications Commission (FCC) Year 2000 home page: http://www.fcc.gov/year2000/.
- Federal Emergency Management Agency (FEMA) Year 2000 Initiative: http://www.fema.gov/y2k/.
- Social Security Administration (SSA) Y2K information: http://www.ssa.gov/facts/y2knotic.html.

Our favorite Y2K sites on the Internet:

- For a general "information portal" on Y2K, try http://www.y2k.com, which should lead you to many other sources of information.
- A good clearinghouse for information, articles, and Y2K solutions can be found at http://www.year2000.com.
- Some of the best articles on Y2K were published by the *New York Times* and are available on one convenient website. (A free registration is required to view this site: http://www.nytimes.com/library/tech/reference/millennium-index.html.
- One of the best places to find out Y2K information on electric utilities is the website of Y2K guru Rick Cowles, which can be found at http://www.euy2k.com.
- Dr. Ed Yardeni's website contains great facts on Y2K's likely economic impact. It can be found at http://www.yardeni.com/cyber.html.
- For information on health care and Y2K, visit the Rx2000 website at http://www/rx2000.org.
- For a Y2K "the-sky-is-falling" view, check out http://www.garynorth.com. While we don't agree with everything Mr. North has to say, he has an excellently arranged website with terrific links.

NOTES

Introduction

1. Reported in a summary of the industrial and Process Control Systems Conference held in Houston, Texas, from May 18–20, 1998. Remarks by Evan Hand, as reported by John Huntress, Year2000.com Partnership.

2. Gene Bylinsky, "Industry Wakes Up to Year 2000 Menace," *Fortune* (April 27, 1998); Rachel Konrad, "Suppliers' Computers a Worry to Carmakers," *Detroit Free Press* (April 23, 1998).

3. Katie Merx, "Warren Store Wins First Year 2000 Suit," *Detroit News* (September 15, 1998); see also Rajiv Chandrasekaran, "Year 2000 Bug Could Bring Flood of Lawsuits," *Washington Post* (May 3, 1998); Douglas Stanglin and Shaheena Ahmad, "Year 2000 Time Bomb: Prevailing Myths Deter Managers From Debugging Computers," *U.S. News & World Report* (June 8, 1998).

4. Scott Thurm, "A Blitz of Fixes Helps Factories Prepare for Year-2000 Problem," *Wall Street Journal* (January 5, 1999). Experts also warn that some programs mistakenly believe that the year 2000, like the year 1900, is *not* a leap year, since it is a year ending in "00." But every 400 years there is an exception to the rule. Thus, 1600 was a leap year, and 2000 also will be a leap year, but 1700, 1800, and 1900 were not.

5. Id.

6. Id.

7. Will Lester, "Most Americans Believe Y2K Bug Will Cause Minor Problems at Most," Associated Press (January 2, 1999).

8. See Dr. Edward Yardeni, *Year 2000 Recession? Prepare For the Worst, Hope For the Best,* available at www.yardeni.com. Dr. Yardeni is the chief economist at Deutsche Bank Securities for North America, and has predicted a 70 percent chance of a global recession resulting from Y2K.

9. See Chris O'Malley, "Apocalypse Not," *Time* (June 15, 1998). Other examples include James Annable, chief economist at First Chicago NBD, and Steve Roach, chief economist of Morgan Stanley Dean Witter, both of whom have dismissed the idea of a Y2K recession. See "Economists Debate Global Impact of Year 2000," R. Schilhab, Fox News (July 1, 1998).

10. The best-known fence-sitter is John Koskinen, special assistant to the president on Year 2000 conversion, who insisted as late as the end of the second quarter of 1998 that "there's not enough real hard data (yet) to make estimates." B. Belton, "Wall St. Forecast: Increased Chance of Y2K Recession," *USA Today* (July 1, 1998).

11. See Edward Yourdon and Jennifer Yourdon, *Time Bomb 2000* in Appendix A (Prentice Hall, 1998).

12. Barnaby J. Feder and Andrew Pollack, "Computers and Year 2000: A Race for Security (and Against Time)," *New York Times* (December 27, 1998).

13. Chris Allbritton, "The Latest Y2K Bug Worry: Checking the Fixes," Associated Press (January 2, 1999) (quoting chief technical officer of Sapiens, a leading international Y2K fix-it company).

14. "Microsoft Says It Can Correct Y2K Bug in Windows 98 System," *St. Louis Post-Dispatch* (courtesy of *Bloomberg News*) (December 8, 1998). The company has made free software available on the Net and on CD-ROM to correct the problem.

15. For a humorous survey of Y2K hysteria, see Patrick O'Driscoll, "Y2K Bug Could Be a Plague, Many Warn," *USA Today* (July 1, 1998) (describing survivalist websites that have sprung up on the net).

16. Feder and Pollack, note 12.

17. Rod Newing, "The Millennium 'Bomb': Systems Are Already Failing," *Financial Times* (July 1, 1998).

18. Raina Grossman, "Percentage of Major Corporations Launching Year 2000 Strategy; As Corporations Add Staff and Increase Budgets for Year 2000 Work, More Than a Third Have Experienced a Year 2000 Failure," Cap Gemini America (Press Release, April 8, 1998), available at www.usa.capgemini.com/services/y2k.

19. See Erich Luening, "Reports of Y2K Failures on the Rise," CNET News.com (December 30, 1998) (citing Cap Gemini

America 1998 Q4 survey of 110 corporations, twelve industrial sectors, and twelve government agencies).

20. "Y2K '99 Preview Reveals Weaknesses," MSNN (January 5, 1999).

21. In fact, some analysts have pointed out that we may get a taste of what's in store when certain computers fail on April 9, 1999—the ninety-ninth day of 1999—which translates into an internal computer message as "9999" on some computers and means "end of data file" in many computing languages. This problem is mentioned in the guidelines prepared by the Federal Financial Institutions Examination Council. Apparently, the same problem may occur on September 9, 1999, which may be read by some computers as "9/9/99." The FFIEC guidance document can be found at www.ffiec.gov/y2k/guidance.htm. Another day to watch out for is August 22, 1999, when the U.S. Navy's global position system, which is used by the world's planes and ships to navigate and by multinational banks to calculate overnight interest, will reset itself. (According to the navy, the system began to count out weeks on January 5, 1980, but only counts up to 1,024 before starting over. See www.tycho.usno.navy.mil/gps_week.html.)

Chapter One: The Missing Nail

1. Daniel Howes, "Flint GM Workers Go On Strike," *Detroit News* (June 5, 1998).

2. "Facts and Figures About the General Motors Strikes," Associated Press (July 11, 1998).

3. "Union Says GM and UAW Reach a Strike Settlement," *Wall Street Journal Interactive Edition* (July 28, 1998).

4. See Tom Wickham and Richard C. Noble, "Second Strike at Flint Plant Could Cripple GM Production," *Flint Journal* (June 11, 1998).

5. Gene Bylinsky, "Industry Wakes Up to Year 2000 Menace," *Fortune* (April 27, 1998).

6. Rachel Konrad, "Suppliers' Computers a Worry to Carmakers," *Detroit Free Press* (April 23, 1998).

7. Steven Levy and Katie Hafner, "The Day the World Shuts Down," *Newsweek* (June 2, 1998). The details were related by Edward Yourdan in an interview with Scott Rosenburg, printed in *The Year 2000 Computer Glitch—And a Great Crash?* available at www.salon1999.com.

8. Konrad, note 6.

9. Sandeep Junnarkar, "GM Offers EDS Rare Y2K Bonus," CNET News.com (November 20, 1998).

10. Matt Hamblen, "Seeking Truth in

Millennium Planning: GM's Y2K Assurances Come Under Scrutiny," *Computer World* (June 22, 1998).

11. In fact, GM has recently faced other crippling strikes where a single choke point caused the whole company to shut down. In 1996, a seventeen-day walkout by workers at two brake plants in Dayton, Ohio, idled 178,000 workers and cost GM over $900 million. Indeed, GM should be no stranger to UAW strikes; the union had previously struck the company nine times since early 1996. See Wickham and Noble, note 4.

12. Ironically, GM's efforts to eliminate possible production bottlenecks and flash points may have been the catalyst for the two Flint strikes. Since 1978, when GM employed nearly 77,000 in the Flint area, employment has dropped to less than half that number, to around 33,000 today. Subcontracting and outsourcing threatened to eliminate another 50 percent of the jobs over the next few years. Id. Over the Memorial Day weekend, just before the strike, GM quietly removed stamping dies for its new 1999 Chevrolet Silverado and GMC Sierra pickups from the plant in Flint and sent them to its plants in Mansfield, Ohio, and Marion, Indiana, all in an effort to ensure that growing labor troubles in Flint did not affect the launch of its new pickup lines in the fall. See Howes, note 1. Alarmed workers saw this move as a breach of GM's promise to improve conditions and productivity at the Flint plant rather than ship jobs elsewhere. The decision was to strike before the jobs got shipped out, too.

13. Frances Cairncross, "Time Runs Out," *Economist* (September 19, 1998).

14. Sara Kehaulani Goo, "Strike or No, Some Analysts Are Stumping for GM Stock," *Wall Street Journal* (July 28, 1998). The article notes, "The thinking is that all of this adds up to one imperative for GM: a thorough restructuring that will finally make the company's North American operations lean, competitive, and profitable. Some analysts are sensing that the strike doesn't reflect GM's same old labor problems so much as a paradigm shift in the direction of serious, urgent change among top GM management." Some analysts were unimpressed with the terms of the settlement, however, saying that GM had gotten little by way of concessions and would have a tough time making up for the losses. See, e.g., "GM Finds Peace Isn't Cheap: After Billions of Dollars in Losses, GM Settles for Minor Gains From UAW," CNN (July 29, 1998).

15. John Crawley, "UPS Strike Will Hit Economy, Affect Millions," Reuters (August 4, 1998).

16. "Food Catalogers Suffer Heavy Losses as Strike Continues, *Catalog Age Weekly* (August 15, 1997).

17. See, e.g., David Altaner and Tom Stieghorst, "Shippers Cope With Strain of UPS Strike," *Sun Sentinel* (August 4, 1997) (citing medical supply shortages at hospitals in Fort Lauderdale); Larry Lebowitz, "Businesses Celebrate End of Strike," *Sun Sentinel* (August 19, 1997) (discussing problems with delivery by blood plasma company).

18. "UPS Strike Causing Textbook Problems," *USA Today* (August 13, 1997).

19. See, e.g., "Businesses Struggle With Strike Impact," *Chicago Sun-Times* (August 8, 1997) (describing one Evanston, Illinois, business which had 400 pounds of cookies still sitting in its shop waiting to be sent to California Starbucks stores); "Strike Cuts Wide but Not Too Deep," *Washington Post* (August 14, 1997) (relating job cutbacks in businesses in New Jersey and Oregon).

20. Andy Patrizio, Survey Says One in Five Companies Working on Y2K Fix, *TechWeb* (December 19, 1997) (citing statement by Jim Woodward, senior vice president of Cap Gemini's Trans-Millennium Services).

21. Stevenson Swanson and Jim Kirk, "Satellite Outage Felt by Millions," *Chicago Tribune* (May 21, 1998).

22. Lost in Space . . . Company Knew as Late as Last Week That Satellite Had Problems, CNN (May 20, 1998).

23. Swanson and Kirk, note 21 (relat-

ing the "noisy" situation at the University of Pennsylvania's Health System).

24. Michael J. Martinez, "The Satellite Fix Is In," ABC News (May 22, 1998).

25. See "Lost in Space . . . Company Knew as Late as Last Week That Satellite Had Problems," note 22.

26. Swanson and Kirk, note 21.

27. "Satellite Outage Hinders Pagers, TV," USA Today (May 20, 1998).

28. See note 22.

29. "Satellite's Failures Ripple Across USA," USA Today (May 21, 1998).

30. Frank James and Jon Van, "Satellite's Breakdown Highlights Telecom Fragility," Chicago Tribune (May 21, 1998); see also note 22.

31. Swanson and Kirk, note 21.

32. Martinez, note 24.

33. See note 22 (quoting Jay Kitchen of the Personal Communications Industry Association).

34. Martinez, note 24.

35. Eric Luening, "An Optimist's View of Y2K," CNET News.com (July 10, 1998) (citing Merrill Lynch Report).

36. "Y2K Bug Sound Overplayed? Look at Hong Kong's New Airport," Bloomberg Business News (July 13, 1998).

Chapter Two: The Plane Truth

1. Chris Stamper, "Airlines Battle the 2000 Bug," ABC News.com (May 7, 1998).

2. See Barry Tate, "Senior Manager Industry Operations, Year 2000," available at www.iata.org.

3. Id.

4. "Northwest Suffers Losses at HK Airport," Shipping Times (July 20, 1998) (courtesy of Reuters).

5. Tate, note 2.

6. See Erin McCormick, "Computer Bug May Hit Where It Hurts," San Francisco Examiner (November 22, 1998).

7. Andy Patrizio, "Year 2000 Glitch May Ground KLM Flights," TechWeb (November 11, 1997); see also "Insurers Could Nix Millennium Flights," Detroit News (November 4, 1998).

8. David Parsley, "Bug Grounds Tour Flights," (London Sunday) Times (August 9, 1998).

9. Laura Bly, "Y2K Squelching Millennium Travel," USA Today (December 31, 1998). The effect of Y2K fear on travel bookings should not be overstated. Our view is that while many will avoid flying around 1/1/00 due to Y2K, the turn of the millennium will nevertheless see a sharp increase in travel due to the uniqueness of the millennial change. Indications are that reservations for the millennial weekend are up some 300 percent over the same period in 1999. This may have the unfortunate effect, however, of further snarling air traffic as airports and airlines try to cope with both Y2K snafus and the increased passenger traffic.

10. Imtiaz Muqbil, "Airlines Work to Ease Growing Y2K Jitters," Bangkok Post, (May 11, 1998).

11. David L. Mount, "Computer Reservation Systems," available at www. louisville.edu/~dlmoun01/crs.html.

12. Hunter Fulghum, "Air Traffic Upgrade Takes Off," ABC News.com (April 14, 1998).

13. Connie Guglielmo, "Sabre Group's Reservation System Hit by Power Outage," Inter@ctive Week Online (June 24, 1998).

14. Dan Reed, "Sabre Travel Reservation System Grounded for Three Hours," Knight Ridder/Tribune (June 25, 1998).

15. Bob Francis, "Sabre Suffers Second Outage," PC Week Online (July 1, 1998).

16. Dan Reed, "Sabre Reservation System Out Six Hours," Fort Worth Star Telegram (July 1, 1998).

17. Id.

18. Stamper, note 1.

19. Thomas Hoffman, "Sabre Group Hastens Y2K Plans," Computer World (March 2, 1998).

20. "KLM to Fly in Rivals to Thrash

Out Date Bug," *Computer Weekly News* (November 20, 1997).

21. Alan Gersten, "Cargo Carriers Can Handle the Millennium Bug—Fed Ex, *Reuters* (July 13, 1998).

22. "Transportation: Wheels of Commerce," *USA Today* (June 10, 1998).

23. David Gersovitz, "World Airlines to Spend $1.6 Billion to Fix 2000 Bug," Reuters (June 9, 1998).

24. Stamper, note 1; see also, Shade Elam, "Airport Computers Far From Ready," *Atlanta Business Chronicle* (May 18, 1998).

25. Gersovitz, note 23.

26. See Gersten, "Cargo Carriers Can Handle the Millennium Bug—FedEx," Reuters (July 13, 1998).

27. Gene Bylinsky, "Industry Wakes Up to the Year 2000 Menace," *Fortune* (April 27, 1998).

28. Peter Robison, "Boeing Says All Its Suppliers May Not Be Ready for the Millennium Bug," *Seattle Times* (November 7, 1998).

29. Kevin Merrill, "Small Business Susceptible to Year 2000 Problems," *TechWeb* (June 15, 1998).

30. Mary Mosquera, "Small Businesses Are Unprepared for Year 2000," *TechWeb* (May 1, 1998).

31. See Jonathan Make, "Many Small-Business Owners Ambivalent About Y2K Computer Glitch," Bloomberg Business News (July 20, 1998).

32. "Price of Jet Fuel Nosedives," Associated Press (March 29, 1998).

33. "Y2K Computer Problem Has Public Wondering Just How Bad It Will Be," *USA Today* (January 7, 1999) (citing study).

34. See Statement of Texaco to Stockholder or Customer, "Year 2000, The Millennium Change," available at www.texaco.com/irss/y2k.htm.

35. Kevin G. Hall, "Y2K Question: Will the Bug Bite Shipping?" *Journal of Commerce* (June 22, 1998).

36. "Chevron Won't Fix All Y2K Bugs in Time," *Contra Costa Times* (November 7, 1998).

37. See Matthew L. Wald, "Millennium Could Be a Headache for Travelers," *New York Times* (December 28, 1998).

38. Laszlo Buhasz, "Y2K Test Fails," *Globe and Mail* (January 6, 1999).

39. Rebecca Landwehr, "DIA Year 2000 Costs Top $9 Million," *Denver Business Journal* (November 16, 1998).

40. Rebecca Landwehr, "DIA Flunks Year 2000 Compliance Test," *Denver Business Journal* (April 20, 1998).

41. Landwehr, note 39.

42. Elam, note 24.

43. As reported in the *Fort Worth Star Telegram* (March 6, 1998), article copy available at www.garynorth.com/y2k/detail_.cfm/1195.

44. Elam, note 24.

45. Ted Bridis, "FAA Seeks Funds to Sap Y2K Bug," *Journal of Commerce* (courtesy of Associated Press) (October 5, 1998).

46. S. C. Chan, "Further Testing Delays KLIA Until June," *Cargo News Asia* (April 13, 1998).

47. "Problems Plague New Asian Airports," Associated Press (July 7, 1998).

48. Lim Kit Siang, Malaysian parliamentary opposition leader, "Media Statement," (July 4, 1998). This document is available at www.malaysia.net/dap/sg1120.htm.

49. Joel C. Willemssen, director, Civil Agencies Information Systems, "Report to Congressional Requesters: FAA Computer Systems—Limited Progress on Year 2000 Issue Increases Risk Dramatically," Government Accounting Office/AIMD-98-45:6.1 (January 30, 1998). Emphasis added.

50. Kenneth M. Mead, inspector general, U.S. Department of Transportation, "The Year 2000 Presents Significant Challenges for the Air Traffic Control System," Statement before the Subcommittee on Technology, House Committee on Science, Subcommittee on Government Management, Information, and Technology, and the House Committee on Government Reform and Oversight, U.S. House of Representatives (February 4, 1998).

51. Id.

52. Jane F. Garvey, federal aviation administrator, "Concerning the Technology Challenges Presented by the Year 2000," statement before the Committee on Science, Subcommittee on Technology, and the Committee on Government Reform and Oversight, Subcommittee on Management, Information and Technology, U.S. House of Representatives (February 4, 1998).

53. Willemssen, note 49 at 6:1.

54. Rajiv Chandrasekaran, "Air Traffic Control Computer System Cleared for 2000," *Washington Post* (July 22, 1998).

55. "FAA Response to Congressional Year 2000 Inquiry," Representative Stephen Horn, chairman, Subcommittee on Government Management, Information, and Technology, to Michael Huerta, Acting CIO, DOT (January 14, 1997).

56. Id.

57. See Mead, note 50; see also Tim Dobbyn, "U.S. Lawmakers Doubt FAA Can Fix 2000 Glitch," Reuters (February 5, 1998).

58. Nicole Tsong, "FAA Assures Congress Air Traffic Will Be Safe From Y2K Problems," New York Times Syndicate (August 1998).

59. Willemssen, note 49 at 0:2.1.

60. Gerald L. Dillingham, GAO associate director, Transportation Issues, Resources, Community, and Economic Development Division: "Observations on FAA's Modernization Program," GAO/T-RCED/AIMD-98-93, statement before the Subcommittee on Aviation, Committee on Commerce, Science, and Transportation, U.S. Senate (February 26, 1998).

61. Jane F. Garvey, administrator, Federal Aviation Administration, "The Clock Is Ticking," remarks to the International Air Transport Association Annual General Meeting, Montreal, Canada (June 8, 1998), available at www.faay2k.com/html/060898.html.

62. Willemssen, note 49 at 6:2 and note 6. There appears to be confusion over the actual total number of mission-critical systems, which in part is a function of how mission-critical is defined. The *New York Times* reported, for example, that there were only 155 mission-critical systems at the FAA. See Wald, note 37. Our figures are based on what was reported by the GAO.

63. See Mead, note 50.

64. See Garvey, note 52.

65. Nicole Lewis and Colleen O'Hara, "Latest Data Refutes FAA Claims on Year 2000," *Federal Computer Week* (March 2, 1998).

66. "Mainframe Cleared for Y2K Take-off," *Wired News* (July 22, 1998).

67. See McCormick, note 6.

68. Margaret Allen, "D/FW Airport Expects to Fly Through Year 2000," *Dallas Business Journal* (January 4, 1999).

69. Wald, note 37.

70. See Garvey, note 52.

71. See Dobbyn, note 57.

72. This statement is taken from a June 11, 1998, memorandum authored by Daniel G. Thorsen, Contingency Plans/Year 2000 Issues, and Chris Monaldi, Denver ARTCC/facility representative, and is available at www.natca.org. Emphases added.

73. "Insurers Could Nix Millennium Flights," note 7.

74. Erich Luening, "Y2K Threatens U.S. Transportation," CNETNews.com (September 11, 1998).

75. Gersten, note 26.

76. See "Management's Discussion and Analysis of Results of Operations and Financial Condition," available at www.fdxcorp.com.

77. See "Year 2000 Project," available at www.airborne.com.

78. See "BAX Global's Year 2000 Compliance Program," available at www.baxworld.com.

79. See "About Atlas Air," available at www.atlasair.com. Emphasis added.

80. See 1997 Annual Report of UAL.

81. Available at www.nwa.com/lb/corpinfo/profi/facts.shtml.

82. See "Scope of Operations," at www.flycontinental.com.

83. See "September 1998 Quarterly

Results Summary, Delta Airlines," at www.delta-air.com.

84. Other foreign airlines trading on U.S. exchanges tend not to have significant around-the-world operations, but rather are limited to service between the home country and the United States.

85. See "Partnerships," available at www.british-airways.com/inside/ world wide/partners/partners.shtml.

86. See "Counteracting the Millennium Bug: The Challenge We Face," available at www.british-airways.com/inside/year 2000/docs/cwf.shtml.

87. "Insurers Could Nix Millennium Flights," note 7.

88. Susan Emmett, "Travel Insurers Wash Their Hands of the 2000 Bug," (London Sunday) *Times* (July 25, 1998).

Chapter Three: Critical Condition: The Health Care Industry and Y2K

1. M. J. Zuckerman, "Medical Industry's Y2K Woes in Spotlight," *USA Today* (July 23, 1998).

2. Miguel Llanos, "Year 2000 Bug Could Bite Hospitals Hard," MSNBC (July 23, 1998).

3. Joe Manning, "Year 2000 Problem a Medical Menace," *Milwaukee Journal Sentinel* (July 28, 1998).

4. Senator Bob Bennett, "Will the Health Care Industry Be Prepared for the Year 2000?" Statement before the Special Senate Committee on the Year 2000 Technology Problem (July 23, 1998).

5. Hakhi Alakhun El, "Insurers May Deny Y2K Coverage," *TechWeb* (August 10, 1998) (quoting study by Gartner Group, Inc.).

6. Roger Croteau, "Hospital's Electronic Equipment Tested for Electronic Problems," *San Antonio Express News* (October 10, 1998).

7. Eric Luening, "How Will Y2K Hit Hospitals?," CNET News.com (July 23, 1998); M. J. Zuckerman, "Y2K Glitch Could Spark Health Crisis," *USA Today* (July 23, 1998).

8. Joel M. Ackerman, executive director, Rx2000 Solutions Institute, Presentation to the U.S. Senate Special Committee on the Year 2000 Technology Problem (July 23, 1998).

9. Zuckerman, note 7.

10. Susan Parrott, "Area Hospitals Brace for Computer Epidemic," *Oklahoman* (June 25, 1998).

11. Robert Lemos, "Senate Hearing to Discuss Y2K Medical Cures," ZDNN (July 22, 1998).

12. Elizabeth McCarthy, "Hospital Systems Brace for Year 2000 Problems," *Sacramento Business Journal* (October 5, 1998).

13. Sylvia Dennis, "Year 2000 Crisis Main Issue for Health Network Managers," CNN ONLINE (July 23, 1998).

14. Robert Lemos, "Y2K Tops Health Care To-Do List," ZDNN (July 22, 1998).

15. Lemos, note 11.

16. Nancy Weil, "Year-2000 Compliance Pace to Quicken Next Year, Cap Gemini Finds," *Info World Electric* (August 12, 1998).

17. Zuckerman, note 7.

18. Rebecca Landwehr, "Hospitals Seek 'Bug' Cure," *Denver Business Journal* (August 3, 1998).

19. This example, which we have taken the liberty of expanding, can be found in an article by Erich Luening, "How Will Y2K Hit Hospitals," note 7.

20. Marlene Cimons, "Doctors Fear Patients Will Suffers Ills of the Millennium Bug," *Los Angeles Times* (January 5, 1999).

21. Andrea Rock and Tripp Reynolds, "The Year 2000: The Year 2000 Bug; It's Time to Check Your Investments, Funds, Bank, Credit Cards, Home Computer, and More to Avoid the Worst Of," *Money* (February 1, 1998).

22. Bob Wilson, "AV Hospital Gears Up for Millennium Bug," *Antelope Valley Press* (October 8, 1998).

23. McCarthy, note 12.

24. Cimons, note 10.

25. Avram Goldstein, "Company Erroneously Denies Federal Workers" Drug Benefits," *Washington Post* (January 5, 1999).

26. Zuckerman, note 1.

27. Cimons, note 10.

28. See Jim Lord, "Y2K Life-Threatening for Some Users of Prescription Medications" (June 8, 1998), available at www.y2ktimebomb.com.

29. Paula D. Gordon, Ph.D., "A Call to Action: The National and Global Implications of the Year 2000 Embedded Systems Crisis," available at www.year2000.com (citing Gartner Group study).

30. Croteau, note 6.

31. Landwehr, note 18.

32. Mike Berry, "Kansas Hospitals Brace for 'Millennium Bug,'" *Wichita Eagle* (July 19, 1998).

33. Parrott, note 10.

34. Tracy Correa, "Hospitals Run Into Y2K Early; FDA Warning Alerted the Facilities to Y99 Problems," *Fresno Bee* (January 1, 1999)

35. Robert MacMillan, "FDA Issues Y2K Medical Device Warning," *Newsbytes* (December 30, 1998).

36. Correa, note 34.

37. Lemos, note 14.

38. Ackerman, note 8.

39. McCarthy, note 12.

40. Llanos, note 2.

41. Dr. Kenneth Kizer, undersecretary of veteran affairs, testimony before the U.S. Senate Special Committee on the Year 2000 Technology Problem (July 23, 1998).

42. Steve Alexander, "Year 2000 Problem Affects Medical-Emergency Equipment," *Minneapolis/St. Paul Star Tribune* (July 27, 1998).

43. Id.

44. Ackerman, note 8. A spokesperson for Medtronic, Inc., of Minneapolis, which is one of the largest manufacturers of pacemakers in the U.S., agrees that the problem lies with equipment used to monitor and reprogram the implanted heart stimulators. He asserts that Med-

tronic, however, has replaced or upgraded its domestically sold programmers. See Mark Perkiss, note 24. "Hospitals Try Inoculation Against the Millennium Bug," *Times (New Jersey Online)* (March 16, 1998).

45. The President's Council on the Year 2000 specifically warns doctors on its website that while pacemakers are not at risk, software used to program them may contain Y2K glitches and should be tested. See www.y2k.gov/java/whatsnew.

46. Kizer, note 45.

47. This document is available at www.Rx2000.org.zella.html.

48. Jonathan Seff, "Be Still, My Heart: It's the New Millennium," *PC World Online* (July 9, 1998) (quoting Donald J. Palmisano, trustee for the AMA).

49. Michael A. Friedman, M.D., acting commissioner, Food and Drug Administration. Statement before the Special Senate Committee on the Year 2000 Technology Problem (July 23, 1998).

50. Brian L. Thompson, "Hospitals Trailing in Y2000 Bug Fix," *Jacksonville Business Journal* (February 23, 1998).

51. Perkiss, note 44.

52. Id.

53. Rajiv Chandrasekaran, "Health Coalition Warns of Year 2000 Crisis in Medical Devices," *Washington Post* (July 10, 1998).

54. Parrott, note 10.

55. "Doctors Want List of Y2K-Affected Devices," Associated Press (July 24, 1998). Senator Christopher Dodd faulted the FDA for failing to inform Congress of the depth of the nonresponse rate, saying that the FDA "ought to be banging the table." Stephen Barr, "Health Industry 'Not Ready' for 2000," *Washington Post* (July 24, 1998).

56. MacMillan, note 35 (citing the *Gray Sheet*, a medical devices newsletter published by Elsevier Science Inc.).

57. Orlando DeBruce, "Y2K Bug May Affect VA Health," *Federal Computer Weekly* (July 27, 1998).

58. McCarthy, note 12.

59. MacMillan, note 35.

60. "Year 2000 Computer Problem,"

Food and Drug Administration (June 25, 1997). This document is available at www.fda.gov.

61. Kevin Thurm, deputy secretary, U.S. Department of Health and Human Services, letter to manufacturers (January 21, 1998).

62. Lemos, note 14.

63. Barr, note 55.

64. "Doctors Want List of Y2K-Affected Devices," note 35.

65. DeBruce, note 37.

66. Jennifer Jackson, general counsel and vice president, clinical services, Connecticut Hospital Association on behalf of the American Hospital Association. Testimony before the Subcommittee on Oversight of the House Committee on Ways and Means, hearing on the year 2000 computer problem (May 7, 1998).

67. Parrot, note 10.

68. Landwehr, note 18.

69. Robert J. Hammell, "Investigating Embedded Systems for Y2K Compliance," (July 24, 1998). This document is available at www.y2ktimebomb.com/ Computech/Management/rhamm9829.

70. Nancy-Ann de Parle, administrator, Health Care Financing Administration, U.S. Department of Health and Human Services, testimony before the Senate Special Committee on the Year 2000 Technology Problem (July 23, 1998).

71. Matt Hamblen, "Doctors Feel Feds' Y2K Pain," *Computerworld* (August 3, 1998).

72. Medicare Transaction System: Success Depends Upon Correcting Critical Managerial and Technical Weaknesses, GAO/AIMD-97-78 (May 16, 1997).

73. The depth of HHS's problems are not apparent at first blush, and HHS's "progress" on the Y2K problem needs some amount of explanation. In its February 1998 report to Congress, HHS had identified 491 mission critical systems, of which 187 were considered Y2K compliant. In its subsequent May 1998 report, HHS had "reclassified" its mission critical systems so that there were only a total of 289 systems to test and renovate, of which 108 were already compliant. See

John Callahan, CIO, U.S. Department of Health and Human Services, statement before the House Subcommittee on Government Management, Information, and Technology, Government Reform Oversight Committee (June 10, 1998). In other words, they made the problem smaller by simply saying that the problem was smaller. The good news is, systems related to Medicare claims typically were not reclassified as nonmission critical. At least they seem to know where the real problems and dangers lie.

74. Stephen Barr, "Hurdles in Medicare's Race for Y2K Fix," *Washington Post* (January 4, 1999).

75. Joel C. Willemssen, director, Civil Agencies Information Systems, Accounting and Information Management Division, U.S. General Accounting Office, Testimony before the Subcommittee on Oversight of the House Committee on Ways and Means, Hearing on the Year 2000 computer problem (May 7, 1998).

76. Barr, note 74.

77. Id.

78. Mary Nell Lehnhard, senior vice president, policy and representation, Blue Cross and Blue Shield Association, testimony before the Subcommittee on Oversight of the House Committee on Ways and Means, hearing on the Year 2000 computer problem (May 7, 1998).

79. Barr, note 74.

80. Id.

81. Id.

82. de Parle, note 70.

83. Bennett, note 4.

84. See Kaiser Family Foundation website, available at www.kff. org/state_ health/states/ca.html.

85. "States Lag in Fixing Year 2000 Computer Glitch," *New York Times* (reprinted in the *San Francisco Chronicle* at A3, November 27, 1998).

86. "Letter to State Medicaid Directors," Health Care Finance Administration, March 6, 1998.

87. See 1997 annual report of Columbia-HCA, available at www.columbia-hca.com.

88. See Management Discussion and

Analysis of Financial Condition and Results of Operation, August 1998, 10-Q filed by Tenet Health Corporation.

89. Id.

90. See 1997 annual report of United Health Services, Inc.

91. See Management's Discussion and Analysis of Financial Condition of Operations, June 1998, quarterly report (SEC Form 10-Q), Province Healthcare Company.

92. See Overview: Health Management Associates (provided by Hoover, Inc.), available at www.msn.investor.com.

93. Form 10-K for Fiscal Year Ended December 31, 1997, AmSurg Corp at 7.

94. See 1997 Annual Report of Beverly Enterprises.

95. See Mariner Post-Acute Network 1996 Annual Report, Selected Operating Data.

96. See notes to consolidated financial statements, Form 10-Q, note 11, filed by Integrated Health Services, Inc., June 1998.

97. See 1997 annual reports of HCR Manor Care, Sun Healthcare Group, Generis Health Ventures and Assisted Living Concepts.

98. See 1997 annual report, National HealthCare Corp.; 1997 annual report of Vencor, Inc.

Chapter Four: Will Y2K Leave Investor-Owned Utilities in the Dark?

1. "North American Power Council Sees Year 2000 Readiness," Reuters (July 28, 1998).

2. Rich Miller, "Race Goes On to Keep Power From Going Off," *Times* (Trenton) (August 10, 1998).

3. SEC Form 10-Q, filed by Conectiv, Inc., September 30, 1998.

4. Alan Boyle and Miguel Llanos, "Y2K Bug Energizes Power Companies," MSNBC (August 11, 1998).

5. From www.sdge.com/VPPT/vppt_2001.html.

6. See www.euy2k.com.

7. See Rick Cowles, "Electric Utilities and Y2K, a Practical Guide to the Year 2000 Computer Problem in the Electric Utility Industry," (1998), 10.

8. As reported in the *Orlando Sentinel* (May 25, 1998), originally available at www.orlandosentinel.com/news/0525bug.htm. Copy of article available at www.garynorth.com/y2k/detail_.cfm/1661.

9. Miguel Helft, "Power Utilities Try to Manage Year 2000 Bug," *San Jose Mercury News* (August 1, 1998).

10. See www.euy2k.com, Electric Power Research Institute, proceedings from EPRI Embedded Systems Workshop (October 4, 1997).

11. "Preparing the Electric Power Systems of North America for Transition to the Year 2000, A Status Report and Work Plan," North American Electric Reliability Council (September 17, 1998), 5. This document is available at ftp://ftp.nerc.com/pub/sys/all_updl/docs/y2k/y2kreport-doe.pdf.

12. Helft, note 9.

13. See, e.g., Dick Mills, "Another Myth: SCADA and EMS Failures Would Crash the Grid" (October 8, 1998), available at www.y2ktimebomb.com.

14. The exception is the high-voltage direct-current tie lines from Hydro-Quebec, which would have a substantial impact on power delivery in the northeastern United States if facilities there go down.

15. Y2K Coordination Plan for the Electricity Production and Delivery Systems of North America, North American Electric Reliability Council (June 12, 1998).

16. The NERC notes, however, that the very diversity of components among vendors, and even within a single vendor's products, has reduced the likelihood of common mode failures. NERC status report, note 11, 40.

17. Edison Electric Institute, March 1998.

18. Boyle and Llanos, note 4.

19. "Hundreds of Thousands Without Power in the West," Associated Press (July 3, 1996). The spokesperson's comments related to a massive power outage across the western United States in the summer of 1996.

20. Boyle and Llanos, note 4.

21. Minnesota Department of Public Service Year 2000 Survey, Docket No. U999/DI-98-430.

22. Boyle and Llanos, note 4.

23. Id.

24. Michael Overall, "D-Day Looms for Y2K," *Tulsa World* (August 19, 1998).

25. "PacifiCorp Readies Plans to Counter Any Y2K Outages," Associated Press (August 21, 1998).

26. As reported in the *Pittsburgh Tribune Review* (July 12, 1998), originally available at www.triblive.com/news/ry2kc712.html, copy of article still available at www.garynorth.com/y2k/detail_.cfm/2029. Some smaller utilities disagree with the charge that they will be less prepared than the big utilities. Noted one systems administrator for Kootenai Electric Company in Hayden, Idaho, "We have been working on the Y2K problem for more than two years and have it under control as much as possible. As a 'smaller' utility, we can react more quickly than the giant mega-utilities. Most smaller utilities do not generate their own power, but purchase it from a large supplier. We get our power from the Bonneville Power Association, which has been working on Y2K for several years. I think that readiness for Y2K depends not so much on the size of your staff as on how seriously you take the problem." Art Malin, "Letters," *Computerworld* (August 17, 1998).

27. See www.euy2k.com.

28. NERC status report, note 11, 16.

29. NERC status report, note 11, 16.

30. Helft, note 9.

31. Senator Bob Bennett, "Hearing on the Risks of Y2K on the Nation's Power Grid," statement before the Senate Special Committee on the Year 2000 Technology Problem (June 12, 1998).

32. Nancy Weil, "Year-2000 Compliance Pace to Quicken Next Year, Cap Gemini Finds," *Info World Electric* (August 12, 1998). Transportation was tied with utilities as the second-to-least prepared of sectors.

33. James J. Hoecker, chairman, Federal Energy Regulatory Commission, testimony before the Senate Special Committee on the Year 2000 Technology Problem (June 12, 1998).

34. Peter Durantine, "PUC Fears Y2K Could Put the Lights Out in the State in 2000," Associated Press (July 10, 1998).

35. Andrew Brownstein, "PUC Opens Probe Into Utilities' Readiness for Millennium Bug," *Bangor Daily News* (September 2, 1998). It was not clear, however, how many of the respondents were electric utilities as opposed to water or communications utilities.

36. NERC status report, note 11, 8.

37. Id.

38. Senator Bob Bennett, remarks before the National Press Club (July 15, 1998), transcript on file with authors.

39. NERC Y2K Coordination Plan, note 15.

40. NERC status report, note 11, 6.

41. H. Josef Hebert, "Utilities Call Y2K a Minimal Impact," Associated Press (January 12, 1999).

42. "Year 2000 Council Kicks Off 'National Campaign for Year 2000 Solutions' by Focusing on Challenges Facing Electric Power Industry," (July 28, 1998), available at www.y2k.gov/new/prel728.htm.

43. NERC status report, note 11, 27. See also, Declan McCullagh, Bankers: Prepared for a Panic?, *Wired News* (December 3, 1998).

44. McCullagh, note 43.

45. Id.

46. NERC Y2K coordination plan, note 15.

47. Terry Shropshire, "Officials Wary of Edison's 2000 Readiness," *Detroit Free Press* (July 10, 1998).

48. Id., 5.

49. "Y2K Problem Not as Bad as

Feared," *Electricity Daily* (September 21, 1998).

50. See AAR's website at www.aar.org/comm/statfact.nsf.

51. "Y2K Computer Problem Has Public Wondering Just How Bad It Will Be," *USA Today* (January 7, 1999).

52. See Union Pacific's website at www.uprr.com/y2k/2kprojct.shtml.

53. See Burlington Northern Santa Fe's website at www.wm7d.net/bnsf/1998/bnsf-090898.html.

54. Christopher Dinsmore, "Norfolk Southern Gets Its Y2K Tracks Straight, Hopes Other Business Partners Are Doing the Same," *Virginian-Pilot* (July 13, 1998).

55. Id.

56. See www.euy2k.com.

57. NERC status report, note 11, 35.

58. U.S. Nuclear Regulatory Commission, Office of Nuclear Materials Safety and Safeguards, NRC Generic Letter 98-03: NMSS Licensees' and Certificate Holders' Year 2000 Readiness Programs (June 22, 1998).

59. NRC/NEI meeting, October 7, 1997.

60. Erich Luening, "Nuke Plants Prepare for Y2K," CNET News.com (August 19, 1998).

61. "Sweden May Close Nuclear Plants for Year 2000 Bug," Reuters (July 24, 1998).

62. Our thanks and the credit goes to Rick Cowles, whose book on the subject and clear examples made this section possible. See Cowles, note 7, 19–20.

63. Shirley Ann Jackson, chairman, Nuclear Regulatory Commission, testimony before the Senate Special Committee on the Year 2000 Technology Problem (June 12, 1998).

64. See NRC Generic Letter 98-03 (June 22, 1998), available at www.nrc.gov/NRC/GENACT/GC/GL/1998/gl98003.html.

65. Luening, note 60.

66. Jackson, note 63.

67. See www.duke-energy.com/units/dukepow2.htm.

68. See www.southernco.com/site/.

69. See www.tu.com/energy/index.htm.

Chapter Five: Don't Bank On It: How Y2K Could Impact Bank Equities

1. If this sounds far-fetched, it is what got Bank of America tuned in to the Y2K problem back in the 1970s when thirty-year mortgages expiring past 2000 couldn't be calculated correctly. See www.bankamerica.com.

2. Rich Miller, "Banks Stress Y2K Readiness," *Times* (Trenton) (October 12, 1998).

3. *Federal Reserve Purposes and Functions,* chapter 3, 53, available at www.federalreserve.gov.

4. "Fed Banks on Y2K Currency Run," *Wired News* (August 20, 1998).

5. "Fed Plans Cash Reserve for 1999," Associated Press (August 20, 1998), available at http://cnn.com/ALLPOLITICS/1998/08/20/ap/federal/.

6. Beth Belton, "A Stash of Cash for Y2K," *USA Today* (August 20, 1998).

7. Thomas Hoffman, "Banks Gird for Runs on ATMs New Year's Eve '99," *Computerworld* (August 24, 1998).

8. Craig Menefee, "Year 2000 Bug? What's That? Say 38 percent in U.S. Survey," *Newsbytes* (June 12, 1998), available at www.cnnfn.com/digitaljam/newsbytes/113250.html; see also www.cio.com/marketing/releases/y2k_awareness.html (CIO poll).

9. Id.

10. "Stockpiling Threat Looms Over Millennium," *Electronic Telegraph* (July 11, 1998), available at www.telegraph.co.uk/et?ac=000158118408973&&pg=/et/98/7/9/ecfbug09.html.

11. Spencer E. Ante, "Banks Bullish on Y2K," *Wired News* (August 21, 1998).

12. Bill Burke, "Banks Busy Preparing for Millennium Bug Bites," *Business Today* (July 20, 1998).

13. "U.S. Bankers Seek to Calm Year 2000 Consumer Fears," Reuters (November 20, 1998).

14. See the Fed's website, www.bog. frb.fed.us/y2k/howcompu.html.

15. See GAO/T-AIMD-98-116, "Year 2000 Computing Crisis: Federal Regulatory Efforts to Ensure Financial Institution Systems Are Year 2000 Compliant" (March 24, 1998), chapter 0:2.

16. "Year 2000 Readiness in the Financial Industry in Japan," Bank of Japan (August 14, 1998), available at www. boj.or.jp/en/seisaku/sei9806.htm.

17. Federal Reserve Governor Edward W. Kelley, Jr., remarks before the Florida International Bankers Association and the Miami Bond Club (February 11, 1998), available at www.bog.frb.fed.us/BOARD DOCS/SPEECHES/19980211.

18. Peter Stinton, "Banks Spending Billions to Avoid 2000 Snafu," San Francisco Chronicle (December 31, 1997).

19. See www.bankboston.com/today/ about/address_to_senate.asp.

20. Andrew C. Hove, Jr., acting chairman, FDIC, "The Year 2000 Problem," statement before the Committee on Banking and Financial Services, U.S. House of Representatives (November 4, 1997).

21. "Year 2000 Readiness in the Financial Industry in Japan," note 16.

22. Elizabeth de Bony, "Global Banking Group to Require Y2K Testing," Info World Electric (April 2, 1998).

23. "Will Your Bank Live to See the Millennium?" Business Week (January 19, 1998).

24. Jane J. Kim, "Will Borrowers Drop Y2K Bomb on Banks?" Business Today. com (August 11, 1998).

25. Id.

26. Id.

27. Lawrence Summers, deputy treasury secretary, remarks before the Senate Special Committee on the Year 2000 Technology Problem (July 7, 1998).

28. See www.bankboston.com/today/ about/address_to_senate.asp.

29. See, e.g., Tracy Corrigan, "Banks in 'Good Shape' for Millennium Bug,"

Financial Times (August 21, 1998) (citing Goldman Sachs report on Year 2000 preparedness in the financial services industry). Cap Gemini also places banks and financial institutions at the top of its list of prepared sectors.

30. See Kathleen Burke, president, California Bankers Association, "Don't Worry About Y2K, Banks Have It All Under Control," San Francisco Business Times (September 7, 1998).

31. See "An Overview of Chase Manhattan's Year 2000 Program," available at www.chase.com/inside/y2k/overview.ht ml#anchor829036.

32. Rich Brooks, "Many U.S. Banks Raise Estimates for Year 2000 Adjustment Costs," Wall Street Journal (November 18, 1998).

33. Id.

34. Ante, note 11.

35. "Citicorp Raises Its Y2K Estimates," Reuters (August 14, 1998), available at news.com/News/Item/ 0,4,25285,00.html.

36. See www.citibank.com/corporate_ affairs/cbworld/1297/maryal.htm.

37. Corrigan, note 29 (citing Gartner Group estimates).

38. Stinton, note 19.

39. Brooks, note 32.

40. "Some Banks Lag in 2000 Fix," Augusta Chronicle (November 14, 1998).

41. John P. McDermott, "Banks Investing Time, Money on Y2K Problem," Charleston Post and Courier (August 2, 1998).

42. "Japan and Germany Face Huge Millennium Problem, Says Expert," Star Online (November 16, 1998).

43. "At Press Time: Texas Leads in NCUA's Y2K 'Needs Improvement' Rating," Credit Union Times (December 9, 1998).

44. "FDIC Unprepared for 2000 Glitch?" Associated Press (February 10, 1998).

45. See generally, American Banker (February 19, 1998).

46. "FDIC Announced Results of Year 2000 On-Site Reviews" (June 1, 1998),

available at www.fdic.gov/publish/newprs/1998/pr9837.html.

47. See "Year 2000 Assessment Ratings" (July 8, 1998) (letter to chief executive officers), available at www.fdic.gov/banknews/fils/1998/fil9874.html.

48. Stephanie Neil, "Y2K Ripple Effect," *PC Week Online* (April 13, 1998).

49. "Frequently Asked Questions," Year 2000 Readiness and Fannie Mae, available at www.fanniemae.com/year2000/faq.html. Fannie Mae isn't limiting compliance to loan servicing systems. A lender's origination systems, many of which Fannie Mae helped pioneer, must also be compliant, or "that lender would not be able to deliver any new loans to us until it could provide Year 2000-compliant origination and delivery data." Id.

50. Nam In Soo, "Banks With Y2K Problems to Be Banned From Interbank Electronic Settlements," *Korea Herald* (August 18, 1998).

51. Tony Munroe, "Regulators Craft Y2K 'Plan B' for Banks," Business Today.com (July 31, 1998).

52. Neil, note 48.

53. Chris Mahoney, "State's Banking Officials Aim to Draw the Line on Y2K Compliance," *Boston Business Journal* (January 4, 1999).

54. "The First Victim of the Year 2000 Bug," *Philadelphia Inquirer* (March 4, 1998).

55. "Interagency Statement, Guidance Concerning Testing for Year 2000 Readiness," FFIEC (April 10, 1998), available at www.ffiec.gov/y2k/guidance.htm.

56. Kelley, note 16.

57. Christopher Price and Avi Machlis, "Flaws Found in Y2K Conversions," *Financial Times* (November 20, 1998).

58. Id.

59. "Year 2000 Problem Hits Early for Annapolis Bank," *Washington Times* (August 8, 1998). Other banks have experienced difficulties in converting their ATM systems to Y2K compliant ones. For example, some customers of First National Bank of Chicago, which is owned by Bank One, found that they could not use ATMs to transfer funds between their primary and secondary accounts. First Chicago explained that the problem was caused by the conversion to a new Y2K-compliant ATM system, and that the problem was temporary. See Eddie Baeb, "First Chicago Says ATM Problem Is Limited, Temporary," *Daily Southtown* (December 31, 1998).

60. See discussion in Kevin Maney, "Can Banks Merge and Nip Y2K Bug?" *USA Today* (August 3, 1998).

61. Brad Hoeschen, "Lower Share Prices,Y2K Worries Bring Bank Buying Binge to a Halt," *Business Journal* (Milwaukee) (November 16, 1998).

62. Rich Miller, "Fed Official Expects Bumpy Y2K Road," *USA Today* (August 12, 1998).

63. Wayne Arnold, "Asian Banks Are Light Years From Solution as 2000 Nears," *Wall Street Journal Interactive Edition* (November 18, 1998).

64. Michael Markowitz, "Defusing the Time Bomb," *Record Online* (May 17, 1998).

65. "Experts Wonder If Japan Is Prepared for Y2K Bug," *San Jose Mercury News* (courtesy of Associated Press) (August 3, 1998).

66. Adam Gifford, "The Reality of a Millennium Meltdown," *Business Herald* (April 25, 1998).

67. Shingo Ito, "Japan's Premier Steps Up Fight Against Millennium Bug," *Agence France Presse* (August 21, 1998).

68. "Japan Warns Small Firms Not Ready for Millennium Bug," Reuters (September 7, 1998).

69. Henry Dubroff, "Alan Greenspan: Few Worries Over Banks' Y2K Problems," *Denver Business Journal* (April 13, 1998).

70. Roger W. Ferguson, "Remarks at the Global Year 2000 Summit in London" (October 16, 1998), available at www.bis.org/review/index.htm.

71. Edgar Meister, "Luncheon Speech at Year 2000 Meeting of European Central Banks," available at www.bis.org/review/index.htm.

72. Patricia Lamiell, "Large U.S. Regional Banks May Have the Edge on Year 2000, Study Says," *Business Today* (August 24, 1998).

73. See Citibank Press Release (October

21, 1998), available at www.citibank.com/citigroup/pr72.htm.

74. See www.chase.com/global/pres ence.html.

75. The Chase Manhattan Corporation, summary of Selected Financial Highlights, Credit Related Information, 10.

76. Bank of America 1997 annual report, average balances and rates.

77. BankAmerica Second Quarter Earnings, Table 15, available at www.bankamerica.com/batoday/earnings_2q9 8.html.

78. Consolidated balance sheet, Bank of New York Company, Inc.

79. Bank of New York Company, Inc., 1997 annual report, 8.

80. J. P. Morgan, Business Sector Analysis (1997), 11, available at www.jpmorgan.com.

81. BankBoston 1997 annual report Table 5.

82. Bankers Trust reports third quarter results (October 22, 1998), available at www.bankerstrust.com/corpcomm/finhigh/3q98epr.doc.

83. Republic New York Corporation and subsidiaries, Form 10-Q for the period ended September 30, 1998.

84. Barclays PLC 1997 annual report, available at www.investor.barclays.com/results/97_1-62.html.

Chapter Six: Answering the Call? Y2K and the Telephone Companies

1. Honorable Michael K. Powell, commissioner, Federal Communications Commission, "Hearing on the Year 2000 Computer Problem and Telecommunication Systems," testimony before the Subcommittee on Oversight of the House Committee on Ways and Means (June 16, 1998).

2. See generally, A. Gerard Roth, vice president, technology programs, GTE, "Hearing on the Year 2000 Computer Problem and Telecommunication Systems," testimony before the Subcommittee on Oversight of the House Committee on Ways and Means (June 16, 1998).

3. Michael K. Powell, commissioner, Federal Communications Commission, statement before the Senate Special Committee on the Year 2000 Technology Problem (July 31, 1998).

4. "AT&T Has New Approach for Year 2000 Computer Problem," *New Jersey Star-Ledger* (June 13, 1998).

5. See Margie Semilof and Edward F. Moltzen, "The Clock Is Ticking: Carriers Claim to Be Far Along in Y2K Work but Caution Users to Test, Test, Test," *Computer Reseller News* (October 19, 1998), available at www.techweb.com/se/direct link.cgi?CRN19981019S0017

6. Dr. Judith List, vice president and general manager, Integrated Technology Solutions, Bellcore, "Communicating the Challenge of the Year 2000," statement before the Special Senate Committee on the Year 2000 Technology Problem (July 31, 1998).

7. Graphic provided by Roth, note 2.

8. Joseph Castellano, president, network and corporate systems, Bell Atlantic Corporation, testimony before the United States Special Senate Committee on the Year 2000 Technology Problem (July 31, 1998).

9. Honorable Michael K. Powell, commissioner, Federal Communications Commission, "Year 2000 Problem and the Communications Industry," remarks Before the Year 2000 Contingency Planning for Government Conference (November 16, 1998).

10. See Roth, note 2.

11. See, e.g., A. John Pasqua, program management vice president, AT&T Year 2000 Program, "Hearing on the Year 2000 Computer Problem and Telecommunication Systems," testimony before the Subcommittee on Oversight of the House Committee on Ways and Means (June 16, 1998).

12. Castellano, note 8.

13. Mary E. Thyfault and Bruce Caldwell, "Are Telcos Ready for Year 2000?" *CMPNet* (June 22, 1998).

14. "AT&T Raises Its Forecast of '98 Year 2000 Spending," *Wall Street Journal Interactive Edition* (November 18, 1998).

15. Pasqua, note 11.

16. Andy Peters, "Phone Companies 'Fess Up to Feds About 2000 Bug," *Atlanta Business Chronicle* (August 24, 1998).

17. Kate Gerwig, "MCI Gets Serious With SNA," *Internet Week* (July 8, 1998), available at www.techweb.com/se/directlink.cgi? INW19980706S0017.

18. See www.sprint.com/y2k/sprinty2k.doc.

19. See www.sbc.com/News/y2k.html.

20. See www.bell-atl.com/year2000/pdf/faqs.pdf.

21. "Firms Lag in Y2K Readiness," Reuters (January 4, 1999).

22. Matt Hamblen, "Telco CEOs Stress Year 2000 Readiness," *Computerworld* (October 12, 1998).

23. List, note 6.

24. Sylvia Dennis, "Bellcore Tackles Year 2000 Problem Head On," *Newsbytes* (June 30, 1998).

25. "Report—Nation's Phone System in Good Shape for Y2K," CNN Financial News (courtesy of *Newsbytes*) (October 23, 1998).

26. To specifically address the Y2K networking problem, the Network Reliability and Interoperability Council was also established in 1998, headed by C. Michael Armstrong, chairman and CEO of AT&T. Powell statement (July 1998), note 3. This brings the total number of U.S. telcom coordinating bodies to three.

27. See Francis Cairncross, "Bare Essentials," *Economist* (September 19, 1998) (discussing how certain sectors that depend on networks tend to emphasize continuity and reliability).

28. Mary Mosquera, "The Fed Warns of Millennium Bug's Economic Cost," *TechWeb* (April 28, 1998).

29. Powell testimony (June 1998), note 1.

30. Powell statement (July 1998), note 3.

31. As reported by Frances Cairncross, "Bare Essentials," *Economist* (September 19, 1998).

32. Roth, note 2.

33. Senator Jeff Bingaman, "Communicating the Challenge of the Year 2000," statement before the Senate Special Committee on the Year 2000 Technology Problem (July 31, 1998), citing *Critical Foundations: Protecting America's Critical Infrastructures,* the President's Commission on Critical Infrastructure Protection, October 1997.

34. Year 2000 Readiness Disclosure Under the Year 2000 Information and Readiness Disclosure Act, available at www.sprint.com/y2k/ sprinty2k.doc.

35. See the SBC website at www.sbc.com/News/y2k.html.

36. Id. (emphasis added).

37. Gerwig, note 17.

38. Pasqua, note 11.

39. Powell remarks (November 1998), note 9.

40. "Report on Survey of the Electric and Telecommunications Industries Preparation for the Year 2000," Texas Public Utilities Commission, available at www.puc.state.tx.us/projects/18491rpt.htm#_Toc418645024.

41. Brad Bass, "Feds Say Vendors Are Stonewalling Requests for Compliance Info," *Federal Computer Weekly* (May 4, 1998).

42. Id.

43. Powell testimony (June 1998), note 1.

44. Thyfault and Caldwell, note 13.

45. "Report on Survey of the Electric and Telecommunications Industries Preparation for the Year 2000," note 40.

46. Id.

47. Id.

48. Powell testimony (June 1998), note 1.

49. List, note 6.

50. Hamblen, note 22.

51. Charles Dervarics, "More Companies Need Y2K Phone Help," *Y2K Today* (November 13, 1998), available at www.y2ktoday.com/modules/home/default.asp?id=522.

52. Powell testimony (June 1998), note 1.

53. Hamblen, note 22.

54. "Battle Plans Agreed to Tackle the Problems Related to the Year 2000 in the Area of Telecommunications," ITU press release (May 29, 1998), available at www.itu.int/newsroom/.

55. Margaret Banaghan, "Out of the Telecoms Cacophony, an Order of Sorts Takes Shape," *Business Review Weekly* (June 22, 1998).

56. "Telecoms Firms Fear Network Failures," *Computer Weekly News* (October 1, 1998).

57. Powell statement (July 1998), note 3.

58. Ian Hugo, "Year 2000 and International Telecommunications," available at www.y2ktimebomb.com.

59. ITU press release, note 54.

60. Neil Winton, "Telephone Companies Claim to Have Exterminated the Bug," Reuters (November 5, 1998).

61. Matt Hamblen, "U.S. Companies Sweat Foreign Telco Y2K Readiness," *Computerworld* (July 13, 1998).

62. Id.

63. See www.primustel.com/about.html.

64. See www.sternco.com/pr/vytl/vytl.html#releases.

Chapter Seven: The Global Economic Implications of Y2K

1. M. J. Zuckerman, "U.N. Confronts Global Shortfalls on Y2K," *USA Today* (December 10, 1998).

2. Valerie Putchaven and Susan Dziubinsk, Make Sure Your Funds Are Prepared for Y2K," *Morningstar* (courtesy of the *Detroit News*) (November 2, 1998).

3. Merrill Lynch Singapore's South Asia research group singles these countries out as more likely to survive the bug threat. It also mentions India, Taiwan, and the Philippines as countries that might be relatively better off. See "Asia at Risk From Millennium Bug," *Straits Times* (courtesy of Reuters) (July 20, 1998).

4. Edward Davies, "Millennium—Asia Utilities Hope Bug Won't Bite," Reuters (August 27, 1998).

5. "Antidote Needed—Asia Has No Time to Lose Fighting the Millennium Bug," *Asia Week* (July 24, 1998).

6. Bill Burke, "Japan Slow to Take Precautions," *Business Today* (August 24, 1998).

7. Christina Toh-Pantin, "Business Battens Down for Millennium Bug," Reuters (July 18, 1998).

8. "Got Y2K Problems? Firms in Taiwan Not Ready Either," *Journal of Commerce* (courtesy of Reuters) (January 5, 1999).

9. "Analysis—Japan Disquietingly Quiet on Year 2000 Problem," *Asia Pulse* (July 16, 1998).

10. Shingo Ito, "Japan's Premier Steps Up Fight Against Millennium Bug," *Agence France Presse* (August 21, 1998).

11. "Analysis—Japan Walking Into Year 2000 Hornet's Nest," *Asia Pulse* (July 28, 1998).

12. See, e.g., Asahi Shimbun, "Y2K Bug Still out There and Clock Is Still Ticking," Asahi News Service (August 14, 1998).

13. "Survey: Japan Not Ready for Y2K," Associated Press (August 27, 1998).

14. Toh-Pantin, note 6.

15. "Japan MITI to Extend Loan Aid for Millennium Bug," Reuters (July 20, 1998).

16. Yoshifumi Takemoto, "Japan Is Slow to Tackle Y2K Bug, Software Exec Says," *Bloomberg Business News* (July 22, 1998).

17. Id.

18. *Australian Financial Review* (May 11, 1998).

19. See "Asia at Risk From Millennium Bug," *Straits Times* (July 20, 1998), note 2.

20. Toh-Pantin, note 7.

21. Andrew Mollison, "Delays Abroad May Hurt Millennium Bug Efforts," *American-Statesman* (June 29, 1998).

22. See "Asia at Risk From Millennium Bug," note 19.

23. "Millennium Bug Chaos Looms as Time Runs Out on Y2K," *South China Morning Post* (September 10, 1998).

24. Anastasia Stanmeyey, "Y2K and China," Newsweek.com (November 9, 1998).

25. Davies, note 4.

26. "Millennium—Asian Airlines Take Off to Fight Bug," Reuters (September 4, 1998).

27. Alicia Seow, "Millennium—Asian Shipping Industry Divided on Bug," Reuters (September 10, 1998).

28. Nam In-soo, "Business Needs 49.7 Trillion Won to Solve Millennium Bug, Survey Says," *Korea Herald* (August 5, 1998).

29. Id.

30. "'Y2K' Could Trigger Another Recession, FKI Says," *Korea Herald* (November 3, 1998).

31. Mark Hollands, "SE Asia Lags in Y2K Plans," *Australian* (July 14, 1998).

32. David Fogarty, "Millennium—Asia Phone Firms Battle Bug, Face Hurdles," Reuters (August 19, 1998) (citing Merrill Lynch analysis).

33. Tony Waltham, "Seminar Speakers Highlight the Enormous Gravity of Y2K Issue," *Bangkok Post* (December 24, 1997).

34. "Computer Experts Propose Holiday in Singapore to Beat 'Y2K' Bug," *Deutche Presse-Agentur* (August 11, 1998).

35. Mark Henderson, "Four-Day Break Planned for the Millennium," *Times* (London) (April 17, 1998).

36. See "Asia at Risk From Millennium Bug," note 19.

37. Davies, note 4.

38. William Hoke, "Latin America's Delay in Tackling Year 2000 May Be Costly," *Business Times* (November 21, 1998).

39. Id.

40. See generally, William Hoke, "Year 2000 Computer Problem Could Be Another Brazil Crisis," *Wall Street Journal Interactive Edition* (November 5, 1998).

41. Matt Hamblen, "U.S. Firms Sweat Foreign Telco Readiness," *Computerworld* (July 13, 1998).

42. Hoke et al., Argentina Leads Latin America in Tackling Year 2000 Problem," *Wall Street Journal Interactive Edition* (October 29, 1998).

43. See generally, William Hoke, "Chile Has Been Slow to Tackle Year 2000 Problem," *Wall Street Journal Interactive Edition* (November 4, 1998).

44. Morris et al., "Though Late, Venezuela and Colombia Work Hard to Tackle Year-2000 Bug," Dow Jones newswires (November 3, 1998).

45. Id.

46. Andrew Craig, "Year 2000 Campaigner Says Delay the Euro," *TechWeb* (February 24, 1998).

47. Id.

48. Steve Ranger and Nick Farrell, "BT Could Spend More on Euro Than Y2K," *Computing* (November 1998), available at http://webserv.vnunet.com/www_user/plsql/pkg_vnu_news.right_frame?p_story=67125.

49. "U.S. Leads Europe on Y2K Spending, but Not Confidence," Reuters (November 10, 1998).

50. Id.

51. "Europe Lags on Y2K Issue," CNET News.com (courtesy of Reuters) (November 4, 1998).

52. Phillip Johnston, "Business Ignores the Countdown to Chaos," *Daily Telegraph* (November 5, 1998).

53. Roland Watson, "Beckett Admits Possible Snags Ahead," *The Sunday Times* (London) (November 6, 1998).

54. Bill Goodwin, "Year 2000 Noose Tightens Round Government's Neck," *Computer Weekly* (November 19, 1998).

55. "British Government Leak Shows Year 2000 Problem," *Newsbytes* (November 6, 1998).

56. Jonathan Prynn, "United Utilities in 2000 Bug Chaos Alert," *This Is London* (November 20, 1998).

57. "Millennium Bugs Utilities," BBC News (November 20, 1998), available at http://news.bbc.co.U.K./hi/english/business/the_com-pany_file/newsid_218000/218347.stm.

58. Tara Fitzgerald, "U.K. Mid-Sized Firms Face Year 2000 Bug Problems," Reuters (October 22, 1998).

59. Id.

60. Johnston, note 51.

61. Pete Danko, "All Is Not A-OK on Y2K," *Wired News* (August 5, 1998).

62. Donna Rosato, "Outside USA, Year 2000 Computer Glitch Ignored," *USA Today* (April 13, 1998).

63. "Japan and Germany Face Huge Millennium Problem, Says Expert," *Star Online* (November 16, 1998).

64. Frances Cairncross, "Countries That Count," *Economist* (September 19, 1998).

65. Id.

66. MSNBC (July 20, 1998), available at www.msnbc.com/news/181448.asp.

67. "Russia Has Y2K Fix Doubts," ABC News (June 26, 1998).

68. "Russia Not Taking Y2K Seriously," CNET News.com (courtesy of Reuters) (June 17, 1998).

69. Zuckerman, note 1.

Chapter Eight: The Economics of Y2K

1. David Hayes, "Experts Disagree on Effects of Year 2000 Computer Problem," *Kansas City Star* (December 4, 1998).

2. Id.

3. Id.

4. Federal Reserve Governor Edward W. Kelley, Jr., remarks at the Annual Economic Symposium, Houston Baptist University (October 29, 1998).

5. Declan McCullagh, "Bankers: Prepared for a Panic?" *Wired News* (December 3, 1998).

6. "Coke Says Has Y2K Contingency In Place," *Yahoo! News* (courtesy of Reuters) (December 30, 1998).

7. Bill Barnhart, "Y2K Costs Threaten Profits, Exec Says," *Chicago Tribune* (November 17, 1998). Whether it is pure coincidence or a human aversion to ends of centuries, the fact remains that at the end of each century we have seen significant declines in stock markets as investors cash out of positions. In 1899, the Dow Jones fell 23 percent between December 2 and December 18 and then continued to decline significantly through mid-1900. Similarly, British and Dutch stock markets in 1699 and 1799 show a pattern of significant share price drops. While this alone would be cause for some reflection by investors, when Y2K is

added to the brew it is a potent combination of psychological factors.

8. *Purposes and Functions of the Federal Reserve,* chapter 2, 25, available at www.federalreserve.gov.

9. "Y2K Will Bring Lower Lending Rates," Reuters (November 2, 1998).

10. Roger W. Ferguson, remarks at the Global Year 2000 Summit in London (October 16, 1998), available at www.bis.org/review/index.htm.

11. See *Purposes and Functions of the Federal Reserve,* note 3, chapter 2, 21.

12. Id. at chapter 3, 38.

13. Ellen Perlman, "Y2K Bugs the Muni Bond Business," *Governing Magazine* (September 1998).

14. Elizabeth MacDonald, "Local Governments Must Disclose Efforts to Solve Year 2000 Problem," *Wall Street Journal* (November 4, 1998).

15. Perlman, note 13.

16. Official statement, State Public Works Board of the State of California, $32,630,000 lease revenue refunding bonds (Department of Corrections) 1998 Series C (California State Prison-Monterey County, Soledad 2).

17. MacDonald, note 14; "Illinois Puts $114 Million Estimate on Fixing Year 2000 Computer Bug," *PostNet* (cour-

tesy of Associated Press) (November 20, 1998).

18. Lisa M. Bowman, "California Out Ahead on Y2K," ZDNN (December 10, 1998).

19. "Illinois Puts $114 Million Estimate on Fixing Year 2000 Computer Bug," note 17.

20. Tom Diederich, "Study Eyes New York's Y2K Readiness," *Computerworld* (September 11, 1998).

21. "State: New York Emergency Services Not Ready for 2000," Reuters (September 10, 1998).

22. Ron Southwick, "Towns Seek Antidote for Y2K Computer Ills," *Times* (Trenton) (August 23, 1998).

23. Eric Young, "Y2K Plans About But Funding Is Lacking: Cities, Counties Urged to Commit to Fix Bug," *Sacramento Bee* (November 17, 1998).

24. Id.

25. "Counties Face 911 Crisis Due to Year 2000 Problem," *Wall Street Journal Interactive Edition* (courtesy of Associated Press) (December 9, 1998).

26. Eric Young, "Y2K Plans About but Funding Is Lacking: Cities, Counties Urged to Commit to Fix Bug," *Sacramento Bee* (November 17, 1998).

27. Id.

28. Bowman, note 18.

29. Eric Lipton, "Two-Digit Problem Means Nine-Digit Bill for Local Governments," *Washington Post* (August 2, 1998).

30. Id.

31. Id.

32. Ann Imse, "Denver Flinches at Y2K Cost to City," *Rocky Mountain News* (August 19, 1998).

33. Julia C. Martinez, "City's Y2K Tab: $44 Million," *Denver Post* (August 19, 1998).

34. Kevin Duchschere and Mark Brunswick, "Local Governments Are Confronting Y2K Problems," *Star Tribune* (August 24, 1998).

35. Id.

36. Deborah Sullivan, "LAPD Gears Up for Y2K Computer Chaos," *Los Angeles Daily News* (January 2, 1999).

37. Stephen Barr, "Emergency Centers to Battle Bug," *Washington Post* (January 8, 1999).

Chapter Nine: Y2K Investment Opportunities

1. Bill Lane, "Better Safe Than Sorry," *Boston Business Journal* (July 27, 1998).

2. See, e.g., Andrew Hay, "Year 2000 Companies—Stocks With Expiration Dates?" *Reuters* (June 4, 1998).

3. See, e.g., Tony Keyes, "*The Year 2000 Computer Crisis: An Investor's Survival Guide* (Edwards Brothers Printing, 1997), 64–67. Other Y2K remediation firms recommended by Keyes and other analysts, such as Data Dimensions of Bellevue, Washington, suffered similar share-price catastrophes.

4. As reported in *Business Week* (June 16, 1997), 98.

5. "Viasoft Off on Loss Forecast, Job Cuts," *Reuters* (October 5, 1998).

6. See www.year2000.com/y2kstock.html.

7. See "Press Digest," *Washington Post* (July 23, 1998).

8. "Research Alert—HP Earnings Threat," Reuters (November 17, 1998).

9. See company press release, "Morgan Stanley Dean Witter Survey Forecasts Moderate Corporate Information Technology Spending Growth in 1999" (November 19, 1998).

Chapter Ten: Protecting Assets

1. John P. McDermott, "Banks Investing Time, Money on Y2K Problem," *Charleston Post and Courier* (August 2, 1998).

2. Cohen et al., *Investment Analysis and Portfolio Management* (Burr Ridge, Ill.: Irwin, 1987), 412.

INDEX

ABOUT THE AUTHORS

L. Jay Kuo is an attorney and international business consultant with an emphasis on automated processes. He served on the board of two manufacturing companies in Asia and is currently employed by Third Millennium Advisors, a San Francisco financial consulting firm. Mr. Kuo obtained his bachelor's degree in political science from Stanford University and his law degree from the University of California, Berkeley.

Edward M. Dua has extensive experience in both investment management and computer systems development. Early in his career, he designed and developed a wide-range of mainframe-based financial and system software solutions for Young & Rubicam.

He served as an investment banker for Thomson McKinnon Securities, a New York-based brokerage firm, and was a portfolio manager for Dominion Ventures, an early-stage investment company. He currently is a principal with Third Millennium Advisors, a San Francisco financial consulting firm. Mr. Dua holds a bachelor's degree in economics from Gettysburg College and a master's in business administration from Duke University.

To reach either L. Jay Kuo or Edward M. Dua, please contact:

Third Millennium Advisors
450 Mission Street, 5th Floor
San Francisco, CA 94105

E-mail: info@tmadvisors.com
Website: www.tmadvisors.com